VOYAGE

OF FAITH

*The Catholic Church
in Transition
by*

GEORGE CORNELL

*ODYSSEY
NEW YORK*

For a sunny sister,
Martha Marie

"For he has made known to us in all wisdom and insight the mystery of his will, according to his purpose which he set forth in Christ as a plan for the fullness of time, to unite all things in him, things in heaven and things on earth."

—EPHESIANS 1:9–10.

CONTENTS

PART ONE

Patterns and Pontiffs

In the present order of things, Divine Providence is leading us to a new order of human relations which, by men's own efforts and even beyond their very expectations, are directed towards the fulfillment of God's superior and inscrutable designs.

—POPE JOHN XXIII
Opening session, Second Vatican Council,
October 11, 1962.

The work begins today and never comes to an end. This is the law of our temporal, earthly pilgrimage.

—POPE PAUL VI
Ecclesiam Suam *(Paths of the Church),*
August 10, 1964.

CHAPTER *1*

The Fraternal Awakening

In the fairy tale of the sleeping beauty, a benumbing trance fell upon the princess and all the occupants of the palace, leaving them for many years in a state of rigid immobility. Nothing moved. Nothing changed. Officers, chamberlains, and ministers, in their archaic livery, reposed statue-like in their places, and the transfixed guards lined the parapets. Decades passed. Dust gathered and thorny brambles surrounded the castle, enclosing forbiddingly its medieval styles, its moldering appurtenances, its captive court. A deadly sameness gripped it. Then, in an instant, with a kiss of selfless love, the whole household awoke and immediately surged into a whirl of affectionate alliances and engagement with life.

This, in the view of the great old French Catholic philosopher Francois Mauriac, depicts what has happened to the Roman Catholic Church. Suddenly it has aroused, cast off its chains, and gone into motion. It has reached "the end of a bewitchment," he says. It has broken free of a prolonged, isolating enthrallment during which "the Vatican had become congealed in motionlessness as though a magician had condemned it to an eternal and incurable ceremony," stultified by ancient formularies and baroque splendors, inflexible, withdrawn, jealously preserving its doctrines as if calcified in stone, suspicious of the evolving world around.[1] But now abruptly, the spell had lifted. The heavy bronze doors swung open; the drawbridge came down, and robust currents issued from that high-walled, gray bastion west of the Tiber, redounding throughout the arteries of Christendom.

A different day dawned for St. Peter's, and beyond.

Assessing the situation as of 1965, an American theologian and editor, Father Ralph Gorman, said that in six years, "there have been more changes in the Catholic Church than in the preceding three or four hundred years." Along with the wave of reforms has come a new freedom of speech and criticism which "would have shocked Catholics a few years ago" [2] but which hardly rates a lifted eyebrow today."

With the touch of that adventuresome and warmly wise old man, the late John XXIII, the entire establishment had blinked, bestirred itself, and breathed a liberating air. Old restraints and barriers began falling away. Old rigidities dissolved. Precedents toppled, one after

2

another, and fresh affinities formed with other Christians, other peoples. By the further leading of the Pope who came afterward, the
practical and purposeful Paul VI, the tempo increased. The roads
lengthened and the horizons widened. Something decisive and unstop-
pable had occurred. The time of seclusion had come to an end. The
slumberer had arisen and strode unfettered and friend-making in the
streets of the present age. "You have before you an humble man, your
brother," Pope Paul told the United Nations, on his epochal peace
mission to America in 1965. He had ventured forth from his sequestered
"spiritual city," as he termed it, to share the mixed "terrestial city" of
men. To the assembled diplomats from around the earth, believers and
atheists, white, yellow, and black men, Communists, monarchists, and
democratic representatives, he said the church at long last was joining in
"conversation with the entire world." It was a strange, new way. A
fuller consciousness "has reawakened in us," Pope Paul observed at the
Vatican Council's concluding 1965 session. It "has dislodged us from
the torpor of ordinary life." Earlier, musing about his unexampled
trip to the Holy Land in 1964, he said it might be likened to the fable
of Rip Van Winkle who appeared in his native land after his long sleep,
unknown and unknowing. Yet there was a difference in the papal
experience.

"We must take note of a very strange thing," he told a general audience later in the Vatican Hall of Benedictions. "Instead of awakening in an incomprehensible world, instead of being a stranger and unknown—think how much time has passed and how many radically
changing events have occurred—we were recognized perfectly
there. . . ."[3]

The newly launched series of papal trips, although only brief episodes
in themselves and doubtless to be followed by additional travels, provided a striking sign and image of the total phenomenon, with all its
varied facets, its expanding dimensions, its many impulses and monumental possibilities. The significance of these stretched beyond any
time-bracketed event or geography. Yet those swift "journeys by jet"
to the United States, to India, and particularly that first precedent-
setting flight to the Holy Land, proclaimed a pivotal point: That what
had seemed immovable could move, and was doing so; that a centuries-
old fixed and self-enclosed stance was giving way to a greater adaptability
and breadth of action and interest; that a previously stationary, hemmed-
about institution was venturing out to meet those beyond its bounds;
that it was setting forth on a roomier way, at a gentler step, hand-in-
hand with others whose faith also sprang from that land of the covenant,
the commandments, and the cross.

In short, Rome changed.

It was becoming less Roman, more catholic, Austria's Franziskus Cardinal Koenig told me as we strolled in a garden behind his apartment. It was dispelling the stereotyped view of the church as a "unilateral bloc," he said, and developing more versatile, internationalized lines of direction, more responsive to varying regions, peoples, and conditions. "We are at the beginning," he said, "of a new stage of wider Christian collaboration." The implications stirred sensations in many quarters. Protestants "have been living in clichés under the assumption that Rome does not change," observed Lutheran theologian Warren A. Quanbeck of St. Paul, Minnesota. "Now we know that Rome is changing, and these changes can be ascribed to nothing less than the work of the Holy Spirit." [4] The turn had come in a span of only six years.

In that period, the Roman Catholic Church had entered into a far-spread and hitherto untraveled frontier of practice and outlook. With a burst of pent-up energies, unleashed at the Second Vatican Council, it had plunged into a vast reorientation which was bringing it closer to other churches and which was drawing other churches closer to it. Methodist Bishop Fred Pierce Corson of Philadelphia, a Protestant delegate-observer at the council, termed it "the most important and most outstanding world event in this century." [5] The effects radiated around the earth. At an interdenominational gathering, one of many such affairs spreading in this country and abroad, Boston's incisive old Richard Cardinal Cushing commented: "We are in the springtime of new discovery of one another and of wonder at the myriad links which bind us together after centuries of separation." [6] No prophets had foreseen the magnitude of the affair. No advance indications had suggested its vigor. Yet it came, an unanticipated tide of spirit, heart, and method which swept the Church of Rome out of its protective fastnesses and into encounter with others and the world.

"*Aggiornamento,*" Pope John called it. An "up-to-dating."

"Reform," Pope Paul said. A carrying out of the church's duty "to reform, correct, and set herself aright in conformity with her divine model." [7]

The objective struck an old chord: *Ecclesia semper reformanda.* This is a standard Protestant watchword, meaning "the church is always in need of reform." It had not been commonly used among Roman Catholics for centuries, largely because of its associations with the rise of Protestantism, but in the wave of change in the 1960's, the term rapidly regained currency among Catholic leaders. John Baptist Montini had asserted it strongly even before he became Pope Paul. "Reform, the program of the saints and the trumpet of rebels, has been through the centuries the renewing ferment of Catholic tradition," he declared while still Archbishop of Milan.[8] And as pope, he voiced the theme repeatedly in pungent discourses both to the Roman Curia, the Church's hoary, formality-laden central administrative organs, and to the global assembly of bishops at the Vatican Council. Before them he set three basic goals for the good of the church: "Its reform; the bringing together of all Christians in unity; the dialogue of the church with the contemporary world."[9]

It was a far, wide vision.

It faced a long road, through difficult terrain strewn with time-encrusted obstacles, misunderstandings, and hostilities. The final destination lay in the haze of distance. But the expedition was under way. And the giant strides already taken brought a transformation in religious relationships and a mounting church solidarity amid the massed, corporate influences of the times. A "new epoch" has begun, says the famed German Catholic theologian Hans Küng, "a new epoch in the history of the Catholic Church and of the whole of Christendom."[10]

With it came an altering church landscape. Unexpected new approaches unfolded. Partitions came down. Connections formed. After centuries of conflict and non-communication, Roman Catholic, Protestant, and Orthodox followers were meeting together, conferring together, praying together, often working together. Christianity also stressed increasingly its roots in Judaism, the joint spiritual patrimony. Closer associations developed in scholarship and in dealing with community problems.

In a modern world, compressed by technology and confronted with common potentialities and perils, the forces of faith recognized more clearly a mutual responsibility, a crucial interdependence. "And if a house is divided against itself, that house will not be able to stand," Jesus had said,[11] and now Rome had declared its wider kinship, its intensified program of propitiation. "We promise our collaboration," Pope Paul assured American Protestant, Eastern Orthodox, and Jewish representatives on October 4, 1965, during his dramatic one-day peace mission to New York. They met with him in a small church near the United Nations to show their mutual dedication to his purpose. Rome's new approach involved not only a reciprocal search for unity with other Christians, but also a readiness for converse with other ideologies, other religions. "All men are brothers under the Fatherhood of the Divinity," Pope Paul emphasized on his December, 1964, visit to India, deep in the mysterious and multi-religious East. "We must come closer together," he told an intimate gathering of the Moslem imams, Hindu pundits, Jains, Sikhs, Buddhist bhikkus, and Zoroastrian Parsees. "We must also begin to work together . . . Are we not all one in this struggle for a better world . . . ?" He recited Hindu Scripture and prayers, commending them. The closer identification, however, was within the Judeo-Christian heritage. *"Shalom, shalom,"* Paul VI had said as he set foot earlier in Israel, the first pope ever to travel from Rome to the region from which Judaism and all Christianity stemmed. "Peace, peace."

It was the old Hebraic salutation; it was the exhortation of Christ. It was a word, a signal of reconciliation—of an "ecumenical age." The church compass was pointed in a new direction. The age-old winds of division had shifted. Disintegration had turned to integration.

From the Middle Ages until the present era, for more than one thousand years, Christianity had been breaking up, torn by a succession of quarrels and cleavages. It had been a weary, wounding cycle. The first massive rupture, aggravated over a long period by political and religious rivalries and preliminary clashes, came to a head in 1054, when the Great Schism ripped the church in half, separating the East from the West. A heavy curtain of enmity and silence fell between Rome and Constantinople, hardened by the Crusades and impervious to time or tactics.

But now at last, it seemed to be rising.

"We greet you with exultation . . .," the Ecumenical Patriarch of Constantinople, Athenagoras I, told Pope Paul as they embraced in Jerusalem on January 5, 1964.

"Great is our emotion and profound our joy . . .," said the Pope.

Then, in that hour of endings and beginnings, the chief leaders of Eastern Orthodoxy and Roman Catholicism prayed for concord in Christ—for a more comradely future whose exact contours none knew, but for which there now was fresh hope.

Even more extensively among the churches of the West, the barricades and battlements were coming down, those angry walls reared in the wake of the Protestant Reformation of the sixteenth century. For 450 years, the harsh warfare had gone on, while the chain reaction of division lengthened and spread, splintering Western churchdom into more than three hundred different denominations—Lutherans, Baptists, Presbyterians, Congregationalists, Anglicans, Methodists, and a maze of subdivisional offshoots born more out of class, race, nation, and language than theology.

"Heretics," Rome excoriated. "Anathema."

"Popism." Protestants accused. "The Roman Babylon."

But the mood has changed radically, and it has done so with amazing speed and sweep. "We have seen things happen in a few years that we had not expected to see in a lifetime," United Presbyterian leader Eugene Carson Blake told me. Rome for centuries had avoided official dealings with Protestants, but now serious interchange proliferated from St. Peter's to Kansas City. Christianity has entered what Catholic philosopher Jean Guitton calls an astonishingly accelerated phase of history in which "the impossible becomes possible in a short time." [12]

The depth of the change was dramatized when the late Pope John, and later Pope Paul, sat down with Protestant representatives and conversed with them as "brothers in Christ." It was voiced when Pope John, at the opening of the Second Vatican Council on October 11, 1962, declared that the Roman Catholic Church nowadays "prefers to make use of the medicine of mercy rather than that of . . . condemnations." It resounded as a pervasive theme by the time of the final 1965 session of that council, when Pope Paul summed up the "recurring and moving note" of its four years of deliberation as work toward "the reintegrating of all Christians in the unity willed by Christ." It was expressed, too, on a chill autumn night of 1965 in New York's Yankee Stadium by the presence of three thousand Protestants and Jews among the ninety thousand there in that huge, prayerful gathering led by Pope Paul, whose words, like the occasion, bespoke transdenominational kinship and affection. It was demonstrated when six major American Catholic publishers announced in December, 1964, that they were revising all textbooks to eliminate "negative images" or "outright distortions" about Protestants and Jews. It was displayed in the increasing joint devotionals of Roman Catholics and other Christians. It was affirmed when the World Council of Churches, responding to the changes, authorized in 1965 the start of the first continuing talks in history between representatives of Protestant and Eastern Orthodox bodies and the Vatican. It was legislated in nearly every paragraph of the Vatican Council's November 21, 1964, *Decree on Ecumenism*, approving common worship services with other Christians, urging co-operation with them, asserting that "both sides were to blame" for the split in the church, and asking and extending forgiveness. That same disposition had been expressed earlier when Pope Paul, on September 29, 1963, turned to the delegate-observers from other churches, seated in a place of honor at the Vatican Council, and pleaded for mutual pardon for past faults which had split Christianity apart.

"If we are in any way to blame for that separation," he said, "we humbly beg God's forgiveness and ask pardon, too, of our brethren who feel themselves to have been injured by us. For our part, we willingly forgive the injuries which the Catholic Church has suffered, and forget the grief endured during the long series of dissensions and separations."

Never before had a pope asked pardon for past offenses to Protestants, and at the same time declared that the Roman Catholic Church no longer holds their defection against them. Several Protestant leaders observed that their churches also should recognize their part of the blame, and ask forgiveness and extend it. Some did.

In Germany, where the breakup started in 1517 when the priest-theologian Martin Luther challenged certain church practices of that time, bishops of the present-day United Evangelical Lutheran Church declared their grateful acceptance of the Pope's plea. They said all separated churches could move toward each other if they would join in a mutual "movement of penance." An essential of Christianity, they said, is "admitting and forgiving sins."[13]

And that was an element of the contemporary movement among Christians to come to terms with each other, and with the needs of an intermingling, colliding world. They recognized that something was wrong in their dismemberment and distrust, that a divided Christianity was hard put to attest to an undivided Lord or to heal a divided humanity. They sought to better manifest their faith, to set a clearer standard for modern man. Says British Jesuit theologian Bernard Leeming: "The shame of our divisions must afflict us and urge us in contrition and humility to work with Christ for reconciliation."[14]

This did not mean that all of the ineptness had been remedied, or that all of the entrenched obstacles had been overcome or canceled out. Far from it. Nor did it mean any glossing over or dilution of basic principle for the sake of general congeniality. In fact, just the opposite. As viewed by Catholic, Protestant, and Orthodox leaders, it meant an overriding loyalty to principle, a dedication to a fuller comprehension of truth wherever it may be found, regardless of past self-justification and self-absorption. It meant abandoning egocentricities and confessing mistakes. It meant a readiness to be corrected. It meant listening to others, learning, improving, or as Pope John once put it, letting in "some fresh air."

It "admonishes us to bear in mind the limitations of our knowledge and recognize also that side of truth which others see, without denying, however, that which we ourselves really know about truth," says Augustin Cardinal Bea, the great old Biblical scholar who heads the Vatican Secretariat for Christian Unity.

"The real love of truth requires us to recognize it wherever we come across it, wherever it may come from."[15]

Rome had opened the doors to this wider orb, not only to other churches, but to the practical realities and experiences of the modern age—its natural sciences, its social and psychological explorations, its interpenetrating cultures. The church had joined in energetic colloquy with other communities of believers and with realms of thought outside itself.

This was the basic metamorphosis.

"This is the day which we have desired for centuries!," Pope Paul told the rapt throng of ninety thousand in Yankee Stadium on that first papal visit in history to the Western Hemisphere. And the Pope, to an overwhelming extent on that October day of 1965, voiced the combined concern of men of many creeds. "Jamais plus la guerre!," he cried in French before the United Nations General Assembly. "No more war, war never again!" The church, which for centuries had held back in lofty, detached judgment of nations and cultures, had plunged into the very thick of the struggle for international concord. And the Pope voiced the universal yearning of a war-weary humanity. "If you wish to be brothers, let the arms fall from your hands; one cannot love while holding offensive arms." In the same cause, he conferred for forty-six minutes with United States President Lyndon B. Johnson in suite 35H of the Waldorf Towers—a remarkable and harmonious confrontation between the world's most powerful spiritual and temporal leaders. And nearly four million Americans watched and cheered the Pope's passage through the nation's mightiest metropolis, its suburbs, Harlem slums, and gilded midtown.

His appeal before the global parliament of the United Nations was a revealing "way station" in the church's new direct approach to modern societies and its joint exertions with others in behalf of international stability. His other journeys, and the accompanying developments, more graphically pointed up the underlying quest for reconciliation among people, at the deep and intimate levels of faith, across the borders of governments, races, and precise theologies—for active partnership among the diverse family of God.

This marked an emergence from the long period of "fortress Catholicism," during which the church had increasingly shut itself off in guarded isolation from others. For nearly five centuries, as a result of the shuddering wave of divisions set off in the sixteenth century, Rome had braced itself, built up its defenses, tightened its lines of authority, and centralized controls in the Vatican. The process had begun at the Council of Trent (1545 to 1563), aimed at reforming abuses and resisting Protestantism. The church tended to draw within a disciplined, closed stronghold, prohibiting religious fraternizations. Teachings, intent on controverting any deviations, developed an exacting, defensive tone known as "Post-Tridentine" (after Trent) or "Counter-Reformation theology." It "has been more anti-Protestant than Catholic," writes American Catholic theologian Herbert McCabe.[16] At the same time, Protestantism blazed back with anit-Roman strictures and slogans.

Thus was stamped a prolonged, bitter chapter in the Christian record, steeped with rancor, suspicion, and mutual misconceptions, perpetuated by superficial generalities and lack of acquaintanceship. Neither side sought consistently to understand the concepts or terms of the other, the reasons for them, or values in them. Each proclaimed its own dicta, virtually deaf to the other.

Siege sank into stalemate.

But Vatican II, and the powerful wells it uncapped, mellowed the whole landscape. It swept aside "the Tridentine policy of fortress Catholicism," says Archbishop Denis E. Hurley of Durban, South Africa.[17] It "administered a death blow to Counter-Reformation theology," says the keenly discerning American Paulist scholar, John B. Sheerin.[18]

Today a new ingredient, a healing tonic, flowed through the broken body of Christianity. It was an impulse for unity.

Called the "ecumenical movement," it originated in Protestantism about fifty years ago, and has gathered momentum ever since then. Particularly since World War II, it has quickened and swelled into enormous proportions, producing a vast, interlinking webwork of interdenominational co-operative agencies, programs, projects, and church mergers, as well as a humming theological concourse, seeking to cure the old ruptures and rancors.

It has spawned numerous operating organizations. Chief of these is the World Council of Churches formed in 1948 and made up of 215 Protestant, Old Catholic, Eastern Orthodox, and Anglican Church bodies with a total of approximately 350 million members in eighty countries. It carries on wide-scale co-operative work, blunting the old sharp rivalries. Regional and national councils also have burgeoned around the globe, including the 1950-founded National Council of Churches in the United States of America.

Until about 1960, however, Rome stood aloof from such interchurch affairs, warning its 550 million faithful against involvement. A 1929 encyclical, *Mortalium Animos,* had discounted the interdenominational activities as not for Catholics. The view was softened somewhat in a 1949 encyclical. But as recently as 1954, Catholics were instructed to stay away from the World Council's general assembly in Evanston, Illinois.

But then along came an old peasant-born prelate, Angelo Giuseppe

Roncalli, confident, soft-spoken, quick, revolutionary. And all at once the walls came tumbling down. Two months after his election as Pope John XXIII, he said in his Christmas message of 1958 that only a rebuilt unity of "true human and Christian brotherhood will be able to check the grave dangers that overhang the world."

Swiftly thereafter, this so-called "interim pope" went at the job.

To stunned Curia cardinals, he dropped his January 25, 1959, bombshell—there would be a world-wide council of bishops to renovate the church and clear the way toward eventual unity. His conciliatory messages drew a stream of Orthodox and Protestant visitors to the Vatican, the first in history to enter those moldering, Renaissance-embellished confines. They included Greek Orthodox, Lutheran, Anglican, Baptist, Presbyterian, Episcopal, and Methodist dignitaries.

A long-embattled Christendom marveled and wondered.

First of the callers, on March 17, 1959, was Archbishop Iakovos, head of Greek Orthodoxy in America and a close associate of all Orthodoxy's Ecumenical Patriarch, Athenagoras I of Constantinople. Part of the conversation between him and the Pope included this exchange:

"My wish," Pope John said, "would be to prove myself a forerunner for the coming of church unity."

"In what sense do you understand this unity?" the Archbishop asked.

The Pope responded, "Unity is that which can be effected only by and through love."

"Therefore I presume," the Archbishop said, "that unity in your mind cannot be understood in terms of submission of each church to the Roman Catholic Church."

"Of course not," the Pope said. "I don't believe that unity can be promoted unless we promote it through equality, fraternity, and freedom of expression. In this way only can unity of the church be founded on a solid base and therefore be a realistic and lasting one."

A parade of other visitors, including the former Archbishop of Canterbury, Geoffrey Francis Fisher, followed.

In mid-1960, Pope John set up the Vatican Secretariat for Christian Unity, to initiate and maintain liaison with other churches. Rome had never before had such an agency, or engaged in regular interchange with denominations outside the Roman fold. Named to head it was Augustin Cardinal Bea, the thin, stooped old German scholar who previously had fired a Biblical resurgence in his church, paralleling Protestant activity in the field.

"Both Catholics and non-Catholics are victims of prejudice and misunderstanding," he told me in an interview in his office-apartment in Rome. "We must get behind the different terminologies to meanings. There are plain misunderstandings, and also real problems." Resolving them, he added, will take much time, hard work, patience, humility, reciprocal esteem, and careful listening to one another.

Bea's constant theme has been that all validly baptized Christians are organically bound to Christ, and thus to each other as brothers, and that Christians outside Roman Catholicism are also members in part of Christ's mystical body, the church. He considers the Bible, and growing mutual study of it, to be the fruitful soil of unity. Through it, he told a Protestant-Catholic-Orthodox colloquium at Harvard University in March, 1963, all Christians "will not only be drawn closer to Christ, but inevitably closer to one another."

With the establishment of the Unity Secretariat, Roman Catholic emissaries began frequenting Protestant and Orthodox centers— Geneva, Constantinople, the See of Canterbury. Bea himself roamed that circuit, meeting with Lutheran and Reformed leaders in Europe, becoming a friend of World Council officials in Geneva and America, calling on the Archbishop of Canterbury, A.M. Ramsey, spiritual leader of the world's Anglicans. Bea was the first Roman Catholic cardinal to visit Lambeth Palace since 1560.

Crowning these preliminaries, an historic and decisive undertaking began in 1965. The Roman Catholic Church and the World Council of Churches authorized the start of regular, continuing consultations on co-operative action and doctrine. Not since the Western rifts in Christianity more than four hundred years ago had there been a permanent, joint forum for developing and carrying on mutual work by Rome and most major Protestant and Eastern Orthodox bodies. Cardinal Bea joined with leaders of other churches in Geneva, Switzerland, the headquarters of the World Council and the historic citadel of Protestantism, in formally launching the plan. He said Rome "greets with joy and fully accepts" it. It had been approved a month earlier by the World Council's Central Committee, meeting in Enugu, Nigeria.

The eighty-three-year-old Cardinal Bea and another venerable Christian statesman, the Rev. Dr. Marc Boegner, eighty-four, dean of French Protestantism, headed the Geneva proceedings, which brought together 2,500 Protestants and Catholics on February 19, 1965. Seated with Bea on the stage of the Salle de la Réformation (Reformation Hall), the white-mustached Boegner called the step "a real miracle of the grace of God" and the first such broad, mutual undertaking since the Protestant Reformation. Cardinal Bea said that for the task ahead, "we all have a basis in common: the word of God in the Holy Scripture." Added the World Council's long-time chief executive, W. A. Visser 't Hooft: "Now the work can begin."

It obviously faced a mountain of obstacles and difficulties, accumulated and hardened by time, but the effort to surmount them had begun. This was the crucial difference. "Now we are on the road to reconciliation," commented Catholic Bishop Francois, of Lausanne and Geneva, at the Geneva gathering. The start of the endeavor was accompanied by many similar supplementary efforts, such as the opening of official, regular talks in the United States in 1965 between American Roman Catholic and Lutheran, Episcopalian and Presbyterian leaders. These moves and the conclusion of the more widely encompassing arrangements begun in Geneva came as a somewhat normal development to the gathering tide of previous contacts. These arose over a period of about five years, by various means and with increasing frequency.

Roman Catholic observers became a regular feature of major Protestant-Orthodox gatherings: at the World Council's central committee meeting in St. Andrews, Scotland, in 1960; at its general assembly in New Delhi, India, in 1961; again at its central committee meetings in Paris in 1962; in Rochester, New York, in 1963; at the 1963 general assembly of the National Council of Churches in Philadelphia; at the Fourth World Conference on Faith and Order in Montreal, Canada, in the summer of 1963; at the U.S. Conference of the World Council in 1964, at other meetings in 1965, and thereafter.

At the latter affairs, Roman Catholic theologians delivered papers and took part in the programs. This participation in the World Faith and Order Conference, involving doctrinal analysis and discussion among Christians of every major church, made it the most widely representative theological parley to date in history. Also, in connection with it, a gathering of fifteen hundred Roman Catholics, Presbyterians, Baptists, Methodists, Congregationalists, and Lutherans joined in a service of litanies, hymns, and common prayers for unity.

Paul-Emile Cardinal Léger, Archbishop of Montreal, called it a "family reunion"—a "sign of the times." Such joint devotional services have become increasingly frequent across America and elsewhere, a product of the ecumenical movement. Rome had cast off its past wariness and entered that movement with industry and verve.

"It is the work of God," says Bishop John J. Wright of Pittsburgh.

Other Catholic leaders, up to Pope Paul and the late John, offered similar appraisals of the movement.

"A great and welcome change has taken place," says W. A. Visser 't Hooft, the veteran General Secretary of the World Council. "We must respond to it hopefully."

"Ecumenical" means literally world-wide. As currently used, it refers chiefly to the efforts and organizations dedicated to furthering Christian unity. In a general sense, it also implies the ideal of pooling insights and endowments for mutual improvement and the better enlightenment of all. In specific connection with Roman Catholic "ecumenical" councils, it denotes the geographical extension of the church, involving its global episcopacy. The word itself derives from a term in Greek manuscripts of the New Testament, *oikumene*, meaning "the whole inhabited world"—the planetary parish to which Jesus directed that his gospel be given.

In him, Christians find the compelling nucleus and motive of the reunion movement. On the night before he was crucified, he prayed that "they may all be one; even as thou, Father, art in me, and I in thee, that they also may be in us, so that the world may believe that thou hast sent me." [19] This prayer and other pleas for unity and brotherhood throughout the Bible constitute the underlying drive of the present endeavor. It is grounded in theology and its source, Christ. "We, though many, are one body in Christ," the Apostle Paul wrote long ago. [20] Since Christians have one Lord, they realize that if they adhere more closely to him, they automatically adhere to one another. Their distance apart, driving wedges between them in ministry, work, membership, and communion, indicates that some of them, or perhaps all of them, to large or small degrees, somehow must fall short of the common center to which all aspire. Reaching it, they inevitably would reach one another. And they seek that mutually professed ground, staked out by the Prince of Peace.

His is the unitary, rallying summons to the churches.

"In their conversations the churches are moving from the periphery to the center," says Lutheran Bishop Anders Nygren of Sweden. [21]

Pope Paul VI told the Vatican Council: "May the living church be conformed to the living Christ." [22] That is the sought-for meeting point.

But the movement also had practical overtones. In a civilization closely knit by technology, governmental activity, and mass communications, Christianity faced crippling handicaps in its divisions and discord. A broken voice often was lost among the more coherent voices of the times. Says Catholic Bishop Russel J. McVinney of Providence, Rhode Island: "If we do not stand together by a bond of love we will die." [23]

That bond was reviving and multiplying in many ways. Protestants and Catholic clergy went on joint spiritual retreats, spoke before each other's congregations and conferences, taught in each other's classrooms. Protestant theologians became regular contributors to Catholic publications, and vice versa. Observed church historian Norman V. Hope, with a wry irony: "The relations between Protestants and Roman Catholics have become almost Christian in character." [24]

The "common Bible" enterprise caught on and thrived, with the Protestant-produced Revised Standard Version widely used in Catholic seminaries, and a Catholic edition already bearing an imprimatur in the United States, Scotland and England. African Christians got out an early combined version in Swahili. Common versions were also in preparation elsewhere. "The scholars maintain that there is no more sense to a Protestant or Catholic Bible than there is to a Protestant or Catholic Shakespeare, Milton, or Dante," writes Monsignor George W. Casey. [25]

Not only in scholarship, but in action, the alliances strengthened. After an historic 1963 conference in Chicago of Catholic, Protestant, and Jewish leaders on race relationships, the first such interreligious action front in American history, similar local councils sprang up across the country. Priests, rabbis, nuns, and ministers marched together in 1965 in Selma, Alabama and elsewhere. On other issues, the National Conference of Christians and Jews sparked a growing network of local interfaith consultation groups.

Among Christians, modes of worship and theological developments showed the converging trend.

Protestants, reared on the Reformation motto of *sola Scriptura* (only the Bible), increasingly recognized the importance of extra-Biblical church tradition, the long stream of Christian insights and experiences through the ages. At the same time, Roman Catholicism, with its firm regard for tradition, stirred with a mounting emphasis on the Bible. Pope Paul, citing the church improvements needed, said:

"The first requirement of this reform will certainly be a more diligent study and a more intensive proclamation of the Word of God." [26]

Many Catholic theologians now taught that tradition must be rooted in Scripture, directly or indirectly, and not divorced from it. On the other hand, Protestants increasingly recognized that the Bible itself, compiled by second century church fathers who winnowed out spurious materials, had been upheld, preserved, and honored by tradition, and that even the legacies of the Protestant Reformation, including its methods and maxims, such as *sola Scriptura*, had themselves become part of tradition. So were the great confessions of faith, the Nicene and Apostles' creeds widely used in Protestantism.

In other ways, too, the churches moved toward each other. Among Protestants, the conventionally plain, pulpit-centered worship gave way to more symbolism and stress on communion around the altar. On the other hand, altar-centered Catholic worship accorded growing attention to the pulpit and preaching. "Protestant and Catholic structures are getting harder and harder to distinguish," comments Jesuit theologian C. J. McNaspy.[27]

Of even more immeasurable consequences, Catholics, Protestants, and Orthodox joined in serious conversation, mutually listening, criticizing, and admittedly learning from one another.

Church monologue had become dialogue.

"The ecumenical dialogue has initiated a transformation in Christian theology," says the perceptive Catholic theologian, Gregory Baum, a consultant to the Vatican's Unity Secretariat. "Each tradition has become aware of its own limitations, imposed on it by past controversies, and hence it reaches out, by greater fidelity to the sources of revelation, to attain a more balanced and more universal vision of the gospel. . . . We have much to discover in areas as yet unexplored."[28]

Among Roman Catholic scholars, the approach became known as the "théologie nouvelle," the "new theology"; and as "ecumenical theology," the "théologie engagé"—an extrapolation of truth "engaged" with other Christians and with the pluralistic society of today.

No longer did leading Catholics speak of a one-way "return to Rome" as the essential of unity, but of a movement toward one another. Pope Paul referred to it variously as a "restoration of unity," a "coming together," a "recomposition of Christians." Comments Archbishop Edward D. Howard of Portland, Oregon: "Reunion will be neither a Protestant 'return' nor a Catholic 'capitulation,' but a brotherly approach on both sides."[29] Neither company stood still. Both moved.

This did not mean sacrifice of principle or compromise of integrity. Rome held fast to its teaching that essential doctrine was unchangeable. In actuality, all churches maintain that the rudiments of faith are unwavering—a fixed, changeless star amidst the vicissitudes of men's ideas. But the dynamic new element in the Roman Catholic Church was that doctrine could be better understood, more fully expressed, more deeply comprehended and interpreted. Pope John publicly introduced that thesis, and it swirled through the church.

"A dogma as such is not finally synonymous with divine truth, but only incompletely expresses the wealth of divine truth because it sees revelation in human terms," Germany's Julius Cardinal Döpfner of Munich told a large gathering of Protestants and Catholics. He added that new aspects of truth can be discovered, and that illumination may come from outside the church. In the past, he said, the church has seemed to stay within a "self-imposed ghetto, trying to build its own small world adjoining the big world." But the view has changed. "The recognition of the Holy Spirit outside the limits of the Catholic Church establishes a bridge to our 'separated brethren' and enlarges the order of the church as such."[30]

Not all Catholics or Protestants approved of the present cross-currents. Some were disturbed, some scornful, some horrified.

"All the church would have to do now is canonize Martin Luther and I'd give up," a Boston priest commented wryly.[31]

Among some Catholics, "the phrase 'black Protestants' comes easily to their lips," says Jesuit Biblical scholar Walter M. Abbott. "For them the Christian unity movement is a warfare, with unconditional surrender to the Catholic Church as the only outcome. If you see it in any other terms . . . they call you a Communist or a member of what they refer to as the 'world conspiracy.' "[32]

Such attitudes have their Protestant counterparts.

Radio preacher Carl McIntire, who carries on a running attack on major churches and the Christian unity movement, says it is a "drive to build the one-world church, to return the Protestants to Rome, and to co-operate with the Communist-controlled churches."[33]

Others also heaped on coals. "Brainwashed by apostate theology and counterfeit ecumenicity, there are those today who may be quite ready to applaud this new look at Rome . . .," says a Reformed minister, John Vander Ploeg. "They are agreeable, meek, and docile folk eager to persuade others also to be agreeable, meek, and docile like themselves. . . . Much of Protestantism has been disarmed."[34]

Despite the denunciations and the demurrers, however, the peace-building tide flowed on, occasionally impeded by embankments and accumulated debris, running through rocky shoals and precipitous gorges, yet going on, swelling, gathering force and direction.

Rather than being a matter of mushy theology or mere good will, says Archbishop Gabriel Garrone of Toulouse, the movement strengthens and intensifies the light of faith, "permitting us to see the treasures of truth guarded by non-Catholics which we have perhaps chosen not to examine precisely because they are found among others. Ecumenism favors the spirit of poverty because it banishes the spirit of proprietorship of truth." Addressing the Vatican Council, he added:

"Ecumenism, then, is a providential event, overturning barriers and dissipating the night which covers the world. Because the night has come, God shows us the stars which we had not noticed up to now. These will guide us to the dawn of the day in which all Christians will be one." [35] This was a recurring theme at the council.

At that august congress of the overseers and chief pastors of the church, Protestant and Eastern Orthodox delegate-observers provided an indirect yet strongly effective influence. Far from being mere silent spectators, they soon were mingling easily with the council fathers and theological experts, the *periti*. Mixed discussion meetings were held regularly, sometimes several of them a week, as a sideline to the council itself.

Presence of the observers has influenced "the course of council debates," says Bishop Francois Charriere of Switzerland. "Contacts between observers and council fathers greatly contributed to the fact that Christian unity was kept constantly in mind during the discussion of each subject." [36] At midmorning council breaks, animated talk between bishops and Protestant scholars went on at the coffee bars, called "Bar-Jonah" (Hebrew for son of John) and "Bar-abbas" (name of the felon freed instead of Jesus), set up under either side of the seating stands in St. Peter's. Those refreshment counters may have altered Christian history.

Out of that council has come a profusion of adjustments which profoundly modify many of the divisive issues and misunderstandings. The full consequences of these still are to be generally realized among ordinary churchgoers. But they stirred searching reappraisals among Protestant scholars.

Karl Barth, widely regarded as Protestantism's greatest contemporary theologian, says that Roman Catholicism may simply "overtake us and place us in the shadows so far as the renewing of the church through the Word and Spirit of the Gospel is concerned. . . . It could very well be possible that we others might find more to learn from the Roman Church than Rome for its part would have to learn from us, as we still assume with undue self-satisfaction." Rome is "making dynamic recovery," he says, and unless Protestantism swings a mighty broom of renewal itself, "we might be left far behind. . . . An exchange of positions and roles is becoming visible today all along the horizon." [37]

The council displayed an aspect of Roman Catholicism unrealized by recent generations—its free and lively community manner of reaching decisions. Although sometimes stalled temporarily by rearguard tactics, a feature of any unshackled representative parliament, the council gradually, step-by-step, reshaped the patterns of the church, remolded outlooks and methods, inaugurated a "new order."

It prescribed a greater stress on the Bible, and more Bible-centered preaching. It overhauled church worship, to make it more an act of the whole congregation, not chiefly of the priest, and authorized expanded use of the people's languages. It enlarged the place of laymen in church services, with related steps contemplated in other spheres. It encouraged more flexibility in the church, repudiating a "rigid uniformity." It shifted tight controls away from the tradition-weighted Curia, and provided for more freedom of territorial episcopal conferences in determining liturgical usages, among other matters.

In its monumental *Constitution on the Church (De Ecclesia)*, the Vatican Council also set a new pattern for collective, or "collegial," church government, balancing out the dogma of "papal infallibility" and declaring that the world-wide episcopate and pope together constitute the "full and supreme" authority over the church. "The head of this body is Christ," the constitution says. It also recognizes the "common priesthood" of lay members, asserting that the entire community of believers share in contributing to the church's understanding, and are guided in faith by God's spirit of truth. Infallibility thus takes on wider connotations, as does the circle of authority and insight. Further moves were in progress to enhance the voice of the laity, and to encourage their initiative and co-responsibility in the church.

All of these actions tended to mitigate old conflicts with Protestantism and Eastern Orthodoxy, and promised greater harmony with them.

"By our attention to the fact of the collegiality of the bishops, we will show the Orthodox that we are thinking along a line that means so much to them," says Leon-Joseph Cardinal Suenens, Archbishop of Malines-Brussels and Primate of Belgium. "By stressing the role of the laity in the church, we will reassure the Protestants that we hold something very dear to them—the sharing of the people in the royal priesthood of Christ." All in all, he added, the shifts not only show greater consideration for Orthodox, Anglicans, and Protestants, but also for Catholics themselves by a "return to the purity of the gospel message." [38]

Even more fundamental, the council refused to endorse Roman Catholicism's long-standing textbook theory of two "sources of revelation," which had regarded church tradition as independent of the Bible. This had been the central conflict in the Protestant Reformation. Developments on both sides have tempered the issue.

The council also declined to single out the Virgin Mary in a special category or to augment her doctrinal status, which would have deepened differences with Protestantism and Orthodoxy, but voted rather to treat her role in subsidiary relations to Christ and his church, relying greatly on the illumination found in Scripture. The concern on this point was indicated in a council address by Archbishop Paul Hallinan of Atlanta. He said:

"To attempt to center our religion in Mary, to exaggerate her cult, to multiply her devotions in such a way that Christ is obscured or forgotten is a blasphemy to the son, an embarrassment to the memory of the mother and a pathetic deviation on the part of the people baptized in Christ."[39] As an upshot of Rome's carefully sensitive approach, numerous Protestant theologians have conceded that their own lack of attention to the place of Mary stands in need of reassessment.

The efforts of both sides at a better, firmer evaluation went unaffected, in the long run, by a temporary, confused furore at the close of the 1964 session over Pope Paul's description of Mary as "mother of the church." Actually, this puts the locale of her work in the human stream, rather than implying a more celestial suzerainty for her, as has been advocated by some Mariologists. Moreover, it was a less striking title than one readily acceptable to Protestants—"mother of Jesus Christ"—mother of one who stands above the church as its source and Lord.

Other mediating steps were in prospect. Roman Catholicism traditionally has taught that it is the "one true church" (which has seemed imperious to other Christians even though intrinsically each also regards his church as the "truest" or else surely he would switch to another), but the council's general tenor on interchurch relations and other matters eased this old irritant to a degree. Roman Catholicism, of course, still regards itself as the "true church," as does Eastern Orthodoxy. But the new Constitution, De Ecclesia, adopted by the Vatican Council's 1964 session, puts greater emphasis on the church's supernatural dimensions, extending beyond juridical lines, and recognizing an authentic zone shared by other baptized Christians. It states that they also are embraced by the Holy Spirit, "for to them, too, he gives his gifts and graces whereby he is operative among them with sanctifying power." The document sees the church as a "people of God," and not just as a structural hierarchy, also a more agreeable note to other churches. "We stand on the threshold of a new era in Catholic ecclesiology," comments Presbyterian Robert McAfee Brown, a council observer.[40]

Christianity's innate ties with Judaism also were being more vigorously affirmed, in Protestantism and Orthodoxy as well as in Roman Catholicism. This deep bond had flamed anew in the Nazi holocaust when rabbis, priests, and ministers shared imprisonment and death. It has strengthened since.

"I am Joseph, your brother," the late Pope John said when receiving a group of Jewish visitors. And he laundered out some old defamatory references to Jews in the church's liturgical books.

Vatican II approved a clear-cut declaration of the church's foundation in Judaism and of Christianity's place as a branch on the Jewish tree through which redemption came. The section points out that Christians, like Jews, are spiritually sons of Abraham, that Jesus, his mother, his apostles, and the earliest Christians were all Jews, and that Christ died because of the collective sin of humanity, not just one segment of it.

This is standard Christian teaching, but its sharp delineation hits at perversions of the faith blaming Jews for Christ's crucifixion. Actually, Jews then were his only followers, and the Roman execution, abetted by a collaborationist Sadducean party and carried out by foreign occupation troops, was carefully timed to avoid an uprising of the masses. So, as Scripture points out, was the arrest and trial. Such details aside, Christianity's entire theology rests on the premise that Christ died on account of the sin of all men at all times—not just a few, at one time. Yet the event has been twisted, by individuals and governments, to engender persecution of Jews. Rome, like other churches, acted to strike down forcefully this anti-Semitic distortion, and to underscore Christianity's basic kinship to Judaism, and the blessings inherited from it. This the Vatican Council did in an historic declaration, approved at its fourth session in 1965, denying collective Jewish responsibility for the crucifixion and deploring "displays of anti-Semiticism directed against Jews at any time and by anyone."

Closer accord also grew apace in other fields. Studies were under way for modified approaches to birth control and mixed marriages. Pope John, and later Pope Paul, put the highest office of their church on record for religious liberty for all men, of whatever faith, everywhere, as a prelude to such action at the Vatican Council's fourth session in 1965, despite a technical snag at the end of the third. Roman Catholicism previously had not taken a definitive stand on the matter, which has been a cause of tension with Protestants and other groups. Now the problem receded.

An array of other possibilities was in the offing as Vatican II moved through its sessions of 1962, 1963, 1964 and 1965, haltingly at times, flashing at moments with lofty oratory and sharp debate, intermittently snagged by procedural intricacies, old-school contraventions, and redrafting delays, yet progressively charting a course that gave new thrust and tone to the church.

It involved a move away "from old forms, from confusing terminology, from customs and habits which have long since become anachronisms," says Bishop John K. Mussio of Steubenville, Ohio.[41] Years would be required before all of the revised norms could be translated into canon law, and fully implemented among the parishes and schools of Catholics around the world. Yet the results already reverberated widely. "Old textbooks and old teaching methods will go," observed Vice-rector Robert F. Coerver of the Roman Catholic Kenrick Seminary in Missouri.[42]

Protestantism also felt the impact. Rome has undertaken a "work of emancipation and resulting reanimation," says Henry Pitt Van Dusen, the keenly analytical President Emeritus of New York's interdenominational Union Theological Seminary. "One may safely forecast that the Roman Catholic Church-in-the-world will present a quite new reality, demanding of Protestants radically altered attitudes."[43]

What had compelled such reconsiderations? What had brought it about? What had kindled this glow, these fertile fires in the Roman Catholic Church? Whence came this sudden commotion, this moving about, this prodigious fraternal awakening? No one can say with exactitude at this point. A "new Pentecost," Pope John had hoped for. Pentecost was the strange and electrifying moment fifty days after Christ's crucifixion when a rushing Spirit like the wind, like tendrils of fire, had swept the bewildered, immobilized apostles, and sent them boldly forth to proclaim the gospel in transformed terms that every man, and all the world, could understand. It was the day when their hesitations, their fears and inertia left them, when they quit their cramped refuge, their anxious isolation, and moved forward into the thick and tumble of life, embracing it, caring about it, serving it.

They had arisen from their torpor and gone to work.

None of them knew then what the eventual results would be, what fates would befall them, what spiritual rivers they would loose on the earth. And no one now can gauge precisely the ultimate import or magnitude of the dynamism stirring in Roman Catholicism and the rest of the Christian domain.

Yet, whatever the outcome, the traditionalist, time-entrenched See of Peter had shaken off its static reserve. It moved. It advanced. It looked outward in its quest. It emerged from its ramparts and offered its goods confidently, amid others, in the broad commune of faith. The pope, regarded as Peter's successor, and the world-wide company of bishops, considered successors of the other apostles, had stepped forth from their sequestered bourns. They walked and talked with their Christian brethren, their fellow men, their implacably confluent world. Like the apostles of old, they had left their cautious retreat. They had arisen, set to work, turning attention to that diaspora con-

sidered alien in the past, that all at once seemed hardly so at all. And
visitors "from every nation under heaven . . . were amazed and wondered,
saying, '. . . we hear them telling in our own tongues the mighty works
of God.' "[44]

Somehow, in the new voices and timbre of these times, the separate
groups, the dedicatedly different groups, which once looked askance
at others, which regarded them with distrust or aversion, or regarded
them not at all, and which found nothing about them intelligible,
had suddenly begun to understand, not entirely, but a little, and more
and more. The Protestant observers at the Vatican Council had that
experience. They caught the rhythms and reasons of Rome. And the
bishops, in turn, also began to discern, to see the Protestant premises,
to grasp the nuances. And often, somewhat surprisingly, the two tendencies
seemed less clashing than complementary.

This, too, was an offspring of that peculiar current, that still
incalculable movement that has risen throughout Protestantism, and
which now struck forcefully in Rome. Ecumenicity, a phenomenon
which is as multisyllabic as it is multiform, has several definitions and
varied connotations, but as Roman Catholicism's pioneering, great
American ecumenist, the late Gustave Weigel, once put it, the thing
can't really be defined at all. "You cannot grab the wind as it passes,"
he said. "What we see happening is something altogether new and
something we believe is of the Holy Spirit."

Whatever its source, it had two powerful outlets, men who bore the
names of the beloved and large-hearted apostle, John, and of the
astute and far-traveling apostle, Paul.

CHAPTER 2

The Responsive Popes

On the first occasion, the host was a short, blocky man who circulated among his guests with an appreciative smile and open gestures of affection. "If you could read my heart," Pope John XXIII told Protestant and Orthodox representatives, "you would perhaps understand much more than words can say."

It was a sentimental, yet determinative evening. It set a style that led to sequels.

When it happened again, the host was a lean, tense man with banked fires of anguish, tenacity, and tenderness in his eyes. Pope Paul VI, mingling with delegates from other churches, said he wanted to receive them "not only at the threshold of our home, but in the very intimacy of our heart."

The speakers differed, yet how alike their words.

Between the times, by death's intervention, the householder at these historically new and hospitable gatherings had changed, even as the practice had barely begun. A different man, a different pope presided. Yet the same spirit.

What Pope John had started, overruling the protocol that would have detracted from it, Pope Paul continued, adding some egalitarian measures of his own. In a personal way, they invited interdenominational companionship, on a Christian-to-Christian level.

John illustrated with a chair.

Paul did it with a simple prayer.

The episodes in themselves produced no specific conclusions, no plans nor pacts, and were not intended to do so. Yet they displayed in a personalized way the moderating outlook in Rome. They dramatized it at one key point, among many. They also shed a light on two men —the receptive popes, the popes who have opened their church to folds beyond its own.

Conventional restraints slid away in those brief interludes. Neither lasted more than an hour, yet already they have spread their imprint and manner through the Christian landscape, tracing lines in the future. The first took place on a memorable October 13, 1962. Never before had a pope sat down in direct confrontation with such a wide cross-section of Christianity, including representatives from most major Protestant churches.

Those present will scarcely forget the quiet of that autumn evening, the curiosity and suspense on the faces of the assorted churchmen as they moved through the labyrinthine recesses of the Vatican; the muted conversation, the shuffle of footsteps on marble floors, the keen sense of an unprecedented moment in the making.

The place, the persons, the hour of day gave a tenuous dreamlike aura to the occasion. Across a stone courtyard, tinted in the reds of twilight, came two bearded Russian Orthodox prelates, sheathed in black. Rounding the corner of an arched passageway appeared two French Protestant monks in snow-white mantles, dark-suited American and European theologians, church officials in cassocks and academic gowns. Lutherans, Presbyterians, Methodists, Congregationalists, Anglicans, Baptists, Orthodox prelates from Egypt and Syria, a Dutch "Old Catholic" whose church split from Rome because of the 1870 declaration of "papal infallibility" on doctrine in specific, extraordinary pronouncements. Gradually, the company converged toward an upper room, their voices low, their glances alert and speculative.

Through the cool corridors they moved, up curving stairs, past niches, friezes, graven doors. Alone, in pairs, in clusters, they filed along, between the shadowy pillars, past statues whose silence breathed of antiquity, across softly lighted Clementine Hall, adorned with murals on walls and ceilings. There, finally, the stillness was broken by the snap of martial commands and the clatter of boots as a squad of Swiss Guards came to attention.

Augustin Cardinal Bea, that wafer-thin old champion of Biblical research, religious liberty, and Christian unity, arrived last, smiling, his head erect above his hunched shoulders, a great scarlet *cappa magna* billowing behind him. One at a time, then, the forty-nine delegate-observers at the Vatican Council were ushered into Consistorial Hall. Bea announced each of them as they entered.

The hall adjoining the papal apartments is one of the Vatican's most beautiful, laid with Oriental carpeting and decorated around and above with Renaissance art, ingeniously lighted by concealed fixtures. Pope John stood at the front, nodding and repeatedly raising a hand in welcome as the guests took their places around a circle of chairs.

It was an acute moment, packed with the cumulative tensions of the past and the swift transmutations of the present. Here, face-to-face with the reigning head of Roman Catholicism, stood the official deputations of those whom the church once lumped in a general classification as "rebels, heretics, apostates, schismatics, and infidels." They, in turn, looked upon the holder of an office which their spiritual forebears had in times past decried as the "murderous pope," the "anti-Christ."

Now they met intimately. "We are very happy to present such an outstanding number of delegate-observers," Cardinal Bea said, "our brethren in the name of Christ."

Once the formal introductions were completed, the rotund, beaming man at the front of the room dispensed with punctilio, and plunged into a buoyant round of individual greetings—a habit of his. Exuberant, pleased, taking his time, he rotated from man to man, chatting with each of them, clasping their hands, patting a shoulder, trading light talk about background and ideas. Laughter interspersed the conversation—laughter and a warmth that gave that regal room a glow brighter than all its masterly lighting and ornamentation.

Then the group sat down.

A throne, upholstered in red damask, stood on a raised dais at the front for the Pope, a mark of his sovereignty over the church. Such symbols and accouterments are an immemorial device of exalted office, of kings and generals and judges, setting the officeholder apart from other men.

But Pope John did not want that. He was a minister among ministers. He turned away from the throne and took an ordinary chair like the rest. That action itself symbolized the readiness to meet others on equal terms.

"May God bless you each and every one," he said.

He sat there, in white cassock and skullcap, a short, corpulent man, with a large, bald head, big ears, a wide nose, and small eyes which shone with an inner grace his body lacked; a kindliness, a brimming love of life. Once, musing about the inelegant physical attributes he brought to the papacy, he remarked, "A conclave is no beauty contest, you know." Now this homely, dumpy old prelate gazed around with the pleasure of newly found friendships.

An aide handed him a manuscript. He held it, not looking at it immediately, as if pausing to drink in more fully his situation there, shoulder-to-shoulder with representatives of most other major church bodies of the world. It was a rare milestone. Only four other newsmen besides myself had been admitted. You could sense, there in that radiant room, a general gratification, an air of relief that an old barrier had come down. A pope had met Protestants and others personally and in force for the first time. And stiffness had melted. Qualms had retreated. The descendants of one-time intransigent foes had looked directly into each other's eyes, and seen mutual esteem and interest. And they were glad.

"The first word which rises up in my heart," the Pope said, "is the prayer taken from the sixty-seventh Psalm, which has a lesson for us all: Blessed be the Lord now and ever, the God who bears our burdens and wins us the victory." He fingered his manuscript, adjusted his glasses, and then went on in an intimately retrospective vein. He recalled events that had brought him to the See of Peter, and his own feelings about it, at the time, that God "carries us, what we are and what we possess; with his treasure in us and with our miseries."

He described the "great emotion" that had moved him in his decision to summon the Vatican Council, and said that, at its opening, from time to time as "my glance rested upon your group, on each of you personally, I drew a special comfort from your presence. I will not say more about that at the moment. . . ." Then he let the papers rest on his knees, and cocking his head to one side, as he characteristically did in moments of fond feelings, he looked about at his guests. "Yet, if you could read my heart, you would perhaps understand much more than words can say."

In plain phrases, using the ordinary "I" instead of the papal "we," he spoke of his thirty years as a Vatican diplomat—ten years in Bulgaria, another ten in Turkey and Greece, and ten more as nuncio in Paris. During those years, he said, he frequently met "with Christians of many different denominations. I cannot remember any occasion on which we were divided on principle nor that there was ever any disagreement on the plane of charity in the common work of helping those in need . . . we did not haggle, we talked together."

And that is part of the fertile chemistry which this farm-reared prelate, who never lost the simple, pragmatic directness of his origins, plowed into the barren soil between Christians. He got them talking. Yet he was not just a benign, gregarious mixer, who prompted easy conversation, although he certainly did that with everyone from premiers to prison inmates. But he also had a courage and shrewdness that guided his bounteous good will. He once said that while he was chronically optimistic about people and events, "I have one eye open to see clearly."

That weather-wise eye gave force and competence to his heart. It enabled him to bypass the age-entrenched routines, restraints, and mechanisms which bound the Vatican, and to call in the church's far-flung forces of renovation. Pope John had that natural gift which no school can teach and which seems so often to inhere in men of rural background—common sense.

He reinforced it with a discerning scholarship, one that illumined the fundamental issues, uncluttered by trivia. He saw the paramount human problems, the critical facts of a revolutionary world in which no nation, or church, could live in insulation. His monumental encyclicals, *Mater et Magistra* (Mother and Teacher) in 1961, and *Pacem in Terris* (Peace on Earth) in 1963, released a reverberating summons to relate Christianity positively to the modern technological age and its intellectual currents, not for the church's special interest, but in service to human well-being and peace as things good in themselves.

In those documents, he sounded a bold and penetrating call to mutual responsibility between industrialists and workers, between the affluent and the hungry, between advanced and underdeveloped societies, between races, political structures, and religions. He recognized values in diverse economic and governing systems, both in private property and in socialization for public welfare, in free initiative and also in social security, health and old-age insurance, fair wage minimums. He maintained that human progress could come through various avenues without any one of them seeking domination.

He sought reconciliation between the world's contending poles of power and function, a collaboration of community with community, religion with religion, labor with management, nation with nation; of combined dedication to lifting the burdens of poverty, injustice, misery, and oppression. He upheld the equal rights of persons, whatever their religion, sex, race, or nationality, and he ringingly defended religious liberty: the freedom of conscience and worship.

He refused to align himself with the rigid blocs of the cold war and the flat portrayals of an evil East and virtuous West, saying that even social movements containing "false philosophical teachings" are subject to profound evolutionary change. He pleaded for an end of the arms race and the building up of a world "public authority," with the United Nations becoming "more equal to the magnitude and nobility of its task" in preserving justice and peace.

Always before, encyclicals have been addressed only to Roman Catholics. But Pope John, unwilling to stay within parochial limits, addressed *Pacem in Terris* to everyone, everywhere. It was acclaimed from Washington to Moscow, and by Protestant, Jewish, and Catholic groups.

Action went with the Pope's words. In keeping with his concept of a deepeningly interwoven civilization, he strove to bring the church into contact with all parts of it, the Christian kin and the secular stranger and sciences, the friendly and hostile, including the Communist East. He abandoned the ironclad militancy of his predecessor, the austere and aristocratic Pius XII, toward Communist governments, and instituted delicate negotiations with them, seeking accommodations for the church to function more fully in Soviet areas —in Poland, Czechoslovakia, Hungary, and elsewhere. He established cordial exchanges with the Russian Orthodox Church, the first such links in history. These were augmented by Pope Paul.

As Pope John interpreted his faith, it was no hothouse plant. It belonged in the midst of the world, involved with life as it is today, with all its compressed, varied, and contending complexities. It was a theme that found an astonishingly similar and amplified continuation in Pope Paul.

For the church to endure and become a "living leaven" in contemporary society, Paul said, it must shed its archaic encrustations and approach others. Otherwise, it is "useless for the priest to ring his bell. Nobody will listen." He says the church must "hear the sirens sounding from the factories" and understand "those temples of technical achievement where the modern world lives and breathes." [1]

The attitude of the two popes, one succeeding the other in this millenial century's third quarter, formed a merged stream, unleashed by John, finding its course, being tapped and harnessed by Paul.

It accepted the inevitable differences in gifts and capacities among men and among Christians, and perceived in them a communal thread, a mandate to "live in communion with one another," as John put it. He was hopeful. "In the present order of things, Divine Providence is leading us to a new order of human relations, which by men's own efforts and even beyond their very expectations, are directed towards the fulfillment of God's superior and inscrutable designs. Everything, even human differences, leads to the greater good of the church. [2]

In particular, Pope John reasoned that differences among Christians should not fence them apart. In his first encyclical as pope in 1959, he served notice on other Christians: "We address you as brothers." The designation, with all it implied, took flourishing root. He (as Pope Paul did later) praised the growing Protestant-Orthodox efforts "to rebuild that visible unity of Christianity which corresponds to the wishes of the Divine Redeemer," and he summoned Roman Catholicism to do its part. [3] He (as did Paul) said doctrine could be better understood and presented. He allowed (as Paul reiterated) that both sides shared faults in causing the separations, and both needed to make amends. "We do not intend to conduct a trial of the past," John declared. "We do not want to prove who was right or wrong. The blame is on both sides. All we want is to say, 'Let us come together. Let us make an end of our division.'" [4]

Beyond his wide-ranging interests, his wisdom and diplomatic lore,

Pope John left an impression on his generation primarily as a man of generous heart. "Good Pope John," he was called. "The people's Pope," a Methodist bishop described him. "He belonged to all Christians." Or as the Italians put it, *un papa simpatico.*

His ways alarmed many of the cautious Curia officials. His irrepressible bonhomie contrasted with the brooding, withdrawn solitude of his predecessor, Pius XII. Too down-to-earth to be swayed by eminence, too sociable to be shut in the Vatican, or to take his meals alone as had been the tradition since 1623 ("I tried to keep the tradition, but it didn't last eight days"), John extended his table, and himself, to others.

When visiting convicts, he told them about a relative who was "caught by the *carabinieri* while hunting without a license and sent to jail for a month." Visiting seminarians, he related that when he was a student, the administrator kept urging "us not to eat too much. Of course, we did not pay attention to him and went on eating." Receiving a group of orphans and war-mutilated children, he wept. "The very young and the very old, they can cry," he said. His compassion, his wit, and his self-effacing geniality are becoming legendary.

In his early days as pope, he warded off tedious questions. "Ask me some other time—I'm not broken in yet." He said he would sometimes awake from troubled dreams, thinking, "I must take that up with the Pope," and then as his head cleared he would realize, "but I am the Pope," and he would sink back on his bed sighing, "I must take that up with the Lord." A light sleeper, and an inveterate walker ("Johnnie Walker," punsters dubbed him), he would often get up at night and pace the floor between bed and study. It bothered him for visitors to kneel before him; he discouraged it but said it was "one of the humiliations we have had to endure." He put up with the papal sedan chair only for crowds to see him better, and told bearers, "You should be paid double for carrying us since we weigh twice as much as Pius the Twelfth." Referring to his World War I days as an army medical corpsman, he told the captain of the papal gendarmes, "Captain, you are a bigger noise than I am, because I was only a sergeant." After a visit with Italy's President, when the Pope dawdled on departure, an impatient aide remarked resignedly, "He will never leave; he wants to say good-bye to every soldier in the President's guard."

He urged, without complete success, that the Vatican newspaper, *L'Osservatore Romano,* drop its papal superlatives such as "the illuminated Holy Father" and "as we gathered from the Supreme Pontiff's august lips." He suggested, "If you would say the Pope has said this, or the Pope has done that, I would certainly prefer it." Breaking with the shut-in habits of his predecessor, he buzzed about Rome and its environs in his black Mercedes, visiting asylums, hospitals, schools, and ailing friends, like a parish pastor. He told Rome's motorcycle-police escorts: "Frankly, I would rather do without you, but you and I are both subject to rules and regulations and must try to make the best of it."

He had a predilection for saying "yes" rather than "no." "Let us say what we are for; rather than what we are against," he said. "We always prefer to underline the things which unite men; and travel with them all the road that can be covered without infringing upon the requirements of justice, nor on the rights of truth."

Projected to the forefront of his church at the age of nearly seventy-seven, surrounded by traditional admonitions and warnings, facing a world beset by tensions and fears, he said: "Cheer up and spread this message around the world."

This was Pope John, the bluff, bustling old man elected on October 28, 1958, as a sort of "stopgap" or "caretaker" pope; expected only to warm the chair of St. Peter until agreement crystallized on a younger man; but who, instead, made his reign the fountainhead of a new epoch in Christianity. He "stands at the end of one era in the life of the church, and at the beginning of another," says Joseph Cardinal Ritter of St. Louis. [5] The World Council of Churches executive, W. A. Visser 't Hooft, says: "He changed the history of Christian relations."

He was the Pope with the peasant's hands, the sunny eyes, the wisdom salted with humor; the Pope whose intuitive quality found truth in experience rather than in abstractions. He was the Pope who dared to consort with the erstwhile "rebels"—the Protestant heirs of Martin Luther, John Calvin, Ulrich Zwingli, John Wesley, and Thomas Cranmer. At the very heart of the papacy, he clasped their hands in friendship, sat and talked with them as "brothers."

At the First Vatican Council, a century ago, a bishop had been criticized for merely mentioning Protestants in a sympathetic way. But John extended to them the hospitality of his house. That gracious evening when he met with them, he paused near the conclusion of his remarks, and looked out at them with fervent resolve, his face pale in the mellow light, shadows underlining his eyes. He said, as if offering a pledge:

"There burns within my heart the intention of working and suffering to hasten the hour when for all men the prayer of Jesus at the Last Supper will have reached its fulfillment." That prayer was that "they all be one."

The Pope then asked God's blessings "upon all of you and all that is yours." And the initial meeting ended. A momentary affair, a courtesy, a single incident—yet a commencement and a promise.

It faced immense obstacles, not the least of which were the flagrant biases and false assumptions that have been generated on both sides: the widespread Protestant fantasies that Roman Catholics worship the Virgin Mary or think priests are the source of forgiveness; the equally general Roman Catholic misconceptions that Protestants deny Christ's guiding action through the church's ministry and think that each man should interpret the Bible to suit himself and "believe whatever he pleases." These and a hundred and one other distortions rankle the Western church scene.

An American expert on comparative doctrine, Douglas Horton, dean emeritus of Harvard Divinity School and a Congregationalist observer at the Vatican Council, told me in an interview in Rome that "many Catholic notions of churches outside the Roman domain and many non-Catholic notions of Rome are sheer mythology, something to be dispelled by contact and more contact."

But the work of clearing the debris, and probing the real causes, has begun. Its Roman Catholic dynamism came through the preeminent act of John's career—the calling of Vatican II, the world-wide council of bishops.

No council had been held for ninety-two years, since Vatican I in 1870, and its definition of "papal infallibility" had left the general impression that no more councils would be held, that the pope and his Vatican bureaus alone ruled, without church-wide assemblies. But Pope John shattered that assumption: the church was no monarchy. Catholic scholars promptly began pointing out that Vatican I, interrupted by the seizure of Rome by Italian nationalists, did not get to finish its intended plan to square papal authority with that of the rest of the bishops and the whole church.

This would temper the issue with Protestantism and Orthodoxy, even though it would not resolve it entirely or at once. But it offered a start.

Pope John said the idea for a council came to him like "the sound of a bell," so suddenly that "to tell about it seems unreal." Shortly after his coronation, he was talking to the late Domenico Cardinal Tardini, then papal Secretary of State, about the threatening antagonisms of the world; its yearning for peace, yet its simultaneous rending dichotomies between East and West; abundance and hunger; "blacks" and "whites"; new nations challenging old orders; dazzling technology obscuring sensitivity to the supernatural; Christian vying against Christian, with many theologians even speaking of a "post-Christian age."

"Our soul," John relates, "was suddenly enlightened by a great idea that occurred to us at that moment and which we received with indescribable trust in the Divine Master. One solemn and binding word came to our lips. Our voice formulated it for the first time—a council." [6]

The decision hit like a thunderclap in the ranks of the Roman Curia, that powerful apparatus of supreme courts and cabinets, developed over the centuries to judge and direct the entire church and prevent deviations from centrally fixed policies. Pope John himself told of the stunned reactions when he announced the plan on January 25, 1959, to a group of eighteen Curia cardinals at the Monastery of St. Paul's Outside-the-Walls. "It was human to believe that, after hearing the speech, the cardinals would surround us to express their approval and good wishes. But there was instead an impressive and devout silence." [7] With sly irony, the Pope added that some of the cardinals a few days later came to him individually with explanations that they had been so moved that they could not find words to express themselves.

That initial shocked silence, however, was only a foretaste of the inner-Vatican opposition to reforms projected by the council—a condition which later provoked Pope Paul into ordering changes in the Curia. Complaints also erupted on the council floor of attempted obstruction by standpat Curia traditionalists, led by Alfredo Cardinal Ottaviani, Secretary of the Holy Office, which rules on matters of doctrine, morals, censorship, and heresy.

Long before, however, the resistance showed up in various ways. The Vatican newspaper, *L'Osservatore Romano,* did not report Pope John's announcement of the council in its next issue, and in the following one, tucked the announcement in between two lesser items. Another semiofficial Vatican publication, the bimonthly *Civilta Cattolica,* did not mention the council announcement for four months. For some reason, too, Rome's bookstores failed to stock the leading reform-minded books prior to the council or during its beginning period.

"I'm in the bag here," Pope John reportedly remarked on one occasion. Of an unnamed Vatican figure, he puzzled, "Sometimes I wonder which of us is pope. I let him talk." [8] He later told bishops at the council of the dismal mood existing among some of his Vatican associates who "see nothing but prevarication and ruin" in modern times, and act as though only the bygone past offered "a full triumph for the Christian idea and life." He added: "We feel we must disagree with these prophets of doom. . . ." [9]

But if some Vatican authorities looked bleakly on the situation,

John and his council had jubilant advance support elsewhere—notably from Giovanni Batista (John Baptist) Montini, Archbishop of Milan, later to be Pope Paul. "A great hope is kindled in the church," he said. "Blessed is he who has made this light of hope shine forth." [10] In three major addresses and in his 1962 Lenten pastoral before the council opened, Montini extolled its possibilities. "We must seek to understand the designs of God, the movement of history, the inspirations of the spirit, the hour of responsibility." [11] Like John, he said the council aimed at "positive reforms" rather than punitive anathemas. "Reform is a perennial effort in the church," he said, to bring "human reality in touch with the divine." [12]

History may some day provide a more detailed picture of the "John-Paul" papal line. But this much is clear: it was an unbroken one. The two men were close. Through the years, they rode some stormy seas together. They shared ideas and co-operated in experimental techniques, which drew Vatican disfavor. They entrusted each other with delicate missions. They made up a church partnership of remarkable facets and far-reaching consequences. They formed a continuum of the church's conciliar age.

John reigned for four years, seven months, and six days, and in the week of pain and hemorrhage before he died on June 3, 1963, at the age of eighty-one, he still prayed, *ut unum sint* (that they all may be one). Then, by the election of the College of Cardinals in conclave on June 21, 1963, the torch passed to a friend and confidant. This was the man who took the name of Paul. He chose it because it signified unity to all Christians. The Apostle Paul was the first-century evangelist who carried Christianity beyond its Jewish confines to the gentiles, beyond its narrow geographical borders to the world. In Christ, the apostle wrote, "all things hold together." [13]

Paul VI became the Pope who literally transported his office beyond the Vatican, beyond Rome, beyond the western hemisphere. He implemented John's yearning for unity with singular and audacious action, by propelling the church into the broad companionship of faith and place.

In physique, upbringing, and demeanor, he differed from his predecessor. John, five-foot-five, weighed 200 pounds; Paul is thin, five-foot-eight, and weighs 154. He has the countenance of an eagle— alert, intense, knowing. His hair is sparse and gray about a high forehead; he has heavy, dark brows; steel-blue eyes; an aquiline nose. The upper lip is thin; the lower one full, above a jutting chin. He has enormous earlobes—which an old Chinese adage regards as a mark of wisdom. But it is his eyes that captivate. In them burn all the realization, hope, and hurt of a lifetime. They can light up with a melting tenderness when he meets a friend or lifts up a child in his arms.

Paul is not casual as John was; yet his consistent and earnest demonstrations of friendliness seem enhanced by his very intensity. It is as if he has a restlessly acute sense of his surroundings, of himself, and of others, so that when he converses with someone, he sees them utterly, hears them utterly, and speaks with words weighed and meant. At the same time, while immersed in the moment, that other introspective quality seems to allow him to stand back and evaluate it all, including himself, to feel both the mutuality and lack of it, the goal and the elusiveness which compound all human relationships.

Paul, like no other pope before him, has pressed out of the tight Vatican ambit to associate first-hand with neighbors distant, as well as near.

To do this, he traveled far and he widened the papal portals. He made known the principle of his acts: "Let the world know this: The church looks at the world with profound understanding, with sincere admiration, and with the sincere intention not of conquering it, but of serving it; not of despising it, but of appreciating it; not of condemning it, but of strengthening it and saving it." [14]

Paul wanted no altitudinal church, looking haughtily down on the rest of humanity; he wanted it in the veins and fiber of these days on earth. And he espoused with fervor the cause that had flared in John— unity among Christians. "We open our arms to all those who glory in the name of Christ," Paul said in his first discourse as pope. "We call them with the sweet name of brothers." [15]

This cementing term has become so common so quickly that it almost obscures just how radically new it is; it was virtually unheard-of in public usage until John and the warming wave he brought with him. He generally used "separated brethren"; Paul went further and dropped the qualifier. The term has deep theological connotations, expressing the bond formed through baptism. And it is the word, more than any other, which has labeled the Roman Catholic shift away from exclusivism.

As on many other occasions, Paul used the salutation on October 17, 1963, when he first met with Protestant and Orthodox delegate-observers at the second session of Vatican II. "Dear brothers in Christ," he addressed them. Again it was a warm, comradely meeting. But this time it went into a deeper give-and-take analysis of objectives and prospects.

The Pope greeted his guests cordially at the door of his library, shaking hands with each of them. Sixty-six were present, compared to the forty-nine of the previous visit. Once more, Cardinal Bea, the doughty old mediator between Rome and Protestantism, introduced the various church representatives. They took seats in an oval of chairs, the Pope along with them.

He said he wanted to welcome them not only in his home but in the "very intimacy of our hearts." It is obvious, he said, that the different Christian communities should get acquainted with one another. "But here there is yet more: to listen to each other, to pray for one another, and after such long years of separation, after such distressing controversy, to begin again loving each other."

Danish Lutheran K. E. Skysdsgaard, a Protestant specialist on Roman Catholicism and organizer of a new Lutheran World Federation research bureau on the subject, told the Pope: "We find ourselves meeting together at the beginning of a road whose end God alone knows. It is for us to walk together in hope because we believe that the crucified and risen Christ is with us on the way." Acting as spokesman for Protestant delegates, he said "much will be required of all of us along this road"—patience, humility, selflessness. "Above all, no divisions can prevent us from loving each other because Christ's love knows no limits. In this love of Christ, we must seek and find the truth."

He complimented Pope Paul for his "sober and realistic" approach to the task, in contrast to the naively "superficial ecumenism" which assumes that "visible union of Christians can be quickly achieved." He added: "It is for us a real relief to know that Your Holiness does not share this opinion." He said Protestants "rejoice wholeheartedly" at Roman Catholicism's "new ecumenical spirit" and are grateful to the Pope and his predecessor for engendering the new "twofold openness to the ecumenical dialogue in truth and love, and openness to the world in humility and service." Christians, he said, are now "walking together, but our path leads us also out of ourselves towards our fellow men."

Pope Paul responded that he agreed fully that "miraculous and immediate solutions" could not be expected. "The fruit for which we hope must mature slowly, by study and prayer. Reconciliations which are only apparent or improvised and which cover up the difficulties instead of resolving them, far from being of any help, rather, retard our advance." However, he said, there are "indications of real progress." He cited Skysdsgaard's remark, "We are together on the way," and added: "We have not yet reached our destination." He said the Roman Catholic Church welcomes the mutual search for common ground in Christ and, rather than standing still, seeks to draw ever deeper into his light. "One must strive ceaselessly to deepen that divine truth so better to possess it and to live it more fully," he said. He added forcefully:

"A true Christian is a stranger to immobility. . . . Let us all give and seek forgiveness."

Conferring there with these one-time aliens and strangers, the Pope spoke with a fraternal warmth and earnestness. Although he sometimes has been portrayed as a spartan intellectual, reserved and efficient, such descriptions miss the compelling, almost plaintive appeal in the man. Fervent emotions burn in him, impulses which have on more than one occasion led him to get down on his knees and kiss the earth, to quit a formal entourage and embrace a humble bystander, to stretch out his hand in friendship to groups of jeering Communist workers in Milan's Sesto San Giovanni (Little Stalingrad) district, to eat with orphan children in the slums of Bombay, to caress a youngster's brown cheek.

He is, of course, a cerebral man, a reader, a thinker. When he moved into the papal apartments he brought ninety cases of books with him. His own published works run to about thirty volumes. He is swiftly, smoothly articulate when using a typewriter or when speaking extemporaneously in French, English, Latin, or Italian. With less facility, he also can handle German, Polish, and Spanish. But intellect notwithstanding, Pope Paul also cares. He sympathizes.

Those who met with him in his huge library knew that. "The esteem which we have for you personally and for the institutions and the Christian values which you represent make easy for us the task of approaching with you in the great dialogue," he said.

Considering his small frame, Pope Paul has a surprisingly powerful voice, but he did not orate. He conversed. "We prefer now to fix our attention on what shall be, rather than on what has been. We are concerned with the birth of something new, the realization of a dream." He quoted St. Paul the Apostle: " 'Forgetting what lies behind and straining forward to what lies ahead, I press on toward the goal. . . .' "[16] At the close of his remarks, he looked about at his guests, the gray-blue embers of his eyes alight with a blend of melancholy and resolve. And again he used words of the apostle whose name he had taken. " 'The grace of the Lord Jesus be with you. My love be with you all in Christ Jesus.' "[17]

What happened next had not been expected by anyone else, and perhaps not even by him. But suddenly he stood and suggested that they all pray together the "Our Father." The circle of Baptists,

Presbyterians, Methodists, Orthodox, Episcopalians, Lutherans, and others arose and, in unison with the Pope, gave the enduring prayer which Jesus taught his followers. ". . . thy kingdom come, thy will be done, on earth as it is in heaven. . . . Forgive us our trespasses, as we forgive others. . . ." They spoke in different languages, but with one heart. "Amen."

Again, at the start of the 1964 Council session, Pope Paul met with the Protestant-Orthodox observers, the numbers of them by then increased to seventy-two from around the earth. As before, he did not simply lecture them, but engaged in give-and-take discussion. He noted "a spiritual growing together that was formerly unknown to us. A new method has been born, a hope has been kindled, a movement is under way." The group joined not only in the "Our Father" but also in invocations from the Anglican *Book of Common Prayer.*

To a fellowship inaugurated by John, Paul had added specific discussion—and common prayer. The spirit was the same; the method was more direct and to the point. This, in part, distinguishes the two men.

Both came from the plains of Lombardy, the vineyard and wheat region at the foot of the Alps in northern Italy. The village of Concesio (near Brescia where Giovanni Montini was born in 1897) is thirty-five miles from Sotto il Monte (Under the Mountain), birthplace of Angelo Roncalli in 1881. Roncalli was one of twelve children of a tenant farmer; Montini's family, including two brothers (one now a doctor, the other a lawyer), was headed by a well-to-do editor, attorney, and member of the Chamber of Deputies. As a boy, Roncalli was healthy, hard-working. Montini was a frail and sickly youngster who got most of his education from a private tutor. After his ordination, he was assigned to the Vatican Secretariat of State in 1923 as a *minutante* (document writer). Roncalli by then was a veteran church diplomat in the Middle East.

In that period, Montini also was spiritual advisor to Rome's Catholic Student Federation, which he kept going in defiance of attempts by the new Fascist government to suppress it. After student headquarters and clubrooms were smashed, he sometimes held meetings in the catacombs of St. Calixtus on the Appian Way, with candles for light.

But it was in the sequestered officialdom of the Vatican that he labored long—for thirty years as a desk man. He became known for his quick, knowledgeable competence, and eventually rose to the position of Pro-secretary of State for Ordinary Affairs under the exacting Pius XII. In his job, Montini came to admire Roncalli, and was considered instrumental in getting him transferred to Paris as nuncio at the end of World War II. Then began an odd series of events.

Many accounts state that Montini lost favor with Pius XII because of his vigorous support of the postwar worker-priest movement in France and for wanting a more flexible strategy for churches behind the Iron Curtain. Such views may have strained the ties with Pius, who in a 1950 encyclical warned against "lovers of novelty." Roncalli and French prelates with whom Montini sympathized also backed the project for priest-workers in factories. But the venture had been suspect from the start in dominant Vatican circles, and it reputedly acquired leftist tendencies which sealed its doom so far as Pius XII was concerned. (However, it has regained vitality under Popes John and Paul, and as of early 1965, France had 350 Roman Catholic worker-priests, with seventy seminarians in training to serve in that field.)

Shortly before phase-out restrictions were clamped on it in 1953, Pope Pius told a consistory for new cardinals that he had wanted to make Montini a cardinal, but the able monsignor turned it down out of his "sense of duty." That same year, Roncalli was shifted to the See of Venice as patriarch, where his first visitor was Montini. Within months, Montini was eased out of the Vatican center of power and made Archbishop of Milan. "Kicked upstairs," some Catholic commentators asserted.

Motives, however, must remain suppositional; only the events are known. The bourgeois Montini, a disciple of the aristocratic Pius and friend of the peasant Roncalli, was sent back to his home territory. He was in tears as he bade farewell to associates. Arriving in Milan on a winter day of sleet and rain, he stepped from his car, dropped to his knees, and pressed his lips to the muddy earth.

In industrial Milan, Montini pursued his penchant for experimental methods—preaching in the streets; visiting jails, hospitals, factories; donning a miner's cap to go down into the pits. In a motorcycle plant, while he was shaking hands with a line of workers, one with a grease-blackened palm suddenly withdrew it. Montini grabbed it anyway. "Be proud of the mark of your labor," he said. Communist workers at first scoffed but came to respect this bishop who could take it, who still came to visit and to listen to their grievances. Montini also sponsored meetings between Catholic and Protestant pastors—a bold innovation in those days.

Although Milan's archdiocese, the largest in Italy, customarily is headed by a cardinal, Montini did not become one until five years later—after the death of Pius XII. When Roncalli became pope, the first red hat he conferred went to his friend Montini.

They had visited each other frequently, and the close alliance continued during John's pontificate. When Montini, as representative of the Pope, received French Premier Charles de Gaulle in 1959, the French press labeled him *le dauphin de Jean*—John's crown prince. In 1960, Montini undertook a mission to the United States presumably to assure American Catholic leaders that a *L'Osservatore Romano* editorial saying the church had a duty to guide Catholics in political matters had no application to the American elections or to the fortunes of John F. Kennedy. In 1962, the Pope sent Montini on a fence-mending tour of new nations in Africa. He traveled a thousand miles by jeep over bumpy roads in Rhodesia, Nigeria, Ghana, and South Africa; rode a canoe down the Niger; listened to drums relaying the word of his coming; worshiped in dirt-floor churches; and ate with tribesmen from a cloth spread on the ground.

When the Vatican Council opened on October 11, 1962, Montini, of all the council fathers, moved in as the guest of Pope John at the Vatican. He reportedly had helped compose John's keynote address to the council, with its stout call for change. In line with John's desire for "free discussion for the good of a free assembly," Montini was said to have privately visited many bishops, accustomed to direction by the Curia, and advised them, "Speak freely, without fear." [18] And these bishops, who had considered Rome the sole source of authority, discovered that they, too, constituted a part of the church's leadership in this new atmosphere.

Montini stayed largely in the background during the first session, reportedly on the advice of John, so as not to upset Montini's chances of becoming his, John's, successor.[19] However, Montini did intervene sharply at one point to criticize a schema as intransigent, incomplete, lacking in ecumenical perspective, and failing to recognize that the church was guided by the whole episcopate and not by the absolute authority of the pope. The draft, sent back for revision, had been prepared by a commission headed by the Holy Office's Cardinal Ottaviani.

As John lay dying, it was Montini who brought the Pope's sister and two brothers to his bedside.

Then, in that fluid interval before the conclave, when it is considered hazardous for anyone considered *papabile* (likely to be elected pope) to commit himself to a definite platform, Montini cast politic discretions aside and made his position crystal clear—the church should "follow the path" set by John. "Death cannot stifle the spirit which he so infused in our era." [20]

However, that course had influential opponents among the cardinals, and it was in the balance. Montini's pre-conclave speaking out for it "was not too popular a thing for him to do," notes Joseph Cardinal Ritter of St. Louis, "because we know that some people thought Pope John was somewhat hasty—an old man who wanted to get things done in a hurry." [21] But it let Montini's fellow cardinals know just where he stood—in advance. The barely begun Vatican Council, automatically suspended by the Pope's death, would not be resumed unless the new Pope reconstituted it. Montini, the Vatican veteran trained by Pius, inspired by John, and elected Pope on June 21, promptly did so.

A revitalizing spiritual lineage went on. Paul not only perpetuated the reforming vigor of his predecessor, but added to the task his special forte for precision and getting down to cases. "He's more progressive than Pope John," said Francis X. Murphy, American Redemptorist priest and noted church historian. Paul also is "more familiar with ecclesiastical procedures and . . . how to get things done." [22] While he continues the spirit, he is his own man in manner, methods, and businesslike proficiency. Three months after his election, he called together members of the Roman Curia, the administrative organs of the papacy, and told them changes must be made.

No longer, he said, is Rome the kind of institution which inflamed the Protestant Reformers in the sixteenth century. "Papal Rome today is quite another affair, and by the grace of God, so much worthier, wiser, and holier, so much more aware of its evangelical vocation, so much more . . . susceptible to perennial renewal." But the internal Vatican machinery has lagged behind the times, he said. "That some reforms must be introduced in the Roman Curia is not only easy to foresee, but is much to be desired." [23] He went on to cite specifics.

Overall, it was a startlingly blunt lecture. Historically, popes who have tangled with the Curia have not fared too well themselves.

The *Curia Romana* (Roman Court), together with the Pope, constitute the "Holy See." Made up of twelve executive branches called sacred congregations, three tribunals (ecclesiastical courts), and a score of other offices and commissions, the Curia's intricate, ponderous procedures and elaborate titles trace back to the Middle Ages. Its motto reflects the scope and finality of the authority it has wielded over the church: *Roma locuta est; cause finita est* ("Rome has spoken; the case is closed").

Manned by about one thousand Vatican employees, the Curia's key posts are held by thirty-one cardinals, most of them aging Italians. Some are men insulated against the changing outside world and instilled with the heritage of combatting Protestantism and condemning "secularism" and "modernism." As Pope John said, they glorify the

past centuries of ecclesiastical prestige and temporal power, while re-
coiling from the present.

However, the Curia is not a solid bloc of reaction. Like any large
administrative organization, it includes a wide spectrum of church
viewpoints, as well as some of the finest minds in the Church. Cardinal Bea and his Unity Secretariat staff are part of the Curia. So is the
pungent, socially conscious Eugene Cardinal Tisserant, French-born
dean of the College of Cardinals. But as in most large establishments,
there are sectors grown adamant in their ways. Pope Paul, in his talk
to the Curia, said the process of church renewal meets "resistance on
the part of the center of the church, the Roman Curia," but parts of
that same Curia are in the forefront of reform.

For years the Curia's most powerful figure has been Alfredo Cardinal Ottaviani, who manages the Supreme Sacred Congregation of the
Holy Office. A gentle, gracious man of seventy-five, almost blind, he
fought the reformist tide. One of a long line of *defensores fidei*
schooled in the Counter-Reformation tradition, he says his duty is "to
keep the deposit of faith intact." [24] The motto on his coat-of-arms reads
Semper Idem (Always the Same).

Shaken by the gales loosed by the Vatican Council, he arose in the
beginning of the 1962 session to demand if it planned a revolution. In
the next session, in 1963, his office came under sharp attack on the
floor. Joseph Cardinal Frings, Archbishop of Cologne, West Germany,
said Holy Office procedures "are out of harmony with modern times,
are a source of harm to the faithful and of scandal to those outside
the church." They should be "basically revised," he said. "No Roman
congregation should have authority to accuse, judge, and condemn an
individual who has had no opportunity to defend himself." [25] The bishops broke in with applause, despite a rule against it.

The Holy Office, known as the Inquisition until 1908, sits in judgment on faith and morals, often silencing theological voices deemed
unacceptable. It has operated in complete secrecy, by unpublished
rules, even using fine sand to blot newly inked documents so that revealing traces would not be left on blotters. Formed in 1542 to com-
bat heresy and the rising blaze of Protestantism, it also handled the
Index of Prohibited Books, and ruled on marriage questions. Smarting
under the criticisms, Ottaviani replied that they stemmed from "lack
of knowledge, not to use a stronger term." He said no Catholic
theologians' works are condemned without "thorough investigation." [26]

Some bishops also charged that the council's theological commission, headed by Ottaviani and functioning somewhat like a congressional committee in drafting proposed legislation, had stalled at

shaping measures in keeping with the majority viewpoint of bishops, particularly in regard to broadening and internationalizing church government. Pope Paul enlarged the commission to shift the scales.

While Paul avoided direct, arbitrary interventions in the council's operations (a policy that aroused some complaints at the close of the 1964 session), he repeatedly stressed that the will of its majority would not be circumvented. In his straight talk to Vatican personnel before the council's second session, he laid down some crisp pointers for the Curia. "It will not," he said, "be miserly of functions that bishops today can exercise better themselves locally," nor will it oppose any council action for representation of the world-wide episcopacy in church government. He complimented the Curia for its dedication, loyalty, hard work, and ability, but said it had shown "at times some amazement and apprehension" at the powerful flux of forces working in the church, and added: "We must accept criticisms that surround us with humility and thoughtful gratitude."

Noting that the latest revisions in Curia norms date back to 1588 and 1717, he said it suffered from "venerable old age," with its practices out of step with "needs of the new times." It must "be simplified, decentralized," and purged of regulations "already perishing and superfluous," he said. "Various reforms are therefore necessary." He spelled out some particulars:

"The Roman Curia will not be frightened, for example, to be recruited with larger supranational vision, nor to be educated by a more careful ecumenical preparation. . . . The Roman Curia will not be jealous of temporal prerogatives belonging to other times, nor of external forms no longer fitted to express and impress true and high religious meaning. . . . Therefore, let the Roman Curia not be a bureaucracy, as some have wrongly judged it, pretentious and apathetic, legalistic and ritualistic, a fighting ground of hidden ambitions and deaf antagonisms, as others accuse it of being." But let it serve—in a "sense of collaboration" with the universal church.

The Pope did not scold; he said: "This is the fatherly exhortation." [27]

He named a committee on Curia reorganization, and by early 1965 had drafted a specific set of reforms. These were said to include requirements that heads of the various Curia congregations be under age sixty-five and that more posts of high responsibility be given to non-Italians so as to make the Curia a broadly international organization, implementing decisions of the pope and the world's bishops instead of making them. Other kindred steps to bring widely representative viewpoints to the Vatican administration, such as an interim governing senate or small council to sit regularly, were being considered, with papal encouragement. In February, 1965, twenty-seven more prelates were elevated to the College of Cardinals, increasing it to an all time high of one hundred and three, changing its proportion of Italian cardinals (there are thirty-two of them) to the lowest level ever, thirty-one per cent.

Paul also clarified his stand in other ways. He sent a message of confidence to the Pontifical Biblical Institute, which had faced past opposition to its scientific research into Scriptural background and meanings—work which has sparked a surging "Biblical theology" in Catholicism akin to that in Protestantism. He also halted pressures against some of the church's leading progressive theologians. He told German Jesuit Karl Rahner, who was once forced to leave Rome because of pressure from the Holy Office: "I know your work. I am very happy with it." [28]

In his 1962 pastoral letter discussing the council, the future Pope had drawn from the works of many reform advocates: Hans Küng, Ives Congar, Henri de Lubac. He also quoted approvingly from a convention-jolting book by Jesuit Ricardo Lombardi, *The Council, a Reform in Charity*, which had been denounced by *L'Osservatore Romano* as "rash and unjust," and removed from circulation.

That Paul took a more tolerant, even respectful view of it, indicates the breadth and resilience of this even-tempered Vatican veteran. A family story recalls that once, on noticing that his brother was carrying a copy of one of Jean-Paul Sartre's anti-ecclesiastical books on existentialism, the pope-to-be advised: "You ought to be careful in reading this book—just as I was." [29] The remark reveals the man—judicious, yet inquiring, realistic, ready to examine ideas from wherever they might come.

This was the mark of the responsive popes. They were open in mind, heart, and arms—to creative thought, to other Christians, to fellow bishops, to better understanding and presentation of doctrine, to the East and West, to old and new friends. They heard mankind's sundry voices, and recognized the mixed, conjunctive timbre of the age. They saw its genius and its relentless interrelationships. They felt the glare of the laboratory, the thunder of the rocket. They sensed the demands and drives of a convulsive world. They realized the intertwining relevance of each nation and group. They accepted it, sought to respond to it, to become part of it.

Pope Paul told the assembled bishops: "You have unexpectedly determined to treat no longer of your own limited affairs, but rather those of the world, no longer to conduct a dialogue among yourselves, but rather to be open, one with the world." And this requires, he said, being guided "by love, the most comprehensive and compelling love, by a love which thinks of others even before it thinks of itself— by the universal love of Christ." [30]

In his first encyclical, *Ecclesiam Suam* (Paths of the Church), on August 10, 1964, he said the church must pursue that "dialogue with the world" in all its varied sectors, near and distant, friendly and hostile. "For the lover of truth, discussion is always possible," he said. And: "Nothing but fervent and unselfish love should motivate our dialogue."

The pope is sometimes called "pontiff," an ancient term meaning bridge-builder. And building bridges is an occupation taken up by the new man in the new Rome—bridges across the age-old escarpments of the church to the further reaches of the human community.

And the swiftly risen, special kind of pope went out to meet that larger neighborhood; out of the medieval compound, the closed rooms. The Vatican bars came down, creakily at times, but down they came.

The Acts of the Apostles tells how the Apostle Peter was once chained in prison, with watchful sentries guarding him. But suddenly in his cell "an angel of the Lord appeared, and a light shone in the cell; and he struck Peter on the side and woke him, saying, 'Get up quickly.' And the chains fell off his hands. And the angel said to him, 'Dress yourself and put on your sandals.' And he did so. And he said to him, 'Wrap your mantle around you and follow me.' And he went out and followed him. . . ." [31]

For a long time, the Roman Catholic leader bearing the title of "successor of Peter" had been almost a recluse, a virtual prisoner of the Vatican. But a lamp flamed in those shadowy chambers, a light lifted up by John and grasped by Paul, and they came down from the compartments of marble and mantles, down from the remote balcony where popes were wont to appear. They put on their sandals and their cloaks and they went out to the hospitals and jails, to the workers with black, calloused hands, to the unbeliever in the marketplace. John went a great distance, and the lamp he carried cast a long beam. Paul went farther, over lands and seas where a pope from Rome had never gone before.

Once started, the paths stretched on—and still other shores beckoned.

CHAPTER 3

Interlude in India

"The truth? That is the question." This impromptu remark came from Pope Paul VI at a news conference in India. Somehow it took on special meaning in that ancient land which calmly accepts questioning as the key to the greatest knowing and which finds the fullest truth in deepest mystery. Pope Paul was reminiscing at the time about his father's journalistic career and about a newsman's basic duty to report the truth. Yet in that particular religious atmosphere, his remark seemed to reflect the new, respectful attentiveness of Roman Catholicism to men's differing insights and varying approaches in their search for ultimate reality. Wooden blades of an old-fashioned ceiling fan rotated monotonously above the hot, crowded lounge in Bombay as the Pope spoke spontaneously in English. "Always be faithful to the truth," he was saying. Then he paused and smiled quizzically as he offered his parenthetical aside. " . . . truth? That is the question."

This was the humble, inquiring mood of the man from the West as a visitor in the distant East, where Christianity is only a droplet in an ocean of many age-old Oriental religions, where populations swell almost immeasurably, where poverty glares stark and massive from the worn acres and littered alleyways.

On his four-day trip to Bombay, the seaport "gateway to India," December 2 to 5, 1964, Pope Paul confronted these things, immersed himself in them with unreserved sympathy, and the imprint went deep. "Unforgettable," he said.

It was a strange excursion, surging with poignant incidents, interspersed with surprises, scattering precedents, and swarming, always swarming, with the compressed brown flesh of the people. Never had a pope traveled so far afield, four thousand miles from Rome; never had a pope ventured into Asia's mystic subcontinent with its time-hidden culture, its profound contemplations, its variegated Eastern religions, and its teeming poor. Into these realms Paul VI moved with forthright acts of concern and words of commitment.

"All men are brothers under the fatherhood of divinity," he said after deplaning from an Air India 707 jet at Bombay's Santa Cruz Airport. On first appearing, he placed his palms together beneath his

46

chin in India's *namaste* greeting, and then amid a roar of delight, pumped his pressed hands up and down heartily so the crowd could see. *"Jai Hind!"* he said over the loudspeaker from a red-draped platform. "Hail India!"

Only a few thousand people had been admitted to the terminal area itself, forming an exuberant crescent around the mixed cluster of welcoming dignitaries, their red Moslem fezzes and Gandhi caps bobbing among the prelatial scarlet zuchettos and military headgear. India's diminutive prime minister, Lal Bahadur Shastri, a Hindu, clad in loose white dhoti, and the goateed vice-president, Zakir Hussain, a Moslem, stood among them as a band played the national anthem, *"Jana Gana Mana"* ("The Morning Song of India"), and a woman in a bright sari hung a wreath of red-and-white tuberoses around the Pope's neck. The airport reception, while impressive, was small compared with that which followed.

Once the Pope moved out of the restricted zone, standing in an open-top white Lincoln convertible, he faced a solid landscape of humanity stretching to either skyline, more than a mile wide, rolling across fields and low hills. It clamped against the winding Gorbanda road and Mahin causeway leading toward the city. *"Che cosa!"* the Pope exclaimed. And it was, indeed, an "extraordinary thing!"

The enveloping tide repeatedly brought the Pope's car to a standstill, as foot police jogged ahead, wielding their lead-tipped bamboo *lathis* to beat a car-wide lane between the walls of human beings. *"Jai! Jai!"* the people cried. "Hail! Hail!" More than a million of them banked the thirteen-mile route to downtown Bombay, an unbroken succession of fascinated Indians, of shouting voices, of finery and rags, of lean-legged children and the withered old, of white-garbed nuns and bespangled, barefoot hill women in Gypsy-like *gujarati* dresses and heavy silver necklaces and ankle bands.

The twenty-seven-car motorcade traversed an outlying stretch of shantytowns, huddled dirty-and-burlap hovels from which rose a smelly haze of smoke from cooking fires fueled with dried dung.

I rode with a truckload of photographers preceding the Pope's car. At one point, a low underpass clipped four men off an accompanying truck's sideracks, killing one of them, Shyam Khilanjar, 24-year-old cameraman from *Asia Magazine.*

The route wound on through cluttered open market places, industrial sections, and tenements. People packed rooftops. They filled balconies and alcoves. They stood atop signboards, walls, and parked vehicles, and perched in trees. The Pope kept waving and gazing about in wonderment, as his car rolled on along the side of Malabar

Hill beneath hanging gardens and, farther up, the Tower of Silence where Zoroastrians expose their dead to scavenger birds. The route emerged on the Arabian Sea, and skirted along the coast, dotted with ancient fishing dhows, their high poops and rigging dark against the orange-red sunset.

Ceaselessly, for a slow-moving hour-and-a-half until the Pope reached the house of Bombay's Roman Catholic archbishop, Valerian Cardinal Gracias, throngs packed the way. The welcome exceeded any accorded a foreigner in Indian history, including the vast outpourings which greeted former United States President Eisenhower, Queen Elizabeth of England, and former Soviet Premier Khrushchev. Even Bombay's pro-Communist weekly, *Blitz*, conceded that "this humble pilgrim of God got a reception that surpassed them all."

Why? Why would the non-Christian masses of India display such fervor over the Catholic Pope? Not religious allegiance nor mere curiosity could have caused such exceptional response. It seems a mystery, in a realm of mysteries. *"Darshan,"* an Indian will explain, and smile because he knows the Western mind won't fully understand. The word is hardly translatable into English, but it means something like goodness, blessedness, or nobility which one supposedly gains through being near or even gazing on some great saintly person. And throughout the Pope's visit, whatever the reason, the Eastern multitudes encompassed the *burra guru*—the "great holy man" from the West—with phenomenal numbers and ardor.

Pope Paul had said he was making the trip in the spirit of a man whom he admired, India's great non-violent revolutionist and father of her independence, Mahatma Gandhi. And not since the Mahatma strode the soil of India had its people reacted with such zealous enormity.

Nothing whatever came of threatened protest demonstrations by a small fanatic society, the Mahasabha, a member of which assassinated Gandhi in 1948, and which called the Pope's trip an "invasion" seeking mass conversions among Hindus. The advance fringe opposition simply collapsed, overwhelmed by the surging approval.

Paul VI returned that warmth in striking ways. While the formal occasion of his visit was the Church's thirty-eighth International Eucharistic Congress, he devoted most of his attention to cementing bonds with his new surroundings. On his second day there, he joined in a fraternal, unprecedented meeting with non-Christian leaders. He cited Hindu Scripture, quoted a Hindu prayer and commended its use. "We must come closer together," he told the intimate gathering of Hindu pundits and swamis, Moslem imams, Buddhist bhikkus with shaven heads, bearded Sikhs, Jainists, and Zoroastrian Parsees. Two white-haired old Eastern sages, Hindu Appa Patwardhan and Moslem Jusef Nazmuddin, introduced the various teachers individually to the Pope. After the salutations, they took seats in the convent-school lounge in the rear courtyard of Bombay's Roman Catholic Cathedral.

Gazing about at the Eastern spiritual mentors, garbed variously in white mantles, embroidered tunics, saffron robes, turbans, and tarbooshes, the Pope said: "Are we not all one in this struggle for a better world, in this effort to make available to all people those goods which are needed to fulfill their human destiny and to lead lives worthy of the children of God?"

It was a dramatic personal overture by the head of the Church of Rome to advance its efforts for fuller concourse with men of sundry cultures and creeds. He extolled India's spiritual heritage, calling it "the cradle of great religions, the home of a nation that has sought God with a relentless desire, in deep meditation and silence, and in hymns of fervent prayer." Drawing from those resources, he quoted a prayer from the Hindu *Bhagavad-Gita:* " 'From the unreal lead me to the real; from darkness lead me to light; from death lead me to immortality.' " That prayer, he said, "belongs to our time" and "should rise from every human heart."

Never before had a pope sat down with such a wide representation of non-Christian religions, and Paul VI said: "We must come together with our hearts, in mutual understanding, esteem, and love. We must also begin to work together to build the common future of the human race. We must find concrete and practical ways of organization and co-operation. . . ."

His appeal echoed both recent administrative innovations by the Vatican and the Vatican Council's draft statement on relations with non-Christian religions, as well as the Pope's August, 1964, encyclical, *Paths of the Church.* In it, he urged deepening ties with all monotheists, and voiced esteem for "the moral and spiritual values of non-Christian religions." He wrote: "We desire to join with them in promoting and defending common ideals of religious liberty, human brotherhood, good culture, social welfare, and civil order. . . . We are ready to enter into discussions on these common ideals, and will not fail to take the initiative where our offer of discussion in genuine mutual respect would be well received." Later, in his 1964 Christmas message, the Pope said the Church wants to promote respect "for whatever is true and good in every religion."

Again, in a public gathering in India, he quoted a maxim from the Hindu *Upanishads:* "Truth alone triumphs, not falsehood." The Vatican Council, in the spring of 1964, already had set up a new Secretariat on Non-Christian Religions to implement understanding and liaison with these faiths.

Its limited aim for practical collaboration, however, differs from the broader objective of restoring internal unity with other Christians. In India, where Christians make up only 2.4 per cent of the vast 480 million population, the need for coherence among them takes on particular urgency. Pope Paul also applied himself to this cause.

Meeting with eight leaders of India's major Protestant, Anglican, and Orthodox denominations, he addressed them as "my dear friends in Christ," and voiced thankfulness for the many steps now being taken to repair the divisions among Christians. Such actions by the Vatican Council, he said, "are not to be made in isolation. Rather it is our hope that our efforts can accompany yours, can mingle with yours so that together we can seek out the ways by which Christ's will 'that all may be one' can one day be fully realized." At the end of the meeting, the group rose and together with the Pope recited the Lord's Prayer.

Although India's Christians are proportionately a scanty minority, they nevertheless number about eleven-and-a-half million, and their faith is a deeply indigenous one, tracing its origins there to the foundations of the Church.

Tradition has it that the Apostle Thomas planted the gospel in India in A.D. 52. Consequently, through the centuries, nearly all the divisions of Christianity have reverberated there, not only separating Protestantism and Orthodoxy from Rome, but also rupturing Orthodoxy. A fragment of its tradition, the Syro-Malabar Catholics, adhere to Rome, yet worship more like Orthodoxy's Malankara Syrian Church than like India's Latin Rite Catholics. Other groups also have arisen, such as the Mar Thoma Syrian Orthodox Church, alongside the larger Orthodox body and Protestants of various denominations. Slightly less than half of India's Christians have ties with Rome.

Despite the maze of divisions—and perhaps because of them— however, the circumstances have stimulated trail-blazing reunion undertakings in India, most notably the United Church in South India, a 1947 merger of a million Presbyterians, Anglicans, Methodists, and Congregationalists. Still broader church mergers in India are in preliminary stages.

Throughout the Pope's steady round of conferences, he stressed the value of diversity in Christian customs, declaring that unity requires no regimented sameness. From the huge outdoor altar of the Eucharistic Congress, set up in the center of an eighty-acre oval ringed by tall palms and flamboyant trees, he underlined this point. "Perhaps in the past the idea of legitimate plurality joined with mutual co-operation may have been obscured at times," he told a hundred thousand Christians gathered there. "But today there must be a new dedication to this idea." Past concepts have equated universality with uniformity, he said. But on the contrary, "multiplicity must be recognized, respected, and indeed promoted and vivified."

One purpose of the Pope's trip was to emphasize that the distinctive Christian ways of the East are just as authentically part of the Church as its Western forms. For centuries, Roman Catholicism and the pope, occupied chiefly with the Latin Rite of the West, have left the Eastern Rites somewhat neglected as if considered a second-class appendage. The effect, aggravated by colonial-era policies, tended to create a one-sided image of Christianity as a Western, white man's religion. This suspicion still lingers in Asia and Africa, although most major churches have striven to overcome it. Pope Paul, by his emphasis and by the trip itself, sought to right the perspective and show that the Church is equally bound to the dark people's East.

He earnestly wooed those people, of all kinds and classes, from the lowly to the great. He clasped hands. He stopped to kiss waifs and hug flower girls. He distributed gifts. He chatted with Naga tribesmen wearing peacock-feather headdresses, and experimentally hefted a spear which these one-time headhunters from northern Assam gave him. He drove seven miles through Bombay to call on India's learned President, Sarvepalli Radhakrishnan, a world-renowned Hindu philosopher. At the stately seafront government mansion, Raj Bhavan, the two sipped soft drinks and talked for half an hour. Radhakrishnan told the Pope that without doubt his outlook in "coming here and trying to find out what non-Christian revelation stands for will ultimately mean that at the top all people will work together . . . as members of one common family of God."

In a contrasting interval, the Pope sat front and center at an Indian ballet performance, depicting the unfolding of divine love in history. Strangely plaintive music accompanied the young dancers, costumed in shimmering saris. Between acts, Pope Paul mounted the stage and, with floodlights streaming down on him, announced he would give commemorative medals to the cast. This set off a hectic scramble. Young dancers converged en masse on the Pope, hands outstretched, locking him in their midst. A dozen security guards charged into the pack, clearing a way for the Pope to get out.

The most touching moments, however, took place away from the bright lights, the decorations, and the diplomacy.

Pope Paul, on the third day of his visit, wept openly as he wandered among the wretchedness and misery of Bombay's Parel district, with its lean, threadbare families, its sick, and its orphans.

"I love you," he said repeatedly as he moved from place to bleak place, the dark, yearning faces encircling him, the thin arms reaching. "Bless you . . ." Compassion etched his countenance, and again and again he dabbed at his misting eyes. At Our Lady's Home, an orphanage adjoining St. Paul's Church, he ate breakfast with thirty of the youngsters there, and then strolled among them, handing out gifts. The boys had toiled to scrub up the place for the visit, but its numerous broken windows, peeling yellowish paint, and floormats for beds showed its sad state. One thirteen-year-old lad, Tony Mascerenas, read a greeting to the Pope, noting that the boys included Hindus and Moslems as well as Christians.

"Many of us have no fathers," the boy said. "Many of us have no mothers. Some, like me, have no one in this world."

Pope Paul wiped a tear from his cheek, and the boy went on. "You have left important people and grand places to see us in our poor home. . . . Since Your Holiness has taken so much trouble to visit us and have given yourself to us, rather than to the rich and great, we know you are a father." The boy then thanked the Pope for the visit and apologized, "We cannot give you anything because we have nothing."

A catch in his voice, the Pope responded, "My dear children, thank you . . . I have come all the way from Rome to see you and tell you how truly I love you." Then the head of the Roman Catholic Church asked the orphans to pray for him and ask God to help him in "carrying out our difficult tasks." One youngster said afterward, "He's a nice man."

Earlier that day the Pope had celebrated Mass, the Church's age-old "great public prayer," in a large outdoor athletic field of St. Xavier School in the same drab, jumbled district.

To the approximately twenty thousand assembled there, most of them destitute odd-job workers or families of mill hands struggling to survive on about twenty-four rupees (five dollars) a week, the Pope declared: "Beloved sons and daughters, and all people of India . . . We do not feel ourself a stranger among you. The pope is at home wherever the church is at home. The church everywhere is closely united to the people. . . ."

He walked along a dusty path to adjoining St. Paul's Church, where two hundred sick people had crowded into the tiny sanctuary, its atmosphere heavy and depressing. The Pope knelt at the altar, praying for the ill, then turned to them. He spoke comfortingly of hope amid pain and adversity, and invoked God's blessing and strength for the pathetic congregation.

Later the Pope rode to the church-run Don Bosco High School, where a crowd estimated at a hundred thousand greeted him with deafening cheers. High school and college students throughout the city had been invited. From a canopied platform, the Pope told them: "I love every human being . . . but above all I love youth. You are the hope of the future. . . . Always try to know Jesus and to know him better." Young girls shrieked in adulation, like American bobby-soxers spellbound by the "Beatles." At one point, the students joined in singing the Credo, Christianity's ancient affirmation of faith, and the Pope lifted his arms in tempo, like a song leader urging them on.

He also visited a hospital, trailed by nurses, doctors, and ambulatory patients, some of them in wheelchairs. He toured an infants' ward, touching pink foreheads and murmuring prayers as he passed. Mothers sidled forward to kiss his ring, and others, probably Hindus or Moslems, edged close to touch his white soutane. In the nurses' quarters, referring to the hospital's works of mercy and healing, he said, "In this we see an example of true brotherhood . . . regardless of race, caste, or creed."

Several hours later, at a civic reception preparatory to the Pope's departure next day, garland after garland was draped on his neck, garlands of jasmine, of golden threads, of roses, of lilies. He had bestowed many gifts—totaling the equivalent of $110,000—including $50,000 to President Radhakrishnan to be distributed to the poor, $10,000 to the orphanage, $5,000 to a seminary, $5,000 to the widow of the photographer killed in covering the Pope's arrival.

The Pope, in turn, had received many tokens of affection—wood carvings, ivory figures, a Kashmir shawl, a silver tea set, and books, some of them commentaries on Oriental religious writings, Islam's Koran, the Buddhist Tripitaka, Zoroastrianism's Zend-Avesta. At one point, Eugene Cardinal Tisserant, the heavyset French prelate who had accompanied the Pope on the trip, stumbled on the stage and fell to his knees. Pope Paul extended a hand to help him up.

Bombay's Mayor B. P. Divgi, a Hindu, called the city the place where India's pulse ticks and its heart throbs, and said that during Pope Paul's visit "never has that pulse ticked more loudly nor that heart throbbed with greater vigor."

The Pope sat facing the assemblage, his eyes deeply thoughtful as he listened to the words, recalling the recent hours, the sights of the haggard ones, the pleading voices. Seated out in the auditorium, I could hear the whispers making the rounds, "He's crying. . . . Look, he's crying." He was. He stepped to the microphone briefly, saying that his experience in India "transcends anything I could have thought when coming here."

He had entered a region of multiple faiths, the oldest, most labyrinthine composite of religions on earth, and he had demonstrated friendship with them, as well as with fellow Christians of various churches. His entire demeanor had served to portray the church as bearer of a universal message that belonged to all men, East and West, dark and white. And he identified that message with justice, compassion for people, and peace.

On his last evening in Bombay, he held his news conference, appealing to the world's governments to convert their expenditures for arms to a "great world fund" to relieve human needs. He had seen those needs. That same night, he carried a two-foot cross in a procession recalling Christ's road to Calvary. And as he left Santa Cruz Airport the next noon, he said: "Here we leave our heart. We feel ourself to share in a moral citizenship with this land which we will ever love."

That unusual journey, however, had been only a sequel, a continuation. It was a characteristic mark of the changing Roman Catholic Church and the man who called himself an "apostle on the move."

Other trips were indicated in the time ahead, to the United States, to the Philippines, to Brazil, and to Australia, as closer communion with all men was sought by a pope named Paul, which also was the name of that tireless first-century apostle, the Jew of Tarsus who became Christianity's most indefatigable missionary and who also roved the known world to give the faith to gentiles and make it universal. Pope Paul took on the ways of his namesake. In India, after consecrating six new bishops from that many continents, he told them, "Go, then, shepherds, on all the roads of the earth." And that was the map he himself followed.

It was a new mobile style, basing the church not just in Rome, but everywhere.

That was the important historical fact.

Yet it did not begin with the trip to India.

That was only another step on the new path. It began with an even more dramatic voyage to where Christianity itself began. That was the signal commencement of the new course. That was the eventful parable of returning to foundations in order to renew a city, of going back in order to go forward. That was the moment of travel that will be recorded in the chronicles of Roman Catholicism as the time its leadership broke free.

The early star shone in the East.

PART TWO

Pilgrimage

"Therefore let us go forth to him outside the camp . . ."

Hebrews 13:13.

CHAPTER *4*

To the Common Heartland

He sat by himself. The regular seats in front of the place he occupied had been removed as had those immediately behind it and across from it. He held a black-bound Roman breviary of prayers and psalms open in his hands. *"Domine, dirige pedes nostros in viam pacis"* . . . "O Lord, guide our feet in the way of peace." He sat quite still, a slightly built man in an ankle-length white cassock and skullcap. Around him and in the cabined air, vibrated the soft, steady whine of the jets. He reached up, adjusting the dark plastic earpieces of his rimless spectacles. *"Et duxit eos via recta ut venirent in civitatem habitabilem"* . . . "And he led them by a direct way to reach an inhabited city."

Paulus VI was going to the homeland of his Lord.

The plane rode at thirty-three thousand feet, a great, white gull of a ship, glinting in the morning sun. There, in the vastness, the graceful, American-built DC-8 seemed barely to move, a pearly wanderer suspended against the blue. Yet distance swam by. The Vatican-chartered Alitalia Flight 180, powered by four streaming jets, covered seven miles each minute. Painted on the rudder of the plane gleamed the white-and-yellow banners of the papacy, and on the left side of the fuselage, beneath the third window from the front, was the crest of the Pope—the dove, the crossed keys topped by the three-tiered tiara. Inside, next to that third port window, Paul sat alone with his book.

The westerner was going east.

A summoner had hearkened to a summons. Rome, in propitiation, was going to Jerusalem. Long ago, another Paul had returned there, determined to convince the other apostles that Christianity should not be locked in a restrictive, possessive system, but should embrace all peoples and knit them into a bond of unity, transcending rites and regulations. For "Christ Jesus . . . has broken down the dividing wall of hostility . . ." the missionary Paul insisted.[1] The council at Jerusalem in A.D. 49 agreed, as recounted in the fifteenth chapter of Acts.

And now, 1,915 years later, in a kindred cause Pope Paul proceeded to the land from which those aspirations sprang. He was going, he said, for "prayer, penance, and renovation, to offer to Christ his church" in concern for those within it and without. He went for "the glory of Christ" and his reconciliation among men. [2] "That all might be one. That was Christ's sublime and final plea before His passion. We make it our own." [3]

"Domine, gressus meo dirige" . . . "O Lord, steady my footsteps." To the rear of the Pope, the cabin held thirty-five other passengers: church diplomats, specialists, secretaries, bodyguards, the Pope's personal doctor, driver, and members of his household staff, a cameraman, the editor of *L'Osservatore Romano,* Raimondo Manzini. Altogether, counting a crew of twelve, there were forty-eight persons aboard. The Pope's party included three cardinals, all of them experts on Eastern-church affairs, particularly the blunt, bearded, seventy-nine-year-old Eugene Tisserant, who speaks a dozen languages, including Hebrew and Arabic.

The other two cardinals were the Vatican Secretary of State, Amleto Cicognani, eighty, a white-haired, soft-voiced prelate who had spent twenty-five years as apostolic delegate in the United States, and Gustavo Testa, seventy-seven, secretary of the Congregation for the Oriental Church. A close friend and one-time seminary classmate of the late Pope John, Testa had served for years in the Holy Land. Also accompanying the Pope were Archbishop Enrico Dante, seventy-nine, the Vatican's master-of-ceremonies whose meticulous sense of papal proprieties would count for little on this excursion, and Jan Willebrands, the able Dutch monsignor who serves as Secretary of the Christian Unity Secretariat, a right-hand man to Cardinal Bea.

The passengers spent the time conversing quietly, reading, ruffling through maps, itineraries, and other papers. Forward, the Pope sat alone. Below, the miles slid away, the humps of the Apennines down the southern boot of Italy, the southeastern coastline, and then the Ionian Sea, giving way to the serrate edge of Greece.

The Pope spent the first hour of the flight in silent meditation. Sometimes he looked out the window beside him, gazing for long intervals at the flowing gridwork of earth or the strangely sculptured fleece of the clouds. He was headed for a place where no pope had gone since the time of Christ and his apostles. "It will be a journey of search and of hope," he had said, "search for all those who are for us sons and brothers in Christ, in the atmosphere of the gospels and as evoked by that land of benediction. . . ." [4] He looked for something there. He went professedly as a searcher, seeking some wider view of mission, some fuller frame of concordance in the Lord. Something was missing, he knew. "Where is the full flock of Christ?" he had asked. "Where are the lambs and sheep of His fold? Are they all here?" [5]

Obviously not. Yet Christ had proclaimed "one flock, one shepherd." [6] There was a gap, something unfinished. So he turned toward the realm where the faith of all who believe in one universal God was born. Would his going there provide some answer? Some guidance, a sign, an indication?

Historic Palestine is only a tiny strip lying on the eastern end of the Mediterranean Sea, not much bigger than the state of Maryland. Yet, more than any continent or culture, it has fed the loftiest ideals, the deepest convictions, and sublimest hopes of the human race.

It had given rise to monotheism. It had cradled the faith of nearly a billion present-day Christians, thirteen million Jews, and almost half a billion Moslems. The strange handiwork wrought there was threaded through the world, through time and distance. It has lifted hearts. It has fired compassion. It has emblazoned justice. It has commanded loyalty, sacrifice, heroism. It also has stirred revolutions, toppled governments, and fixed the borders of nations. Crusaders marched there, and blood flowed. It has produced glaring paradoxes. Its influence sparked printing, literacy, and learning—and also suppressions and executions. Its impact largely drew the national lines of Europe, and sent the pilgrims to America. From it came the Bible. It has seasoned almost every language. It reared the ethical pillars of civilized life—enduring standards of social order, whether in the United Nations, in the law, or in the church, for the non-religious as well as the religious.

Such were the fruits and fascination of the Holy Land. Its influence was utterly odd, out of all proportion to size, wealth, art, or power.

Even in its physical aspects, it has curiously intriguing qualities. It forms the intersection of three continents: Europe, Asia, and Africa. It is situated on the peninsula where archaeologists believe that civilized life began on earth, in the Tigris-Euphrates valley. Its environment presents a collision of opposites, of sea and desert, of mountains and depths, of flood and drought, of hot days and chill nights. Events which happened there provide the point from which we compose our calendars, date our past, and measure our present years.

There, said Pope Paul, in that land where "Christ, the Son of God, came down from heaven . . . we feel that, by uniting ourselves with him in the gospel setting, we shall be able to carry out with greater perfection and success the mission entrusted to us. . . ." [7] A world had found inspiration there. Might not he? His attention stretched not only beyond Rome, but beyond Christianity. "Our heart will reach out also to those outside the fold of Christ. . . . In asking pardon from our Lord, the Merciful One, for all our faults, for all our weaknesses, we will not hesitate to beg for all men mercy and peace and salvation. ' [8]

During the flight, the Pope dispatched messages of greetings to the heads of governments of the countries over which he flew—Greece, and later Cyprus, Lebanon, and Syria, areas of Eastern Orthodoxy and Islam, expressing his esteem and affection for their people, and prayers for their well-being.

In the message to the late King Paul I of Greece, Paul VI recalled "the great apostle whose name we bear"—the indefatigable Paul who roamed the first-century world, extending Christianity into Greece's ancient Ephesus, Philippi, Thessalonica, Corinth, preaching on Mars Hill. "Mindful of all that Greece has contributed to the patrimony of Christian culture in the course of ages," the Pope said, "we express our good wishes for its noble people and we invoke from all our heart upon them and their worthy sovereign an abundance of heavenly favor."

Saluting Orthodox Archbishop Makarios, President of Cyprus, and Mohammed Amine Hafez, President of Syria, the Pope also noted the Apostle Paul's activity in those countries. In the greetings to Lebanon's President Fouad Chehab, he referred to the "great Biblical and Christian traditions" of that land, "which is dear to us and which we would like to visit." Rather than send standardized messages, the Pope included personal references, relevant to individuals and places.

Midway in the flight, the veteran airline pilot, Commander Gian Mario Zuccarini, took the Pope into the cockpit, showing him the instrument panels, the dials, meters, and levers. The Pope slipped on the radio headphones, listening for a while to the calls coming in from checkpoint towers along the way.

He returned to his seat. His private secretary, Monsignor Pasquale Macchi, brought him an attache case of documents, including texts of seven addresses he was to deliver in the Holy Land. He began going through them, occasionally pausing to pen a note between lines.

He could not be sure what experiences lay ahead for him. It was an inaugural day, a new thing in papal annals.

For the Pope, that waking day had begun before dawn, at 5:15. A half-moon rode in the sky outside his window. A cold wind blew. It was Saturday, January 4, 1964.

After dressing, Paul VI entered the papal chapel, along with several other prelates. He recited the age-old prayers and Scriptures of the Mass. "O Lord . . . grant of thy goodness, peace in our days. . . . Regard not my sins but the faith of thy church, and deign to give her peace and unity according to thy will." He tarried that morning in special petitions, and there in the Vatican, and around the world as the day wore on, others joined in the "prayer of the voyager," beseeching for the embarking Pope the protection of the "God who let our fathers pass across the Red Sea, and who carried them across that sea, an immense quantity of waters. . . ."

The first streaks of daybreak fanned above the Tiber as he stepped out into San Damasus courtyard at 7:15 A.M. and slid into a black Mercedes-Benz with the top down. A throng of Vatican employees applauded and cheered. He stood up, arms spread in comradeship. The car rolled out of the gate as a Palatine Guard band played Gounod's pontifical anthem. Swiss Guards in gleaming breastplates and helmets genuflected and dipped their banners in salute.

A tight, minute-by-minute schedule had been worked out for this unprecedented papal outing, but it fell apart from the start.

Pope Paul took his time, frequently stopping or slowing his car to acknowledge the crowds. At the edge of St. Peter's Square, the border between the Vatican city-state and Italy, he left his car briefly for a greeting by a government delegation headed by the Italian Foreign Minister, Giuseppe Saragat. While they shook hands in the street, aides closed the top of the Pope's convertible because of the windy cold—39 degrees Fahrenheit. Then the thirteen-car cavalcade moved on, as the great bell of St. Peter's began booming out a Godspeed.

Paul VI rolled across the Vatican line, out of his embayed domain, out of the 106-acre Vatican territory once considered the "prison of popes," out of the ceremonial casements and into the open air, headed into the chancy, unsheltered expanse of distant places, distant peoples, distant kinds, into the turbulent atmosphere of the farthest, fastest, strangest excursion ever taken by a pope.

He departed along the broad avenue stretching out from St. Peter's Piazza, the Via Della Reconciliazione (the Street of Reconciliation). It was named for the Lateran Treaty of 1929, when the government and the Vatican worked out an agreement, after more than half a century of dispute during which popes remained behind the locked doors, literally confined there. However, the papacy gave up its former territorial claims, retaining independent possession only of its small ecclesiastical enclave, with the pope permitted to go outside it on due notice to civil authorities, and with police escort.

The privilege was seldom exercised, however, until the beloved gadabout, John XXIII, came along. He threw the whole sedate system into virtual turmoil, jaunting about Rome at whim, visiting sick pastors or friends, showing up unexpectedly at churches and other institutions, making about one hundred fifty sorties out of Vatican City. He even made a 450-mile train trip to Loreto and Assisi in 1962, the longest papal journey in 148 years.

Paul VI not only took up the circulatory habits, but surprised those who had considered him a retiring intellectual, by mingling with the *hoi polloi*—the poorest and the lowest. Many incidents had begun to reveal the new Pope as much more sentimentally expressive than early appraisals suggested. But it was not until his journey to Jerusalem that his personality came clearly into public focus.

On the sixteen-mile drive to Rome's airport at Fiumicino, clusters of people dotted the way, carrying signs that read *Buon Viaggio* (Good Voyage) and *Roma Ti Ama* (Rome Loves You). En route, the Pope stopped to talk to a group of nuns, then halted to give souvenir medals to a group of convicts and guards waiting outside Rome's Regina Coeli (Queen of Heaven) Prison, and later paused to bless a crowd of a thousand at a village on the airport road. Italian road police in brown leather military coats stood traffic watch at cutoffs along the blacktop highway. Twenty-seven minutes behind schedule, the Pope's car swung into Leonardo da Vinci Airport.

Diplomats had gathered; spectators lined the terminal roof; familiar shouts went up. *"Viva il Papa!"* Even the old Marxist socialist, Pietro Nenni, the Vice-premier, showed up to grip the Pope's hand and wish him well. In a brief statement, Paul said, "We will present to Christ his universal church in its resolution of loyalty to the commandment of love and of union, which he left to her as his last command."

Then, in brisk step, he moved along the fifty-yard strip of red carpet to the airliner stairway and climbed aboard. He went directly to his seat, and could be seen through the window fastening his seatbelt.

The plane took off at 8:55 A.M. for Amman, Jordan. A squadron of the Italian Air Force Fifth Aero-Brigade F-84 jet pursuit planes flew escort, four on either side of the airliner, until it moved out over the waters of the Ionian Sea.

A pope, for the first time, traveled by plane. For the first time in modern history, a pope left Italy. Not for one hundred and fifty years, when Pius VII in 1814 migrated slowly back to Rome by stagecoach from Fontainebleau, France, where he had been held captive for six years by the Emperor Napoleon, had the presiding head of Roman Catholicism been outside Italian borders. But now, under different circumstances, with the church disentangling itself from imperial courts and crowns, the Pope journeyed freely in the name, not of politics or secular power, but of penance and conciliation. More travel would follow. A new chapter, in the breadth and mobility of the church, had begun.

It was a 1,403-mile flight from Rome to Amman. On the plane with him, Paul took seven suitcases and a trunk, packed with gifts and altar vestments he would use and then leave as presents at churches in Jerusalem, Nazareth, and Bethlehem. As the flight progressed, people almost everywhere spoke of the man and his mission.

The Archbishop of Canterbury, A. M. Ramsey, said the prayers of all

England were that the trip might hasten the advance of Christian unity. In the United States, Presbyterian leader Eugene Carson Blake said the trip illustrates "changes both great and small within the Roman Catholic Church." It may mark "the beginning of a dialogue in mobility," said Protestant Episcopal Bishop James A. Pike of California, and will "strengthen the whole ecumenical movement." Rabbi Joachim Prinz, President of the American Jewish Congress, said it would provide "tangible recognition of the shared roots of the Jewish and Christian tradition" and show an "ecumenical spirit embracing . . . men of all faiths." The spiritual leader of Eastern Orthodoxy, Patriarch Anthenagoras I, said the trip presaged "a new era in the history of Christendom. New shapes and forms will emanate, as well as new methods of Christian Church contributions to world peace." The Patriarch himself was en route to Jerusalem to meet with the Pope. Both Jordan and Israel, each of which holds portions of the Holy Land, warmly welcomed the Pope's coming. Jewish and Moslem leaders alike expressed hope that it would strengthen peace and human solidarity.

Yet around and within this sanguine glow smoldered the torment of men's estrangement from men, the scarring old wounds which marked the distance between reality and the dream.

Just as historic Palestine has in so many ways nurtured the finest and noblest in human life, so it also harbors, in microcosm, the woes and divisions of the world. It is a realm of ultimates, of the best and the worst, of close kinship and bitter enmity, of industrious progress and primitive inertia, of luxurious villas and massive poverty, of gentleness and war. There, where the prophets envisioned the day when men would "beat their swords into ploughshares," the landscape is spotted with armed militia, rusting Renault tanks, and the skeletons of bombed-out buildings. There, where Christ taught that the equivalent of loving God was "to love thy neighbor as thyself," rivalry, suspicions, and jealousies flare—even among his followers. In Bethlehem's Church of the Nativity, the place where he was born, outright scuffles have occurred between Eastern Orthodox and Roman Catholic clergymen over property rights. In the Church of the Holy Sepulchre, traditional site in Jerusalem of his death and resurrection, Moslems stand guard to prevent violence between Christians who disagree over the technical details of theology of the One who commanded love. There, where the Psalmist sang of goodness, mercy, and green pastures, thousands hunger and hate. There, where Jacob caught a glimpse of heaven, are hints of hell.

As in the past, so this land is today—a powder keg, primed with deep and partisan passions.

Although the night raids and gunfire have abated under an uneasy truce, Jordan for sixteen years has maintained its technical state of war against Israel. Gun emplacements dot the border and troops patrol the roads. "Danger," reads a yellow sign marking the line through the "holy city" of Jerusalem. "No Man's Land. Keep Out." On roof-tops on either side, machine guns face each other day and night. Even as the Pope approached, Radio Jordan proclaimed that "he will see the crimes committed by Zionists. No Arab will sleep quiet until justice is restored . . . the Jews are the enemies of God."

A zigzag north-south border separates the two countries under the United Nations decision establishing the nation of Israel in 1948. It received the seaboard portion of formerly British-held Palestine; the eastern sector of old Samaria and the Jordan Valley went to the re-established kingdom of Jordan. In the hostilities that followed, about 900,000 Arabs fled their homes in Israel—a wretched and restive spawn of angers and alarms. Their numbers have since swelled by births to about 1,400,000. Along with Jordan other Arab countries—Syria, Egypt, Iraq, Lebanon, and Saudi Arabia—also pursue economic boycotts and bans against Jews in opposing the state of Israel. At the time of the Pope's trip, new bitterness simmered over an Israeli project for tapping Jordan River headwaters for irrigation.

Long before the present difficulties, however, this crossroads of continents and conscience had been an explosive area, a center of conquests and rebellions dating back thousands of years before Christ, a target of invasions by Babylonians, Assyrians, Persians, Macedonians, Egyptians, Romans, and later, by Moslems, Christian crusaders, and British marines. Again and again, Jerusalem rose and fell, by catapult, fire, and sword. Revolutions, too, flamed here, audacious uprisings of ideals and valor. In the buckling, volcanic hills of Galilee, the ancient Maccabees raised mankind's first armed revolt against tyranny, and with their guerrilla tactics, routed mighty Syria. During the Roman occupation in the time of Jesus, dagger-wielding Zealot bands carried on under-ground resistance. Hundreds were executed; Herod the Great sent the fiery John the Baptist to the gallows and the lowly Nazarene became a wanted man for preaching Godly deliverance. "He has sent me to pro-claim release to the captives . . . to set at liberty those who are op-pressed, to proclaim the acceptable year of the Lord." [9] Olden Israel, finally crushed by Rome in A.D. 70, had no later counterpart until 1948. But the land has remained a tinderbox of staunch belief and recurrent battle.

Pope Paul has stressed the non-political, religious nature of his trip, disassociating it from specific issues of the territorial friction. Yet he went to plead peace. And the volatile atmosphere made up part of the prospect and part of the peril he faced in entering that strangely electric region.

Today, the region is predominately Jewish on the Israeli side, Moslem in Jordan, with Christians comprising only six per cent of the total. A majority of the latter are Eastern Orthodox Christians.

Modern Israel hums with expanding industries; rumbling trucks and tractors; newly productive fields; and large-scale farming, often by community collectives, the kibbutzim. In contrast, Jordan largely maintains its primitive ways, hauling its freight by camel-back; its peasants tilling and sowing tiny plots by hand; its nomadic bedouin clans living in black-hair tents, seeking out pasture and oases for their flocks, riding their proud, graceful Arabian horses.

In Israel, with 2,437,000 people, there are about 70,000 Christians, scarcely three per cent of the population; and 200,000 Moslems, Arabs who stayed there. In Jordan, with its population of 1,785,000, there are about 180,000 Christians, ten per cent of the total. Of the overall Christian population totaling 250,000 in both parts of the Holy Land, about 129,000 are Orthodox (usually called Greeks, but also including Armenian, Syrian, Coptic, and other Orthodox), and about 111,000 Roman Catholics (usually called Latins, but also including Eastern Rite Catholics attached to Rome), and less than 10,000 Protestants.

Thus, Paul winged toward a land which not only was mostly non-Christian, but whose Christian minority was preponderantly non-Roman Catholic.

In this respect, too, the Pope pioneered. He looked not at the wrangling human surface, but at the mystical, overpowering depth of that country. Paul VI said: "Ours is intended to be a return to the cradle of Christianity where the grain of the mustard seed of the evangelical parable sent forth its first roots, extending itself like a leafy tree which by now casts its branches through the world." [10]

It was a return to the fountainhead, to sources, to the springs from which all Christians, as well as Jews, drew their sustenance, and in which Pope Paul sought the guidelines of unity. This has been a hallmark of the Vatican Council, and of the entire ecumenical movement, among Protestants, Orthodox, and Roman Catholics—a sedulous searching of their one past to find the right foundations and directions for a more brotherly future.

As Pope John had put it, the task is "to give back to the face of the church the simpler and purer form of her birth." [11] Paul, by his trip, vivified this determination. It is Christ "by whom we live and toward whom we strive," he said. "Let no other truth be of interest to our minds, but the words of the Lord, our only master. . . . Let no other aspirations guide us, but the desire to be absolutely faithful to him. Let no other hope sustain us, but the one that through mediation of his word, strengthens our pitiful weakness." [12]

This submission and dependence, this testing by the elemental taproots of faith was considered the key to Christian rapprochement—to a solution of the embarrassing dilemma of a religion destructively warring within itself, while a world turns away in disdain.

In the dusk of this present trial, would light yet come out of Zion?

On maps of the Middle Ages, when the earth was considered flat, Jerusalem was pictured as the center of the world. In a primogenitive sense, the old mapmakers were right. For out of this haunting corner of the earth stemmed the first known glimmerings of human enlightenment. Among the oldest discovered implements fabricated by man's hands, there have been unearthed hereabouts and in the adjoining sands of Mesopotamia, artifacts dating back to the Neolithic Age, more than ten thousand years before Christ, seventy or more centuries before the ancient craftsmanship of Minoa, Egypt, or Greece.

It was out of prehistoric Ur of the Chaldees, in Mesopotamia, that the nomadic patriarch, Abraham, brought his flocks to this hallowed region. Here he made his covenant with the one Almighty God through which "all the nations of the earth" would be blessed. [13] Even in the dimmer mists of time, the rainbow of promise shone here after Noah's ark of "gopher wood" had ridden out a calamitous flood (signs of which have been found in the sediments of Mesopotamia). In these deserts and hills and at these immemorial watering places, man first saw the light of unity—of a unitary God over a single human family. It was a place of light. "Surely the Lord is in this place," Jacob said, trembling after his dream on a rock at Beth El of the sparkling stair let down from heaven. "How awesome is this place!" [14]

So steeped is it in mystery and antiquity that tradition holds that the first man, Adam, lies buried at the site of Jerusalem. There, in the Valley of Jehoshaphat outside the city's eastern walls, Old Testament prophecy (also accepted by Moslems) says that mankind will be assembled at the end of time for judgment and resurrection into a timeless dimension. In this realm, the wandering Abraham met the mysterious Melchizedek, the primordial priest of the Most High God. Islam draws its faith from this same time-rooted religious ancestry, regarding the later Mohammed as the last in the prophetic line of Adam, Noah, Abraham, Moses, and Jesus.

To this land, after the enslaved Jewish exile in Egypt, Moses led his people in mankind's first break from bondage. "Let my people go!" And a plume of fiery light guided them. Here, driven by a piercing inner light, the prophets thundered against injustice and oppression. Here the great Shema resounded: "Hear, O Israel, the Lord our God is one Lord." Here, through the eons of kings, judges, war, struggle, and gradually intensifying revelation, the spiritual and moral character of humanity unfolded—for Jew, Moslem, and Christian, all of those whose teachings include Old Testament Scriptures.

To these three great related faiths, Jerusalem is the "holy city." "El Quds," the Arabs call it, which means the same. Literally, the name, Jerusalem, means the "city of God" or "hearth of God."

An old Talmudic legend says that in the creation of the world, when God commanded, "Let there be light," it first shone forth from Mount Moriah, the commanding eminence of the city. There, on that broad height, Abraham had offered to sacrifice his son Isaac for the "glory of the Almighty." There the shepherd-king David had his divine vision and built his threshing floor. There his son Solomon raised his fabulous temple, "the house of the Lord." [15] There the successions of other temples arose. There, on that tall hill, Moslems believe that the Prophet Mohammed mounted his favorite mare before ascending to heaven. And here, to this region, "when the time had fully come, God sent forth his Son, born of woman"—the Jewish rabbi Jesus, who is to Moslems a great prophet, and to Christians, the Messiah, "God with us," the incarnate Lord and Savior. [16] Here he gave his glad tidings. "I came, that they may have life, and have it more abundantly." [17] Here he lived, taught, died, and to his followers, lived again and lives still. "In the world you have tribulation; but be of good cheer, I have overcome the world." [18] To Christians he is "the door," the way, the truth, and the life," "the light of the world."

To the ancient geographers, the cross on which Jesus hung stood at the center of the world. And in a Christian context, that crosspoint does, indeed, mark a universal axis, set in the religious motherland, the trunk of the tree with its many branches. Toward that central zone of faith, the chief representative of the largest body of Christians traveled, in search and homage, meditating with the Psalmist: "I was glad when they said to me, 'Let us go to the house of the Lord'. . . . O Jerusalem!" [19]

Then, as Flight 180 pushed eastward above the Mediterranean, aircraft radio channels came alive with word that the weather had closed in on Amman Airport. The Pope's plane might have to be diverted to Beirut, Lebanon, two hundred miles north of his destination. Lebanese officials hustled frenziedly to the airport to improvise some sort of reception. A second time, Pope Paul entered the flight compartment to listen to the radio communications.

At Amman, meanwhile, it had been a morning of tense nerves, restless crowds, and miserable weather. Dark, blustery clouds hung low over the airfield. A northeast wind turned the temperature of 42 degrees into a biting chill. Newsmen jammed the terminal building, drinking hot coffee, testing telephone lines and radio equipment. In one corner, four little schoolgirls waited with bouquets of flowers to present to the Pope, and two wooden cages of white doves to release as he came down the ramp. Outside, flags and bunting whipped in the cold wind. On a ridge along the east side of the building, and on roads approaching it, crowds of Arabs, nuns, and children stood shivering, their blue fingers gripping horns and pennants. On the second floor of the terminal, Meteorologist Ali Abandah bent over his instruments and isotherm charts. At 11:30 A.M., the clouds began lifting slightly. But not until 12:20 P.M., with the plane less than an hour away, was a decision made that the weather would clear sufficiently to permit a landing there. Walkie-talkies blared back and forth between newsmen outside the terminal building and others handling communication equipment inside.

At 12:45 P.M., the plane passed over the Mediterranean coastal city of Beirut, and with the hopeful word from Amman, swung southward across the snow-capped peaks of Lebanon. As it passed over Damascus in Syria, the airport manager in Amman, Halib Yousif, working in the control tower, got a last visibility reading and radioed the order, "Descend to ten thousand." The plane started down. But anxiety lingered in Amman. A wail of sirens, and Jordan's King Hussein arrived in his cream-colored Rolls-Royce. An experienced flier, he headed for the control tower to direct the final approach himself. An escort of Jordanian Air Force Hawker-Hunter jets joined the approaching airliner. It reached the Jerusalem beacon. "Descend to four thousand."

At this point, Pope Paul may have had his first, hazy view of the rocky hills, the cupped valleys, the sunken seas, and the wide deserts of the Holy Land. *"Innotuit Deus in Iuda . . . et habitatio eius in Sion"* . . . "God is renowned in Juda . . . his dwelling is in Sion."

While the Pope's trip broke with recent restrictive tradition, it revived a freer, older one. Not all popes of the past were stay-at-homes, and the early Christian leaders were irrepressible rovers. Although no pope had left Italy since the early 1800's, this narrow keep had not always been so. Its circumference had drawn tighter simultaneously with the concentration of church power in Rome over the last four and a half centuries. As the circle of authority had contracted, so had papal movement, until it finally became nil. But now, with the shift back toward more dispersion of church government, the pope again, as it were, flew the coop.

In bygone eras, other popes had traveled far—even into the Near East—although none ever had made the trek from Rome to the Holy Land. They did, however, take to the road.

Even the Apostle Peter himself, regarded by Roman Catholicism as the first Pope and Bishop of Rome, had the urge to leave there, but didn't make it, according to a story current in the fourth century. It relates that he was fleeing Rome along the Via Appia to escape Nero's persecutions when he met the Lord walking toward the city, and asked, "*Quo vadis, Domine?*" . . . "Where goest thou, Lord?" "I am going to Rome to be crucified for you again," Christ is said to have replied. At that, the departing Peter turned around and went back, dying on a cross head downward at his own request, in honor to his Lord. Tradition also has it that another first-century Bishop of Rome, Clement I, made a long journey as a prisoner; he reportedly was exiled by the Emperor Trajan to an isolated mountain town on the Crimean peninsula where he was martyred.

Between the fourth and eighth centuries, when the capital of the Roman Empire was in Constantinople (called the "new Rome"), several bishops of Rome journeyed there, either as prisoners of imperial troops, or to negotiate with the Eastern patriarch over theological disputes which finally led to the split between those two Christian centers in A.D. 1054.

In the Middle Ages, popes often traveled beyond the Alps to France and Germany to attend councils or to negotiate with rulers, or to crown kings and emperors. For one seventy-two-year period, from 1305 to 1377, the popes resided in Avignon, France, when that country was in the ascendancy in European power politics. Immediately afterward, a confusing situation developed in which there were separate claimants to the papacy—at one point three of them—in Rome and Avignon, elected by groups of cardinals. For thirty-nine years, from 1378 to 1417, this "western schism" led to a harried coming and going by prelates and popes, a kind of to-and-fro pontifical shuffle, finally straightened out by the Council of Constance. The fuzzy, fluid placement of the papacy was then firmly rewelded to Rome.

There the ensuing popes generally have held fast. Advance tremors of the Protestant Reformation already were being felt in Europe by the early 1400's—through the influence of theologians John Wycliffe of England and John Huss of Prague, who pitted Scripture against church a century before Germany's Martin Luther and Geneva's John Calvin. In the wake of the Protestant upheaval and the later repercussions of the French Revolution, popes became more guardedly entrenched in their Roman redoubt. They stuck close to home port as the battle and breakers rolled. The rare outings usually were uneasy, reluctant, or forced. The latest and most notable occurred at the turn of the last century in a turbulent interval culminating in 1808, when troops of the French emperor Napoleon seized Pope Pius VII and shanghaied him to Fontainebleau, France, where they held him captive for six years until his release in 1814 to return to Rome.

Not since then had a pope ventured out of Italy. The pope became strictly a Roman figure, a static part of the scenery, almost like the Acropolis in Athens or the Eiffel Tower in Paris, riveted, tied down, a "must" tourist sight on that little third-floor Vatican balcony. Over more than four centuries, through pressure and precautions, the pope had withdrawn more and more into the sanctum sanctorum, gathering the reins of rule to that one protected point, shielded against the outlying winds of challenge and change, thundering condemnations against them from behind the thick bronze doors. In the latter part of that period, he had become veritably walled around, sealed in—a condition aggravated most lately by the external conflagration of World War II. In that turmoil, with Italy in the grip of Mussolini's black-shirted Fascists, and with Hitler's abominations desecrating Europe, Pope Pius XII, on June 2, 1943, told Vatican cardinals that he "found himself before a door which no key could open."

But now that key had turned. That door had opened. On a wave of astonishingly sudden and barrier-breaking energies sweeping the church, expanding its perimeters of direction, and extending its concern and understanding to others outside itself, the pope again, like the apostles of old, took to the open trail. It was not actually something new; it was something old, tried, and tested, but which had been lost to these times. Travel had been a mark of the apostles; they fanned through the world, penetrating its farthest places. Tradition has it that the Apostle Thomas even reached India, where Paul VI would later go himself. The apostles traveled, not at the behest of or in links with earthly rulers, but in devotion to their Lord. It was this tradition which the Roman Catholic Church, and its chief pastor, casting off the Constantinian couplings to kings and prime ministers, espoused anew.

So Paul VI went out to meet the world—in a place both of its majesty and its misery.

The plane circled once beneath the low overcast, and then came in from the south against the wind. Its wheels touched down with a puff of dust at 1:15 P.M. Deducting the hour's time differential, it had been a trip of three hours and twenty minutes. As the plane rolled up on the terminal apron, a battery of howitzers barked out a twenty-one gun salute from behind a rocky hill on the eastern edge of the field.

Artillery smoke spiraled above it in the wind. Bagpipes skirled in the distance. Three platoons of military honor guards stood at stiff attention—air force men in gray uniforms, navy men in blue and white, army legionnaires in olive drab with their red-checkered bedouin headdresses, the *kaffiyeh.*

From the place where the plane stopped, a yard-wide crimson carpet stretched one hundred yards to the entrance of the royal reception house, flanked by another platoon of royal cavalry guards, liveried in bright red, with white epaulettes, white belts, and shako-like hats called *kalbaks.* A score of church and government notables formed a double line beside the plane; they included black-robed prelates of the Coptic and Eastern Orthodox churches, disassociated from Rome, as well as patriarchs of Rome's Eastern Rites, some of them in scarlet mantles, and the military and civilian officers of the Jordanian government in frock coats and fezzes, headed by the young King Hussein, whose Hashemite family traces its ancestry back to Islam's prophet, Mohammed. He himself wore a Royal Air Force uniform.

Pope Paul stepped out on the stairway platform, his left hand gripping the edge of his wide-brimmed red hat to keep the wind from taking it, waving repeatedly with his right hand. He wore an ankle-length, double-breasted, white wool overcoat—and a smile. He made no Sign of the Cross, since this was a Moslem land. At the foot of the stairs, he shook hands with King Hussein, then turned to the little girls, bending down to press their hands as they curtsied. The fifteen white doves fluttered briefly, then settled back on the tarmac to huddle together in the cold.

Behind the Pope, Cardinal Cicognani (alert to state protocol) whispered a reminder to him to remove his hat, as the King began introducing him to the line of officials. After taking it off, the Pope still had on a white skullcap, a zucchetto. He waved again at the airport crowds as he and the King moved to a low, wooden dais and stood there, facing the northeast wind, as a band played the Vatican anthem, then the Jordanian anthem. The King, slightly to the rear of the Pope, held his hand in salute, while the Pope, the cold frosting his breath, stood with hands clasped in front of him, holding his red doughboy-shaped hat.

He had arrived, but the elemental moment of his arrival was not yet. Nor had the sharp image of its meaning appeared.

The King led him along the red carpet to the reception house, where they exchanged gifts and each spoke briefly, both in English. "On behalf of the Arab people and all people who believe in God," the King said, "we offer you our deepest gratitude and sincerest welcome to Jordan and the Holy Land." The encircling dignitaries applauded vigorously. "Our visit," the Pope said, "is a spiritual one, an humble pilgrimage to the sacred places made holy by the birth, the life, the passion and death of Jesus Christ, and by his glorious resurrection and ascension. At each of these venerable shrines, we shall pray for that peace which Jesus left to his disciples, that peace which the world cannot give, but which comes from the fulfillment of his commandment to love one another as he loved us." He quoted St. Peter's epistle with its enjoinder to "Honor all men. Love the brotherhood. Fear God. Honor the emperor," [20] and added: "May God grant our prayer that all men of good will . . . may help one another in love and justice, and attain to universal peace in true brotherhood."

Paul presented Hussein with an eighteenth-century watch and a medal bearing the papal profile. He gave the King's English-born wife, Princess Muna, a golden ring studded with small stones; and to the queen mother, Zeine, he gave a brooch set with pearls. The Pope also had shipped ahead a gift of electrocardiograph equipment for a Jordan hospital. The King presented the Pope with a clock of gold and blue lapis lazuli with two figurines on top, an autographed picture in a silver frame, and a plaque cut out of wood from an olive tree in the Garden of Gethsemane. The Pope sipped a cup of thick, black, Arabic coffee, offered by his host.

Niceties of state, similar the world round, prevailed. The real substance of the Pope's arrival still was to come, even in a geographical sense. For the borderland of historic Palestine still lay fifteen miles to the west, along the Jordan Valley.

Twenty-five minutes after the landing, the Pope stepped out of the pavilion and into a waiting black Mercury sedan, with his driver, Franco Ghezzi, at the wheel. Lent by the President of Lebanon, the car had bullet-proof windows. It swung around and started the fifty-four-mile drive to Jerusalem, led by four army jeeps mounted with fifty-caliber machine guns. As it passed through Amman, townspeople lined the route: nuns, blue-skirted schoolgirls, Arabs in blanket-like *haiks,* khaki-clad Boy Scouts wearing red-and-white bedouin headdresses and holding bugles to their lips. The road quickly issued into open country, a dry and pebbled plain which soon reared into the slaggy crests and rifts of the Mountains of Moab.

Clouds still masked the sky, throwing a copper shade over the inclines. Spotted at intervals along the highway, halftracks stood with gun barrels extended, and from high knolls riflemen surveyed the Pope's passing, part of the two brigades of about nine thousand of Jordan's tough desert legionnaires assigned to guard the visitor. Here and there, you also saw a mounted cavalryman, a shepherd leaning on his stick, black goat-wool tents—the "houses of hair" of the desert people—a herd of black goats dotting an embankment, a plowman pausing behind his wooden plow and camel to stare from some terrace high above. The road snaked through the mountains, and then abruptly the valley spread out below.

There, meandering two hundred miles along the length of the valley (sixty-five miles as the crow flies) from the Sea of Galilee in the north to the Dead Sea in the south, the River Jordan formed the central artery of the "promised land." "There is a river whose streams make glad the city of God, the holy habitation of the Most High." [21] From the peak of Mount Nebo, here in the steeply carved range of Moab, the old, white-haired Moses had gazed out over that valley. He died without entering it himself, but he had brought the Israelites at last in sight of their destination. "For the Lord your God is bringing you into a good land, a land of brooks of water, of fountains and springs, flowing forth in valleys and hills, a land of wheat and barley, of vines and fig trees and pomegranates, a land of olive trees and honey." [22] The Pope's car, led by the soldiers and trailed by hundreds of vehicles stretched out over ten miles of highway, began its descent into the valley. "Beulah land" the prophet called it, the beloved bride of God's people. In the heyday of imperial Rome, Mark Antony prized that valley. Cleopatra inveigled him out of it. Herod bought it. Only its Creator owned it. Its Arab name was "el-Ghor."

Territorially, Paul VI was in the Holy Land. But in essence the real moment of his arrival still lay ahead.

Across the highway overhead, banners and arches of foliage, woven as only Middle Easterners can weave them, marked his passage. So did papal colors, strung on pylons, and the flag of Jordan, three horizontal bars of black, white, and green, with a red triangle at the staff surrounding a seven-pointed white star. Some of the wind-whipped streamers carried pathetic—and political—implications. "Palestine Refugees Welcome His Holiness." The lettering and bright rayon-like fabric of the banners seemed unlikely to have come from any of the bleak, impoverished refugee camps.

Winding along narrow ledges beside towering cliffs and along the edges of immense gorges, the road dropped swiftly toward the valley. Off about ten miles to the left, the Pope could see the flat and sticky waters of the Dead Sea, lowest place on earth, 1,286 feet below sea level, 48 miles long, 11 miles wide, 1,319 feet deep, its waters thick and bitter with salts and minerals, lifeless as its name, ringed with dunes, bluffs, and caves. From those caves have come ancient scrolls that enrich and reinforce the Biblical narratives.

The long, honking motorcade following the Pope foretokened the throngs and attention that would surround his visit. Thousands of other pilgrims had flocked here from throughout the world for the occasion, in addition to about fifteen hundred representatives of broadcasting and publishing media. The Associated Press put sixteen newsmen and eleven photographers on the story, a relatively modest team compared to the hefty battalions dispatched by other organizations. The French magazine, *Paris-Match*, sent a crew of sixty in a chartered Caravelle fitted out with a film-processing dark room. RIA, the Italian government's television system, deployed thirty-five vehicles and 235 men.

But the communications personnel were only a part of the influx. Tourists, privately and in groups, had come for the occasion. Jerusalem, on the Jordan side alone, had stretched its normal accommodations of twenty-eight hundred hotel beds to provide room for six thousand visitors. Eastern Orthodox and Protestant, as well as Roman Catholic groups, had organized chartered trips to coincide with the Pope's visit. President Johnson sent an envoy, Peace Corps Director Sargent Shriver, to extend an invitation to the Pope to visit the United States—an invitation which drew an interested response: "We would like that very much." The general incursion, however, was only a minor sidelight to the intent and substance of this unique journey.

Pope Paul's car reached the River Jordan, crossed the Amir Abdullah Bridge, and halted on the west bank. Overhead circled a red-and-white helicopter, piloted by King Hussein, now acting as a sort of airborne host and patrolman, while below a girls' choir sang the traditional Arabic welcoming song, "*Yaish-Yaish* . . . Long live—Long live." It was 3:15 P.M.

The Pope got out. Jerusalem church and civic officials waited there at the river to greet him, but scarcely had the chance. The welcoming committee included Jerusalem's Mayor Al Khayib, waiting to give the Pope a mother-of-pearl medallion bearing the profile of King Hussein on one side and the Pope's on the other. Crowds began closing about the Pope as he slowly made his way down a slanting, roped-off walk of newly oiled gravel to the edge of the muddy river, about fifteen feet below the level of the roadbed. The loose gravel underfoot gave way at one point, and a Moslem soldier steadied the Christian Pope. On a pitted, flat promontory of rock, he halted beside the sluggish, gray waters. He took off his red hat and stood in thought.

Ordinarily these banks are thick with rushes, willows, and tamarisk, but the skeletal trees were leafless and pallid in winter, devoid of the chattering life which swarms through their branches in warmer months. Slightly more than two miles to the north is the river ford where Jesus is believed to have been baptized by John the Baptist, near ancient Beth-barah. And "heaven was opened, and the Holy Spirit descended upon him . . . as a dove, and a voice came from heaven, 'Thou art my beloved Son, with thee I am well pleased.' " [23]

The Pope put his wide-brimmed, red hat back on and lifted his hands in a gesture both glad and reverent, looking upward at the leaden sky, the people along the highway, the spires of the eastern mountains. He climbed back up the slope. Beside him, Jerusalem's apostolic delegate, Monsignor Lino Zainini, and two husky Moslem legionnaires shouldered off the pressing crowds as he re-entered his car. The cavalcade moved on toward Jerusalem, still twenty-eight miles to the west.

It had been a nostalgic pause there on the river bank, but the revealing moment was still to come.

Dust devils twirled out on the tawny, eroded lowlands, its sands sculpted by winds into dunes and hollows. Off five miles to the right was Jericho, oldest city in the world, a city of citrus groves, banana, and date palms. Excavations there have yielded ruins which date back beyond 10,000 B.C., older by seven thousand years than Egypt's pyramids, as determined by Carbon-14 tests. It was there that Joshua's army, after circling Jericho for seven days while blowing continuously on rams' horns, brought down its mud-brick walls with a last mighty combination of shouts and horn blasts. "And the wall fell down flat." [24]

Modern investigators say that unconsolidated sedimentary deposits left beneath the city in Pleistocene times and sometimes shifting like layers of jelly make the phenomenon naturally credible—although divine knowledge of the condition at the time was needed to inspire the tactic.

Jesus also taught in Jericho. On his final trip to Jerusalem before his crucifixion, he passed through the city and stayed overnight there to help a hated publican overcome an obsession with material possessions —the man who climbed a sycamore tree to see Jesus passing by. "Today salvation has come to this house," Jesus told him. "For the Son of man came to seek and to save the lost." [25]

The thirty-car papal motorcade, followed by the long string of traffic, sped along the new blacktop, bearing toward the hills of Judea. Out of the desert, clusters of Bedouins emerged to stare, held at a distance by the legion patrols. Off to the right, scarcely visible in the haze, rose the "mountain of temptation," steep and desolate, with an ancient monastery standing in lonely isolation on its summit. Up in those crags, Jesus spent forty days in solitary fasting and prayer before he began his ministry. There he was tempted by the blandishments of the devil, who offered him wealth, power, and fame—the sought-after objectives of ordinary men. Jesus eschewed those ends. Quoting the

Torah, he said: "Man shall not live by bread alone. . . . You shall worship the Lord your God, and him only shall you serve." [26]

The russet of the landscape dissolved into somber gray as the highway tilted upward, climbing into the *qaltaras*, those weird, barren humps that make up the wilderness of Judea, a moonscape stretching away to the Negev in the south. An empty stillness broods over those rock-ribbed hills; they seem shorn of movement or life, except for an occasional thistle or buckthorn bramble. It is a place of crawlers, jackals, and the circling hawk, an ashen wasteland of hummocks and hogbacks, gashed and gullied by weather, crisscrossed by ridges and rent by ravines. Through these hills Jesus often traveled, sometimes lingering here to rest and pray.

Along the way is the supposed site of the inn to which the "good Samaritan" carried the injured stranger, after men of respected race and rank had passed him by, as related in the parable told by Jesus. The spot, called Khan Hatrur, is now a Jordanian police substation.

Nearing Jerusalem, the hills rose taller, grander, soaring three thousand feet above sea level, four thousand feet higher than the floor of the Jordan rift. The sun broke through the clouds now, gilding the heights in saffron hues. Jutting bands of pink and white limestone, interspersed with patches of vegetation, ringed the mountains. The asphalt highway wound back and forth along the high shoulders, overlooking dizzying dropoffs. On the second leg of a long, horseshoe bend, the Pope reached the village of Bethany, situated on a mountainside two miles from old Jerusalem. Here he stopped again and left his car.

It is a charming, tranquil spot of orange groves, fountains, and gardens in a compound beside the yellow-stone church that marks the site of the home of those two whom Jesus loved—Martha, the bustling one; and Mary, the thoughtful one who preferred to sit and listen to him talk instead of tending household duties. Here Jesus raised their brother Lazarus from death; this was not a resurrection, like that of Christ into a permanent sphere, but a reanimation to live out a normal life. Below a white Moslem minaret, twenty-four twisting steps lead down to the cave-like tomb. "Lazarus, come out!" Jesus had cried in a loud voice. And he came. "Unbind him, and let him go." [27]

Nearby on the slope, sheep milled in dusty pens, and chickens and children dawdled about the stoops of mud-roofed huts. Recorded hymns and chimes poured from a loudspeaker as the Pope mounted the steps to the church. King Hussein's helicopter circled low, dipping and climbing. Pope Paul had coffee offered by the convent's superior, Augustino Patacconi, a genial friar with a pet bird perched on his shoulder. He showed the Pope about the interior, with its arches and

artwork dating back sixteen hundred years. Above a green marble altar glowed the words of Jesus in gold mosaic, "I am the Resurrection
and the Life."

It was nearing sunset, but the muezzin of the tower over the cave,
out of respect to the visitor, deferred the start of the plaintive evening call to prayers to Allah. Pope Paul removed his coat, and over
the shoulders of his white cassock he slipped on a scarlet short cape
with white trimming, in preparation for his entry into Jerusalem.
Friar Patacconi wanted him to stay until sunset to hear the birds sing,
but an aide whispered, "There is no time." He had been there about
thirty minutes.

Outside, a group of sick and lame Arabs had gathered, brought
there by their families, drawn by some ephemeral hope or faith,
unaffected by particular theologies. The Pope saw them and stopped.
He spread his hands toward them, and then with a look of distress
and compassion, he bowed his head. After a few moments he raised
his eyes again, trying to muster a smile, and again lifted his hands in
benediction. A member of his party hurried him to his car.

He was running late. It was 4:30 P.M.

By now Paul VI had gazed on the storied terrain and passed its
outposts. But even at this point, he had yet to confront the stark connotations of his coming to this country, to look it full in the face, to
hear its voice. That consequential moment of arrival still lay ahead—
and near.

Led by the armed jeeps, his black Mercury rounded an elevated
spur, and on the hills across the Kidron Valley the city came in lofty
view. "Awake, awake," the prophet wrote. "Put on your strength, O
Zion; put on your beautiful garments, O Jerusalem, the holy city." [28]
The sun shone brightly now; the earlier clouds had flown; the haze had
spent itself, and in the last hours of afternoon, the sun flung slanting
javelins of gold across the ancient ramparts and towers, shimmered on the
tiers of stone roofs, turrets, and arches arrayed with multi-colored em-
blems, struck fire on the marble facades and gilded chrome cupola of
the "Dome of the Rock" mosque, perched high on the broad plateau
of Mount Moriah where the Jewish temple of old once reached its al-
abastrine magnificence toward the heavens.

"Our feet have been standing within your gates, O Jerusalem!" [29]
So sang the Psalmist in words that Paul VI planned to quote on reaching here. It was a speech text he would never have a chance to utter,
but it contained his sentiments for the occasion. Jerusalem, Jerusalem
. . . "May they prosper who love you! Peace be within your walls, and
security within your towers!" [30]

It must have been a moving moment for the Pope as he rode down the hill, along the edge of the Mount of Olives, approaching the old walled city, so touched at that instant by the soft splendor of declining day.

Down this slope, across this valley, and up to the city gates, Jesus had often walked. And once, the last time, on the way to his death, he had ridden down this trail on the burro's back, receiving the plaudits of the multitude as he wept. Jerusalem, Jerusalem! . . . "Would that even today you knew the things that make for peace!" [31]

And so, Christ's pre-eminent modern apostle traveled that road, its surface now in black macadam, the transport a black automobile.

Once again the populace filled the air with music and acclaim. Young and old, Moslem and Christian, the ragged and richly mantled crowded the roadsides, smiling, pointing, waving, cheering. Nuns in starched white coifs, and swarms of children wigwagged palm branches and tiny papal flags, which fluttered like ranks of yellow-and-white butterflies in the sun. Soldiers stood in close-order file, and brown, shrunken-faced old men and women, veiled and kerchiefed, sat on roadside stools. A conglomeration of instruments played, close by and distant: a throbbing farrago of bells, horns, flutes, tambourines, bagpipes, and the roll of drums. Banners in Arabic, French, German, and Italian welcomed the "Pastor of Peace." Overhead swooped the King's helicopter.

Paul absorbed it, gesturing appreciatively, but with creases of preoccupation deepening between his eyes.

Among reports about this episode, some waxed rather maudlin, comparing the entry of Paul into Jerusalem with that of Jesus. The analogy ran directly contrary to the Pope's avowed purpose; he had come in search, in penance, to offer homage, not to receive it. "Pardon us, O Lord," he would plead later in a Jerusalem tomb. "Have mercy on us." His thoughts must have been divided, both grateful and humbled, as the city packed his way to extol him.

Even so, this still was not the eloquent time, the naked, distinct time of arrival. But it was at hand.

His car pulled up before the Damascus Gate, nearly an hour behind schedule. It was 4:45 P.M.

Then the moment came; then came the salient and telling time. Then he had reached a zone which Jesus had occupied. Then he knew. Then he had arrived. Then came the hour of truth of his entry into this strange vale of the Most High. The Pope fell captive to the chaos of his fellow men.

CHAPTER 5

Saturday

The gentlefolk had prepared to receive him. But he met the people.

The men of station and prestige had arranged for elegant hospitality. But he disappeared in the mob.

The Pope became the possession of the rabble, of the publicans and pariahs.

The honored personages, the emirs, the high ecclesiastics, and the magistrates had planned befitting ceremonies. But the spectacle dissolved in storm.

The Pope who sought contact with a turbulent world found it.

"Yaja baba! Yaja baba!" the nameless ones screamed in Arabic, and swallowed him in their midst. "Long live the father!"

His retinue and ranking hosts recoiled in shocked dismay at the raw confrontation. But Paul VI, that thin, inquisitive man with the deep-set gaze, surrendered to it with a tenacious calm.

The church, he had said before, must confront the realities "that surround us" and "move ahead in the stormy sea of the world." [1] On his trip, he had declared, he would be at one in heart and prayers with the cries "of the sick, the poor, the disinherited, and afflicted . . . those who suffer, those who weep, those who hunger and thirst for justice." [2] The stark blast of those hungers, of those wild yearnings and passions, struck him and engulfed him in the frayed and feverish horde of old Jerusalem.

Pope Paul became one with the uncombed, the unpropertied, the uninvited. It happened unexpectedly—in that land of unexpected happenings. It obliterated the elaborately planned pageantry in an avalanche.

The stage had been set so carefully, so properly. The notables, each in his place according to titular precedence . . . the little Orthodox girls dressed like angels, their censers giving off a delicate fragrance . . . the bright banners and giant photographs of Pope and King draped from walls at the Damascus Gate . . . the oriental rugs spread on the flagstone triangle in front of it . . . the carols and hymns pouring from the amplifiers . . . the garlands of flowers . . . the flags snapping in a late afternoon breeze . . . the nuns with their palm fronds . . . the honor guard of the red-trousered Knights of the Holy

Sepulchre . . . the Knights of Malta in black capes and white pants
. . . the Moslem officials in their red, tasseled tarbooshes . . . the
choirs singing, *"Laude Jerusalem Dominum"* . . . "Glorify the Lord, O
Jerusalem."

It was an impressive tableau before the great northern portal
through which Pope Paul would enter the walled city to traverse the
Via Dolorosa, the Street of Sorrows, trod by Jesus on the way to his
crucifixion, the man condemned because "he stirs up the people." [3]

Encircling the formations of formal welcomers, a tight cordon of
police and army legionnaires manned barriers to hold back a border-
ing swarm, dark and murmurous. Strict security measures had been
imposed to shield the gateway formalities and to limit admission to
the processional route. Everything was to be correct, illustriously devout, and stately.

Along a fifty-yard Persian carpet leading from a microphone to the
wooden gate, the eminent figures stood elbow-to-elbow in a double
lane: the diplomats, the military commanders, the mufti of Jerusalem,
the United Nations emissaries, the patriarchs, abbots, and bishops, the
bearded Greek and Armenian Orthodox prelates, the scarlet-cloaked
Eastern Rite leaders, the heads of religious orders in loose-fitting scap-
ulars, the Anglicans in their four-pointed birettas, the black-gowned
Lutherans and other Protestant representatives, the picked delegations
of Franciscans, Dominicans, Assumptionists, and others. The decorations, the music, the ornate vestments and costumes, the gracious
words to be spoken, the set order of procedure—all these matters had
been worked out in meticulous detail.

But on the edge of that imposing scene, and further within the dim
interstices of the walled city, the man-swarm collected from noon onward, thickening, breathing more heavily, shifting, a rumbling surf of
voices.

The open esplanade before the gate is shaped something like a flat
funnel, more than a hundred yards wide at the outer extremity, but
narrowing sharply as it slants downward between stone parapets to
the gateway.

Beyond that massive door, old Jerusalem remains a reliquary of the
past, separated from the outside world of automobiles and modern hotels. It is a realm of heaped stone, of ancient ruin underlying ancient
ruin, a cavernous labyrinth of cramped, tunnel-like streets, stairs, and
alleys, ordinarily bustling with waifs, travelers, veiled women, bleating
sheep, Arabs in their long *ebayas*, donkeys laden with baled cargoes,
vendors peddling steaming beans. Arches and buttresses overhead
keep the place in perpetual twilight, except for patches of sunlight
breaking through. The cobbled streets, often no more than three yards

wide, wind through huddled stone houses and ancient bazaars, rank with smells, peopled with old men smoking water-pipes, stocked with cheeses, fish, rugs, pottery, caged birds, souvenirs, jewelry, and hung with freshly slaughtered carcasses.

Prior to the Pope's coming, entry into the old city had been tightly restricted so as to keep the scanty streets relatively clear for his processional along the "stations of the cross" to the Church of the Holy Sepulchre, venerated as the site of Christ's crucifixion, burial, and resurrection. Only a limited quota of journalists received passes. But none of this would stay the impending upheaval that day.

Outside the Damascus Gate, the distant sirens heralded the approach of the Pope's car. The music climbed. Sunset and floodlight cast an orange glow over the splendidly marshaled company. Beyond it in the shadows, swollen, undulant, a kind of thunder rolled.

One of the parables of Jesus tells about another gate, the gate of a wealthy nobleman, clothed in purple and fine linen. Outside that gate, in the shadows, "lay a poor man named Lazarus, full of sores, who desired to be fed with what fell from the rich man's table. . . ." [4] Jerusalem today still is a place of many Lazaruses, of the tattered, the scarred, and wretched, scrounging for crusts. It also still has its lame, homeless, and blind, like those who once clustered about the Pool of Bethesda, desperate for some miracle, some flash of hope, some break in the drabness and misery.

And now, a renowned "holy man" of the West entered this domain.

The Pope's car crept slowly along, past the Jerusalem post office, nearing the triangle, pushing through the clogged vehicles and pedestrians. Sirens of the armed jeeps wailed; bells set up a tintinnabulation; a vast Babel of cheering and shouts spiraled into a feverish fortissimo. With their sticks, military officers whacked at the heaving human mass surrounding the reception arena. *"Irja's wara! Irja's wara!"* "Get back! Get back!" Across the street from the gate, the facade of a German-Catholic institution, Schmidt's Girls College, glittered like a Christmas tree with bunting and colored lights, and high up, a giant electric replica of the papal tiara shone against the reddening sky. The King's helicopter whirred low and loud, its blades pounding like the wings of some anxious bird. Below, the cordon of guards bellowed and beat at the tightening coil of the common horde.

The black automobile with the slight, white-mantled figure inside pulled into the arena.

At this point Paul VI reached the precarious, exposed ground familiar to his Lord.

And Lazarus, with a thousand faces, with an exalting, hungering cry, broke through. The lowly, the crude, the unwanted poured like a tidal wave across the barriers, through the flailing, yelling police and military lines, and submerged that courtly assemblage in utter turmoil. The converging flanks of that wave closed on the black car, slammed against it, and spumed over it. *"Baba! Baba!"*

Down went the microphones; helter-skelter went the flower girls and fine rugs; the tidy ranks of ministers, consuls, and knights scattered like tenpins. *"Salvate il papa!"* "Save the Pope!" Shrieks rose in many tongues. The machine gunners gripped their weapons, jerking at the loading bolts. A bearded prelate, hands thrown above his head, tried to flee. The noise became a steady roar. Men and women swarmed over the armed jeeps, over each other. Legionnaires swung rifle butts or grabbed palm branches from the nuns and lashed about with them. A rifle stock jarred off the glasses of the Pope's secretary, Pasquale Macchi. He dived among legs, boots, and sandals trying to retrieve them—to no avail. Another monsignor of the Vatican Secretariat of State was knocked to the pavement. He scrambled back to his feet. The racket reverberated across the mined "No Man's Land" to Israel, where people gathered on rooftops and sentries emerged from behind sandbags to stare across the border in amazement at the orange-hued, ear-piercing pandemonium.

The Pope was trapped in his car, its doors compressed within the sea of bodies, which at moments lapped up on the metal top or hood.

Five thousand . . . ten thousand . . . the estimates of the number of the crowd varied as bewilderingly as it behaved. (Police superintendent Kazem Abu Ghazala said eighty thousand were there.) But its nature, not its number, was what stunned and alarmed. Frenzied, shoving, churning, it roared its hoarse and heavy-breathed acclaim. Its temper bespoke avid affection, but also some ravening want; some wild, forlorn, yet exuberant anticipation. What? Why? These were not just tourists, monks, and reporters, but street Arabs, the fellaheen, the Moslems, the shabby hewers of wood and drawers of water. They were Lazarus, scuffed and scorned, rushing on the Pope with cries, with hot, dark eyes and broken-toothed smiles. "As you did it to one of the least of these my brethren," Jesus said, "you did it to me." [5]

For fifteen minutes, Paul VI remained besieged in the car. Those who saw him through the windows during that interval said he looked perplexed, yet compassionate and undeterred. But surely his nerves must have tightened. The formal welcome and planned speeches were, of course, abandoned. The Pope's prepared text, undelivered, said, "From the depth of our heart, we thank Almighty God for having led us to this place and hour."

Yet what might befall him, if or when he emerged, was uncertain at that point. The gendarmes kept slamming and shoving, trying to make way for him. It was impossible. He finally emerged anyhow, his elbows gripped by Jordanian legionnaires, and immediately the torrent took him, and hauled him, pushed him, carried him down the funnel through the crammed, eight-step spout of Damascus Gate. *"Ha scappa-to alla morte!"* yelled an Italian priest, arms aloft. "He has escaped death!"

But the rampage had only commenced.

The sun sank. It was 5:00 P.M. and in the dusky straits of the walled city, a staggering ordeal began for Paul VI.

He had wanted to walk the Way of the Cross in solemn prayer and meditation. But now he gave himself over to being thrust along, flung this way and that, amid blaring confusion and violence, his life in possible jeopardy. It was not the kind of *Via Crucis* that had been planned, yet in a sense it was more akin to that of Jesus than any of the usual pious and cadenced processionals along those dusty, pinched streets. "If any man would come after me," Jesus had said, "let him deny himself and take up his cross and follow me. For whoever would save his life will lose it. . . ." [6]

Pinned temporarily against a wall myself, I could see the white patch of the Pope's skullcap bobbing along in the roiling human cataract. A crash of splintered glass . . . a black-robed clergyman clambered back out of a shop window. A current of humanity dragged me into the general maelstrom.

For nearly an hour, the Pope joggled along, shoved, gouged, squeezed, separated from his party, clenched in the grip of the lunging herd.

In that crush, you did not go anywhere, you were taken; you did not choose your whereabouts, it was chosen for you; you did not walk, you were tugged, pulled, and pushed one way and then another in a swaying, twisting wedge of bodies. It was pointless to resist. It was a "struggle all against all," the dean of Jordan's Lutherans, Carl Malsch, commented later. The bellowing legionnaires, in their bandana-like desert sudaria, parried and thrust with rifles, clawed at collars, shoved and heaved. *"Khalaf! Khalaf!"* Platoons of them shouted it from assorted directions. "Back up! Back up!" Sometimes you found yourself face-to-face with the Pope; at other times you had no idea where he might be, only that he occupied the vortex of this mass churning through the constricted passageways of old Jerusalem.

"The Pope weeps," said a young, bespectacled Franciscan seminarian, jammed momentarily into a corner with a colleague. "The Pope smiles," said the other. Both were right. In his pitted eyes and drawn face were both joy and distress. " . . . you will be sorrowful," Jesus told his men, "but your sorrow will turn into joy." [7]

Behind the close-pressed tide, the giant Damascus Gate had been forced shut to block the outside crowd from entering. As it gradually dispersed in the twilight, observers said the area remained littered with shoes and strips of clothing which had been ripped from the frenzied ones in the outburst. Wailing ambulances came and went, but Jerusalem officials insisted later there were no serious injuries. *Paris-Match* writer Georges Menant said he found the cuff of his raincoat covered with blood after the melee subsided. Near the gate, two aged nuns stood alone against a dark wall, asking repeatedly as if in a daze, "Where is the Pope? Where is the Pope?" They had never seen the man whom they had come to honor. He was long gone, locked in another, harsher tempest.

Despite strict measures taken to keep the walled city barred and free of crowds during the papal processional through it, the surging multitude had materialized somehow, from somewhere, out of its warren of dark lanes and doors.

But why such delirious interest among a largely Moslem population? Anwar Nuseibeh, present head of the Moslem family which had been keeper of the keys to the Church of the Holy Sepulchre since the time of Saladin in the twelfth century, later told an interviewer that the enthusiasm was "quite natural. We Moslems believe that the Pope is a holy man just as we believe certain of our own teachers are holy." Nuseibeh, who traces his ancestry back to the prophet Mohammed, added: "No one who touches the robe or bends the knee to a holy man can be the loser." [8]

Still, something else must have figured in it; some vague, groping expectancy, some thirst for refreshment in lives surrounded by squalor and the bare struggle to survive. Not in modern history had Jerusalem been the center of such world attention, nor host to such a celebrated personage, and whatever the cause, excitement gripped the plain people. The crowd clutched the Pope.

"*Sara ucciso!*" . . . "He'll be killed!" an Italian priest shouted at a Jordanian police officer, who simply shouted back. Several times the Pope floundered and nearly went down. But he remained upright, his white cap a cork on a wild river. "Let him through! *Imshi, imshi!* . . . Move, move!" But the shouts, whistles, and hammering made no dent in that ungovernable milling pack. So tumultuous did the scene become at some points that the Italian government television system, RIA, cut out parts of its film for showings back in Italy.

The papal entourage had ceased to exist from the start. Disrupted at the Damascus Gate, its members lagged helplessly in the crowd, or gave up altogether. None of the three cardinals who had come with the Pope reached the Church of the Holy Sepulchre with him. Cardinal Cicognani, whipped about in the whirlpool, finally took refuge in the small shop of a Syrian tailor, staying there until the storm passed. Father Pierre Duprey, of the Vatican's Christian Unity Secretariat, escaped into a wayside curio store. So did Archbishop Angelo Dell'-Acqua, of the Secretariat of State. Several times I encountered Cardinal Tisserant laboring along in the ruck, his beard flying, taking punches in his ample girth, shouting commands at the soldiers. Other functionaries and prelates, those charged with tending to ceremonial scruples, straggled behind in bewilderment, the man whom they were supposed to attend wrested from them, a prisoner of the people.

At times, Paul VI looked worried, his smile thin and quavering. But in his eyes shone an unflagging forebearance and love for these obscure ones, a faith beyond fear that all this was right somehow, that he belonged here among the many, in the midst of the paltry and the lowly. "Those who are well have no need of a physician," Jesus had said, "but those who are sick." [9]

Accustomed to the Byzantine orderliness of Vatican protocol, the Pope had been plunged into unexpected and brutal realities, into the middle of the ragtag multitude, the sweat, the rancid smells, the musty street. It was an enviroment seldom frequented by popes through the centuries of the church's temporal power and pomp, but Pope Paul stood there now, pale, prayerful, sorrowing, lifting his hands in blessing.

The crowd, with its sundry dress of the Orient and the West, with its varied voices and skin colors, seemed to represent the whole jumbled, raucous world. Gray faces peered from dark windows above. Droves of urchins leaped from rooftop to rooftop. And below, the Pope inched along in the thick confluence. Dark arms reached to touch him, to clasp his garments. A tattered, barefoot mother squirmed along, one soiled hand holding to her shoulder a baby wrapped in dirty rags. A shriveled old man, bracing himself on a stick, appeared from a side alley and was sucked into the swarm, his eyes wide, startled. "Blessed are you poor . . . are you that hunger . . . are you that weep . . ." said the Galilean who walked these streets long ago. [10]

At some point, Pope Paul leaned down and picked up a little crippled boy, shielding him against the pressing throng until his mother made her way to him. The Pope kissed the boy and handed him to the woman. At another place, a Jerusalem monk slipped the Pope out of the crush into a dark hallway and up a flight of twenty-five stone steps to the dingy hovel of a paralyzed seventy-six-year-old man, Khalil Nhas. Propped on the yellowing sheets of his cot, warming his hands by a lamp, the old man looked up in astonishment as the Pope bent and entered the low door. The Pope knelt briefly in prayer beside him, offered some comforting words, a token gift, and as he left, said, "My friend, pray for me."

The route bypassed the initial two stations of the cross, the pavement or *lithostrotos* where the Roman governor Pilate condemned Jesus, had him flogged and consigned to a squad of soldiers to be crucified—and also the site where Jesus supposedly shouldered his cross. "Greater love has no man than this, that a man lay down his life for his friends." [11]

Pope Paul began the hallowed, winding path at the third station, recalling Jesus' first fall. "Pardon my offenses, O God, and permit me to accompany thee on this journey." This is from a typical meditation, which ordinarily accompanies the "making of the stations," whether in Jerusalem or at symbolic church stations. "I will not refuse the cross . . . I accept it. I embrace it." The fourth station commemorates Christ's meeting with his mother; the fifth, the lifting up of his cross by Simon of Cyrene; the sixth, the wiping of his face with a towel by Veronica; the seventh, his second fall; the eighth, his meeting with the daughters of Jerusalem; the ninth, his third fall. "Adored Jesus, it was not Pilate, no, it was my sins that condemned thee to die." Tablets, monuments, or small chapels mark the nine stations on the quarter-mile walk to the Church of the Holy Sepulchre, in which the remaining five of the fourteen stations are situated—the traditional places where Jesus was stripped, nailed to the cross, crucified; the stone of anointment of his body; and the tomb of burial. "Thou hast made this journey to die for me with love unutterable. . . . May I live and die always united to thee."

The Pope's progress was sometimes halting, sometimes precipitous through the jammed, riotous streets. The course was hung with bunting, flags, and pictures of the Pope and King, and extensive preparations had been made for choir-singing and pageantry along the way by groups depicting the events of the various stations. But these plans, too, vanished in the hubbub and confusion. Instead of the celebration of a rite, the Pope's passage became a traumatic re-evocation of the scene in Jesus' times—the soldiers, the costumes, the hysterical faces, the staring and shouting, the slow, arduous movement through the throng.

Along these same streets, the Apostle Peter, regarded by Roman

Catholicism as the first of the papal line, had wandered in stricken shame after he had fearfully denied Christ and told suspicious questioners that he did not even know the accused man. Forgive him? . . . forgive as many as seven times? Not seven times, Jesus said, "but seventy times seven." [12]

It is questionable whether Pope Paul could have completed the route had it not been for a brace of bodyguards—burly, dark-haired civilians sent with him by the Italian secret service. They managed to stay near him, warding off some of the buffeting. They looked desperately apprehensive and shouted rebukes at the crowd. "*Se ne vada . . . se ne vada!*" . . . "Out of the way!" Much of the time they, too, were hurled aside by the leviathan-like waves of motion which rolled to and fro. Pope Paul, pressing on alone, sometimes appeared strained and melancholy, his face as immobile as pale clay. Yet he continually lifted his thin arms in blessing.

At one juncture I found myself wedged beside a friend, Weldon Wallace of the *Baltimore Sun*. He observed, "I've been in war, but this is scary." By the time the sixth station was reached, the turbulence had become plainly dangerous. Someone was screeching, "*Assassinini! Assassinini!*" The alarmed bodyguards hustled the Pope through a wooden door into a small, cavern-like chapel beside the street, and kept him there for twenty-five minutes while they and the legionnaires battled to ease the crush.

The chapel is maintained by the Little Sisters of Jesus, a community of nuns who labor among the poor—among the Lazaruses of Jerusalem. Garbed in heavy sandals, blue cotton dresses, their sleeves rolled up and kerchiefs on their heads, they look like hard-working domestics. The chamber, four yards wide, was lighted by two sets of smoking candles on a ledge. The Pope, it was learned later, knelt at the altar there, and after a while, got up and took a chair to wait, obviously weary. "My, it's hot in here," he sighed. "Let's open a window." But the place had no windows. A nun offered him some coffee, but he declined with a movement of his hand. "Well then, Holy Father, a lemonade?" He refused that, too.

Outside, the two black-suited civilian bodyguards and soldiers, largely frustrated in their efforts to thin the crowd despite nearly half an hour of storming and heaving at it, finally gave up, and summoned the Pope out anyhow, diving ahead like football linesmen, as the legionnaires punched and parried with their rifles.

Shortly the street widened, relieving the pressure somewhat. As if a dam had broken, the whole mass surged forward, carrying the Pope at a running pace. Excited Arab whistles blew. Ahead, the television floodlights glared blindingly, and from somewhere now, a singing chorus could be heard and bells pealed.

The old basilica of the Holy Sepulchre is a decaying crusader monument of stone and concrete, recently undergoing repairs, with steel girders and wooden scaffolding exposed in its dank interior of somber chambers, stairs, and galleries. It is the most sanctified spot in all Christendom, the most venerable church on earth. Jurisdiction over it is shared by Greek, Armenian, and Coptic Orthodox churches, and Roman Catholics. It is the traditional place of Golgotha, the hill of the skull, where Jesus, beaten, bloodied and crowned with thorns, hung on the cross for three agonized hours, while the Roman soldiers gambled for his garments and mankind jeered. "Father, forgive them for they know not what they do." [13] And he died. "For God so loved the world that he gave his only Son, that whoever believes in him should not perish but have eternal life." [14]

The sprawling church also includes the traditional site of the tomb of Jesus' burial, found empty by the women mourners on that Sunday morning long ago. Mary Magdalene sat grieving in the garden outside, and then all at once someone stood beside her. *"Rabboni!"* . . . "Master!" [15] And she went running to tell the others. "He has risen." [16]

The pressing crowd virtually catapulted Pope Paul through the gate of the church. A giant Moslem and his helpers then threw themselves against it, forcing it closed against the throng. *"Sainteté! Sainteté!"* . . . "Holiness! Holiness!" Then came a bellowing scream of pain. The Moslem guard had got his foot caught in the heavy gate as it shut, and the weight of the mob now struck with crushing force. His scream slackened the onrush somewhat; he freed his foot, groaning and standing on one leg as he locked the gate.

It was 5:50 P.M. A normally slow fifteen-minute walk had taken fifty minutes.

Cardinal Tisserant arrived shortly afterward, panting and expostulating. "This has been a tremendous ordeal for the Holy Father. He has been jostled and pushed all the way through the Via Dolorosa."

But the ordeal had not ended.

Hundreds had invaded the Church of the Holy Sepulchre without authorization, packing its hallowed halls and chapels. A thunder of applause, organ music, glaring television lights, and smothering congestion greeted Pope Paul's entry. He looked tired but tense. Jordanian soldiers slowly carved a path for him through the church's high-domed rotunda, ringed by sixteen columns and overlooked by galleries now crammed with people and flood lamps.

In the middle a stone structure encloses the holy sepulchre. The Pope knelt briefly in front of it. Then he slipped the short red mozzetta off his shoulders, and put on a white, gold-embroidered dalmatic for the celebration of Mass. When he removed his skullcap, one observer said he noted a small cut on the Pope's forehead. A portable wooden altar had been set up outside the tomb.

"*Introibo ad altare Dei*" . . . "I will go to the altar of my God." In a voice tremulous with emotion, he began the solemn words. "Send forth thy light and thy truth; they have led me and brought me to thy holy hill and thy dwelling place." Around him the murmurous, heterogeneous crowd looked on, the bearded Orthodox, the Protestants, the soldiers, the technicians and cameramen perched on the scaffoldings. Television cables slithered among feet, and the arc lamps gave the place the hot brightness of daylight. People kept shuffling about. An aged Franciscan, bearing a container of holy water, collapsed and was carried away moaning, "I can't continue." A brown-uniformed Moslem legionnaire stood staring down at the small kneeling figure in white.

Tears streamed down the Pope's cheeks.

"*Munda cor meum, ac labia mea, omnipotens Deus . . . ut sanctum evangelium tuum digne valeam nuntiare*" . . . "Cleanse my heart and my lips, O Almighty God . . . that I may worthily proclaim thy holy gospel." He read from the gospel of the resurrection. The crowd had become silent. Then in the hush, a cry, "*El kahraba!*" . . . "the electricity!" Up in the iron scaffolding, tongues of flame two feet long leaped out. "Fire!" Cries of fear swept the rotunda.

Pope Paul did not halt or look up. "*Laus tibi, Christe*" . . . "Praise be to thee, O Christ." Waving arms pointed aloft at a tangled pair of cables, which had short-circuited. A Moslem in a red fez tried unsuccessfully to reach up with his silver-tipped staff and pry them apart. Smoke curled through the heavy air. The Pope went on, seemingly oblivious to the disturbance: "In humble spirit and a contrite heart, may we be accepted by thee, O Lord. . . ."

Suddenly the lights went out, plunging the chamber in darkness, pierced by the red flames overhead. A Bedouin soldier handed his headdress up to a technician on the scaffolding to use for snuffing out the fire. It didn't work. "*Oremus*" . . . "Let us pray." Someone reached up with a fire extinguisher. A few squirts, and the blaze went out. The technician pried the smoking cables apart. The room remained in darkness except for ten tall candles burning behind the altar, "Holy, holy, holy, Lord God of Hosts! Heaven and earth are filled with thy glory."

The Mass ended, an hour after it had begun. A nun observed, "It was like a Mass celebrated on a battlefield." Then in that jammed, now silent chamber, with the wavering candlelight and shadows dappling the columns and the miscellaneous sea of faces, Pope Paul led a prayer he had composed especially for the occasion—a supplication for forgiveness, peace, and brotherhood.

"O Lord Jesus . . . we have come to strike our breasts, to ask your pardon, to invoke your mercy. . . ." He spoke in French, a sob in his voice. "O Lord Jesus, Our Redeemer and Teacher, give us strength to forgive others in order that we may be truly forgiven by you. . . . Instill in us the capacity to love, as you would wish that we love you and all our brethren in you. O Lord Jesus, our Redeemer and Shepherd in peace, who has made known to us your supreme desire 'that all may be one,' grant the fulfillment of that same desire which we have made our own prayer: 'that all of us may be one' . . . Omnipotent and eternal God, consolation of the sorrowful, strength of the afflicted, may the prayers of all who suffer tribulations reach you, in order that all may experience your mercy in their necessities. Through Christ our Lord. Amen."

He stood there for a moment, his head bowed. Then he turned and disappeared into the tomb, stooping to go through the low four-foot door. Inside the candlelit crypt, six feet square, he knelt beside the cracked, yellowing marble slab where the body of Christ is believed to have lain in death from Friday until Sunday morning. The incense of time hangs heavy in that tiny vault, the incense of damp rock salt, of dust in an impassioned dialogue with eternity. Pope Paul, his head bent to the stone, prayed. Then he placed there an olive branch which he had brought from Rome, a symbol of peace. He came out, a misty brightness in his eyes.

The crowd churned around him. He made his way, half lifted, half walking, up the eighteen steps to the top of Calvary, now an ornate chamber of black marble, statues, pictures, bronze and silver icons. A cleft in the floor marks the supposed spot where the cross stood. "It is finished," Jesus had said, as his head sagged in death.[17] And the earth had trembled, the sky darkened, and a pagan soldier had gasped, "Truly this was a son of God." [18]

After about five minutes there, the Pope left by the church's west door, and thence out through the walled city's old Dung Gate, through which refuse was removed in ancient times. It was after 7 P.M., windy, dark, and cold.

Behind lay a sharply etched experience, one whose impact would linger on in Pope Paul's mind, as he later related. On that tortuous path he had followed, so freighted with its varied peoples, its yearnings, and disorders, the changing face of the church had become apparent.

On that street Roman Catholicism had displayed through its chief pastor the turning of a corner. The turn had its grounding in many recent events, including the work of the Second Vatican Council, but it was dramatized in human terms there in the Pope's identification with the straining, mixed family of men.

From the time of the Emperor Constantine the Great, who early in the fourth century made Christianity the religion of his empire, history gave rise to a long succession of church-state alliances, including those of the Protestant Reformation in northern Europe. King and ecclesiastics occupied the shared upper estates, set apart from the "lower classes."

The pattern was gradually dissipated in the modern era, although Rome has maintained vestiges of it in some of its pacts and protocol. But on the streets of Jerusalem, those remnants were trampled underfoot. The Pope became literally part of the masses, stripped of regal trappings, unprotected, vulnerable: an admired man who moved intimately and humbly with the people.

It doubtlessly failed to please some old Vatican hands, who had been dubious of the trip in the first place. But Paul didn't mind; he said later that it had filled him with wonder and joy. In leaving his armored hill, in coming down and giving himself to the crowd, no longer a remote figure to be presented for prudent veneration amid soft lights and trumpets, but in unceremonious contact with the people, he had found warmth, exhilaration, and truth.

New insights for the church had shown themselves there, he said later, for those who want to "seek and decipher 'the signs of the times,' as Jesus said." [19] There was discovery on those crowded streets, and also signs of a launching forth, on the level of ordinary people, in their midst, seeing their needs, feeling their rough passions, hearing the cries of Lazarus for succor.

It was only a gesture, some say, a symbol; and that is true. Yet gestures hold meaning—often more than mere words. Providence decreed a powerful gesture there on those troubled streets—and Pope Paul felt it. He also disclosed something of his own character—of courage, patience, sympathy.

The Pope's waiting car took him out of the city and across the Kidron Valley to Jerusalem's Apostolic Delegation quarters. This is a two-story building of yellowish stone situated a mile from the city and about halfway up the 2,700-foot Mount of Olives, not far from the Garden of Gethsemane where Christ prayed on the night before his crucifixion. Pope Paul's room was Number 9, a small, fifteen-by-twelve-foot room on the second floor, furnished with a kneeling bench, an olive-wood crucifix, a single bed, a wardrobe, two straight-back chairs, and two working tables. It adjoins a modern bathroom.

For the Pope's two-night stay, the Franciscan nuns who serve as housekeepers had painted the walls of the room yellow, and the ceiling white—the papal colors. The room's one window, fitted with shutters, overlooks a chicken run and small chicken house.

Across the narrow hall another small room served as the combination lodgings and office for the Pope's secretary, Monsignor Macchi. He and another secretary, Bruno Bossi, were the only two members of the Pope's party staying at the residence of the Jerusalem delegation, headed by Monsignor Lino Zanini. For dinner, near 8 P.M., the housekeeping sisters had consulted a cookbook and boned up on making *risotto alla milanese*, a rich dish of northern Italy and a favorite of the Pope's.

But his arduous first day in the Holy Land was far from finished.

He would be off again in his car at 9 P.M. What little intervening time for rest had been planned went aglimmering when some priests from Milan—a deputation of men who had worked with Paul back in his former archdiocese—appeared for a nostalgic visit. He could not turn them away. Then he received a call from Jerusalem's Greek Orthodox Patriarch Benedictos and Armenian Orthodox Patriarch Derderian, the first such contact between a pope and an Orthodox patriarch since the fifteenth century, and a prelude to his meeting the next night with the leader of all Eastern Orthodoxy, Patriarch Athenagoras of Constantinople. But even later on that first night, on his way to the Garden of Gethsemane, Pope Paul paid a short return call on Benedictos at the nearby Orthodox headquarters, also situated on the Mount of Olives.

With no letup in his pace, the Pope stopped off at Jerusalem's St. Anne's Church, dedicated to the mother of the Virgin Mary, and delivered a discourse to leaders of Oriental Rite Catholics, who recognize the authority of the papacy but maintain their own traditions, local liturgical languages, and worship practices akin to Eastern Orthodoxy. In essence, they constitute fractional sectors of Orthodoxy reunited with Rome, and are in rivalry with the bulk of Orthodoxy, which does not subscribe to papal rule. Pope Paul told the Oriental prelates:

"No one can forget that when God decided to choose for himself a fatherland, a family, and a language in this world, it was from the Orient that he took them." The Pope then injected a point of importance to the entire ecumenical movement—the idea that Christian unity does not demand uniformity. Noting that the first apostles carried the gospel from Palestine throughout the earth, he said:

"Each nation received the good seed of their preaching, according to its proper mentality and culture. Each local church grew with its own personality and customs, its own way of celebrating the divine mysteries, all of which did not, however, harm the unity of faith or the communion of all in charity and in respect of the order established by Christ. In this is the origin of our diversity in unity, our catholicity, that property which was always essential to the church of Christ, and of which the Holy Spirit gives us a new experience in our present time and in the council (Vatican II)."

Rows of torches flamed on the Mount of Olives, fluttering in the chill night wind, as Pope Paul drove back up that sacred hill to the Church of All Nations. It adjoins an ancient olive grove, bright that night with floodlights, the traditional site of the Garden of Gethsemane, the wooded glade to which the armed band came with its flaming torches, clubs, and swords to arrest Jesus. He had stepped forward. "Whom do you seek?" "Jesus of Nazareth." "I am he." [20] Judas planted his identifying kiss, and Peter lashed out with a sword, but Jesus had remonstrated, "Put your sword back into its place; for all who take the sword will perish by the sword." [21] The soldiers seized him, bound his arms, and led him away as the apostles fled in terror.

Some of the eight gnarled olive trees standing there may be the same ones that surrounded that midnight arrest. Botanists say they may be three thousand years old. The whole hill used to be forested with olives, myrtle, and pines. To "Gethsemane," which means olive press, Jesus frequently had brought his apostles for safety and rest. On that last night there, before the soldiers came, he had told them, "My soul is very sorrowful even to death; remain here and watch with me." [22] But they fell asleep. Jesus threw himself on a nearby rock and prayed in agony, "Father, if thou art willing, remove this cup from me, nevertheless not my will, but thine, be done." [23]

A rough outcropping of flinty, white limestone, called *nari*, marks the place. It is inside the adjacent church, railed around with curling spiked iron resembling a hedge of thorns. Jesus knew dread there. Scripture says his sweat became as drops of blood. "Father, the hour has come. . . ." [24]

Several hundred people sang hymns and held their torchlights aloft as Pope Paul arrived at the church about 10:50 P.M. Once again a shoving crowd hemmed him in, and Jordanian troopers forced a path for him up the eleven steps and through the church door. It was promptly barred. Inside another throng of about fifteen hundred filled the church, standing among its ten towering columns crowned with a multi-domed ceiling.

The Pope's face showed dark lines of fatigue, but he raised his arms in greeting. Clad in white skullcap and soutane with a long, crimson cape over his shoulders, he moved down the aisle between rows of security officers, extended arms, pushing bystanders. Some broke through the lines to kiss the papal fingerband, the "ring of the fisherman." He reached the rock, got down on his knees, and pressed his lips to its glinting surface. He then moved to a red-upholstered prie-dieu for a service of prayer and Scripture, recalling Jesus' night of grief.

From outside there came a momentary distraction. Cardinal Tisserant, still trying to keep up with the Pontiff, arrived late, finding himself locked out. He pounded on the tall, copper-sheathed doors. When the Moslem soldiers outside refused to heed his authority as a cardinal, he began giving orders as an ex-French army officer. One young soldier nervously opened the door a crack, and when the cardinal sought to shove his generous torso through the opening, the soldier clouted him on the head with a stick. The cardinal barged in anyhow, growling through his beard. The young soldier later explained with artless innocence: "That priest with the red ribbon on his hat was screaming and trying to get in without even a ticket."

The worship continued with the Pope's prayers interspersed with the singing of priests in various languages—Latin, Greek, Arabic, Armenian, Russian, and Coptic—the gospel accounts of Jesus' prayer for unity. "Holy Father, keep them in thy name which thou hast given me, that they may be one, even as we are one." [25] With Eastern Orthodox and Protestant clergymen present, the use of the different languages again underlined the Pope's broad view of diversity in a unified faith. "They may become perfectly one," Jesus had prayed, "so that the world may know that thou hast sent me. . . ." [26]

Moving back through the crowds, blinking at the television lights, Pope Paul made his way outside at 11:30 P.M. He climbed into his black car and rode across the hill to the Apostolic Delegation building.

He got scant sleep that night. Likely, before he retired, he said the prayers of compline from the Roman breviary. " . . . through the night watches I will meditate on you . . . in the shadow of your wings." And before dawn, another priestly prayer: "Lord, our God, King of heaven and of earth, for this day please direct and sanctify, set right and govern our hearts and our bodies, our sentiments, our words, and our actions in conformity with your law and your commandments."

CHAPTER **6**

Sunday

Shortly after daybreak at 7:02 A.M., Sunday, January 5, the black Mercury sedan pulled out of the steel gate of the Apostolic Delegation yard, rolled down the mountainside, swung around a line of plodding donkeys laden with sacks of beets and cabbages, reached the highway, and headed north toward a border which has been sealed by wrath and war for fifteen years.

A radio jeep and two motorcycle outriders accompanied the Pope's car, in addition to six maroon-hued, machine gun-armed jeeps, three to the rear and three in front. The security escort had been increased, and after the fracas in Jerusalem on the previous day, King Hussein had assigned his own crack royal guard to the job.

Paul VI motored toward a trigger-taut boundary line, and the land beyond it—Galilee. The sixty-seven-mile road to the border ran through the reddish, limestone-fringed mountains of ancient Samaria, ranging the western side of the Jordan Valley. In that roughcast country, the peaks, wooded slopes, caves, and valleys abound with Biblical history. At every bend, from nearly every plateau and winding ledge appear the vistas which formed the stage for the divine drama of warriors, kings, sages, and prophets of old.

The geographical panorama unfolded . . . the hillside town of the Prophet Jeremias, who hurled his invective against injustice . . . the Wadi Farah, a picturesque valley considered the herding ground of David and scene of the beautiful twenty-third psalm, "The Lord is my shepherd, I shall not want" . . . the supposed burial place of the prophet Samuel . . . site of ancient Mispah, where Saul was elected first King of Israel . . . the little hamlet of Bireh, believed to be the spot where Joseph and Mary, en route back to Nazareth, discovered that the twelve-year-old Jesus was missing (later they found him back in Jerusalem conversing with the scholars) . . . Bethel, the place where Jacob dreamed of a ladder to heaven . . . the vicinity where Jeroboam erected a golden calf as an idol . . . Shiloh, where the Ark of the Covenant stood . . . the sweeping "valley of the dancers" from which men of Juda, short on wives, kidnapped young brides by night . . . and the looming crests of Mount Ebal and Mount Gerizim, the holy mountain of the Samaritans, rising above the Mahneh Plain. There be-

95

low stands Jacob's Well, the spot where Jesus met the Samaritan woman who became a fervent disciple. Nearby is a white-domed structure marking the tomb of Joseph, who fed the brothers who sought to kill him. On the edge of that same pass is Shechem, considered built on the "parcel of ground" where Abraham first raised an altar to the Lord.

At times, the "papalcade"—as it came to be known—moved at speeds up to sixty miles an hour, but frequently it slowed to a crawl or halted briefly for the sights or because of roadside clusters of applauding adults and children. Pope Paul is known as a man-in-a-hurry when driving, and often tells his driver, Franco Ghezzi, to step on it. But already, captivated by the storied scenery, the Pope was running considerably behind schedule. It was cloudy, with brisk temperatures in the forties. He had with him a vacuum bottle of hot coffee.

Along the way were the Bedouin tents, the black flocks on the mountainsides, the mud-brick huts with their flat roofs for drying figs. Villagers flocked to the roadsides with banners of greeting. At a refugee settlement, several hundred lined the street. Mingled with the cheering were undertones of strife. At some points Jordanian spectators set up a rhythmic clapping and chanted, "Palestine for Arabs . . . Palestine for Arabs."

Northward the highway runs through Sebastye, where King Herod had a sumptuous retreat, where Salome supposedly danced for John the Baptist's head, and where, as one tradition has it, the Baptist spent his last imprisoned days. A rockhewn underground cell is pointed out as the place of his confinement before execution. Of him, Jesus said that he was "more than a prophet . . . among those born of women none is greater than John . . ." [1] Sebastye now is a place of ruins; of excavations and moldering towers, of unearthed columns and corridors.

At Jenin, the last town in Jordan before reaching the border of Israel, villagers offered a festive reception, including a tooting band of blue-clad boys and other youngsters in red Arab headdresses, waving flags. They made up a gala picture before a grim one.

A long-unused, rutted road led a short distance on to the iron roadblock, Taanack Gate. Not since 1948, when Jordan launched hostilities against what it calls "occupied Palestine," has that border been crossed, except under peril of gunshot, or occasionally by United Nations officials; and only then to return cattle or Arabs strayed into no-man's land. Ordinarily it is a forbidden desert frontier, bristling with barbed-wire entanglements, concrete tank traps, and burned-out, abandoned vehicles. But on this particular day, a pleasant transformation had occurred.

Gone were the dusty blockades, the barbed wire, the scrap; and in their place, long white-and-yellow pennants flew. Jordanian shepherds and Israeli farmers from the nearby kibbutz, Givat Oz, congregated together, applauding unitedly. It was a rare and refreshing pause in the long bitter conflict. The sun came out, the two rusty gates swung open, and at 9:45 A.M., Paul VI drove into Israel.

Before him spread the fertile Plain of Esdraelon, lush and greening in the sun with fresh crops of sugar beets and rutabaga, watered by the Kishon. Despite its richness and beauty, this plain among the mountains—whose name means "God-sown"—has been a field of battle from time immemorial. Probably no other single piece of earth has been stained by so many bloody encounters. Here Gideon's three hundred won their victory; here Saul retreated before the Philistines; here Josiah struggled against Pharaoh-Necoh and fell mortally wounded; here numberless other battles have raged, and here, the seer of the Apocalypse predicted, will the final decisive struggle between good and evil ensue, with "flashes of lightning, loud noises, peals of thunder, and a great earthquake . . ." at the world's Armageddon.[2]

But to Paul's eyes, it stretched peaceful and productive toward the highlands of Galilee.

On a little rise three miles northwest of the frontier, an honor guard of Israeli soldiers saluted as the Pope drove into Megiddo. There, beside the courtyard of a stone building housing a museum and an archaeological research team of the University of Chicago, the smiling, bespectacled President of Israel, Zalman Shazar, stepped forward and gripped the Roman Catholic Pontiff's hand. "Blest be thou in thy coming," Shazar said. Scarred memories of rancor and hurt between Christian and Jew dwindled in that moment.

The Pope stood with Shazar at a battery of microphones, surrounded by prelates, the Israeli cabinet, the top-hatted ambassadors to Israel from Italy, France, Holland, and Belgium, and the dean of the diplomatic corps, Russian Ambassador Mikhail Bodrov. Most of the government officials occupied bleachers set up in the area. Israel's Chief Rabbi, Izhak Nissim, had declined to take part on the ground that spiritual leaders should meet only in a religious setting, without political implications. But he had voiced a welcome to the Pope, saying his work for "mercy and peace among all men is timely indeed. May his coming and his going be blessed with peace."

Shazar, in black coat and striped trousers, hailed the Pope's pilgrimage as "a journey of prayer, to seek mercy, peace and prosperity, freedom and justice," and said: "Surely the devastation of my people during this last generation is a bitter warning of the depths of bestiality and loss of the divine image to which ancient prejudices and racial hatreds can drag men down if a purifying spirit does not come into being while there is yet time to dam up these dangers forever." He added that Israel's hope and confidence is that the ancient vision of her prophets will be realized, that "mankind shall be redeemed from its distress, the world shall be built in righteousness, and our eyes shall behold this. Blessed be our illustrious guest upon his arrival among us."

A slight wind stirred, rustling in the leaves, rippling the papal banners and the blue-and-white flags of Israel bearing the six-pointed Star of David. The Pope wore a long red cloak over his white cassock.

"We come as a pilgrim," he said. He spoke of the common roots of Christians and Jews, and of the great emotions he felt at entering this land of "our fathers in the faith, this land where down through the centuries there resounded the voices of the prophets speaking in the name of the God of Abraham, Isaac, and Jacob," a land which Jesus Christ "blessed and hallowed forever for all Christians, and one might say, for the entire human race."

The words caused a ripple of resentment back in Jordan. King Hussein next day sent his Foreign Minister to Cardinal Cicognani with a discreetly private complaint about the Pope's seeming to imply that Israel was the Holy Land—an indication of the delicately explosive atmosphere in which the Pope moved. He told his Israeli welcomers: "In this land unique in all the world for the greatness of events enacted in it, our humble supplication is raised toward God for all men," for non-believers, believers, Christians, and Jews "whose part in the religious history of mankind can never be forgotten." He added: "We pray before all else for the favor of man's reconciliation with God . . . and true profound concord among all men and all peoples."

He spoke in French. But he concluded with a Hebrew word that covers the gamut of harmonious relationship. Literally it means peace, but it also means friendship, loyalty, hello, good-by, and mutuality of feeling. Declaring that it summarized everything else he felt—"our greeting, our prayers, our wishes"—the Pope said: *"Shalom, shalom."*

You can brush this off as a ceremonial nicety, a mere appropriate courtesy. But if you read the long story of religion, you know it meant that something irrevocable had happened, that something basic and demanding had been recognized, and was being declared, that something true which had often been denied was being asserted in the most personal, most institutionally representative, most understandable, and simplest way. *"Shalom, shalom."*

Here was the earthly head of a church whose members in other times, distant and not so distant, had abetted or countenanced disparagement of Jewry, or even impediments against it, now expressing firm and fond ties to it, in a vivid, universal Hebrew phrase which no one could mistake and which no pope would use casually. The leader of a daughter religion, Christianity, had come paying respects in the household of the parent faith, Judaism. They met in common esteem, and the old alienation could not easily be the same again. While the Second Vatican Council and other developments gave increasing substance to this bond, the direct, intimate word of mutuality, spoken there in that verdant valley of decisive encounters, lifted it to a level beyond treatises or theology, to the point where men look into each other's eyes in peace. *"Shalom, shalom."* The observers burst into loud, sustained applause.

President Shazar presented to the Pope a golden medal engraved with a miniature map of the holy places, and an inscription, "Love thy neighbor as thyself." Also on the edge were the words, "State of Israel." Some Israelis maintained that by the formal exchange with Shazar and his cabinet, on Israeli soil, the Pope had committed the Vatican to all but formal recognition of Israel—a step hotly opposed by the Arab states and thus far avoided by the Vatican because of the unresolved state of war. The Pope presented Shazar with two silver candlesticks, with figurines of angels holding the candleholders.

Among those greeting the Pope was a man who recalled poignant memories—Meir Mendes, deputy director of the Ministry of Religious Affairs, who said his own life and that of his father had been saved in 1939 by Pope Paul, then Monsignor Montini, a Vatican Undersecretary of State. Through Montini's intervention, Mendes said, he and his father had been enabled to leave Italy for Jerusalem, thus avoiding certain arrest and internment in Germany by the Nazis. He and the Pope embraced warmly.

The Pope left Megiddo at 10:18 A.M., an hour and a half behind schedule. It was thirteen miles northwest to his next stop, a town which once had a shabby reputation. As typical Galileans used to put it, "Can anything good come out of Nazareth?" [3] It was the hometown of Jesus.

Nazareth nestles against a crescent-shaped mountainside, a sleepy village of flat, white limestone houses, sloping dusty lanes, stone walks, and surrounding groves of figs, cypresses, and pomegranates. Below it a rocky and wooded gorge between the mountain spurs issues into the Plain of Esdraelon to the south. Here, in the heart of Galilee, Jesus spent his boyhood, learning to fell timber, to use an adze in shaping yokes and plowshares in Joseph's woodworking shop.

From the surrounding high ground, he could look out and see almost the whole country, from the snow-clad Mount Hermon in the north to Mount Tabor on the southern plain and the ranging heights of Carmel on the coast of the great sea to the west. Here in obscurity he grew to manhood and here, after beginning his ministry at the age of about thirty, he came home to preach a sermon. It so aroused the townspeople, who considered it presumptuous of this familiar son of a carpenter, that they sought to hurl him headlong from a precipice. "No prophet is acceptable in his own country," he said. [4] He left, not to return.

In an Israel which swiftly is becoming a nation of modern technology, Nazareth retains its ancient, provincial ways—much as in Jesus' time. Its women still carry water jars and baskets on their heads. Shepherds still drive their flocks along narrow streets. Citizens wear the dark robes and flowing white headdresses of Bedouins. Although in an overwhelmingly Jewish country, Nazareth is a thoroughly Arab town; its Arab people are both Moslems and Christians, and there is a sizable bloc of Communists. Two Communist members of the fifteen-member Nazareth town council had abstained when it voted to name the street on which the Pope would make his entry, "Paulus VI Street." They had argued unsuccessfully to make it "Street of Peace." The two-mile street never had a name before. Formally designating it on the day before the Pope's arrival, Nazareth Mayor Seif Ed Din Zubi, a Moslem, cut a blue-and-white ribbon, the colors of Israel, and said:

"In the name of Allah and the holy Pope Paul VI we name this street." A thirty-foot banner of papal yellow-and-white was raised above the street, proclaiming its new name in Arabic, Hebrew, and English.

It whipped in a twenty-four-mile-an-hour wind, which was piercingly cold despite sunny skies, as Pope Paul rode into town at 10:45 A.M., an hour and five minutes behind his scheduled arrival time. Balconies, store windows, and hotel fronts blazed with pennants and his portrait. Thousands of people, who had waited shiveringly, wrapped in shawls and blankets, or jumping up and down to keep warm, let go with the banked fervors in them, and the waves of applause, cheers, and waggling flags rolled along the street. A specially constructed "Trinity arch" marked the city entrance. Built in three sections, representing God the Father, God the Son, and God the Holy Spirit, it was hung with Vatican and Israeli flags and a thirty-foot banner saying in Arabic, Hebrew, and French: "Greetings from the workers of Nazareth to His Holiness."

The reception had enthusiasm and color, like that in Jerusalem, but it also had a difference—discipline.

Israeli security forces kept things under tight control, as they did throughout the papal tour of Israel. Since the night before, for more than twelve hours, Nazareth had been a closed city, with only officially authorized traffic allowed in or out. Iron barricades lined the streets to hold back the crowds, with white-capped police and green-uniformed frontier guards armed with Uzzi submachine guns standing at close intervals. More than three hundred plainclothesmen were on rooftops along the route into the city.

At the door of the Church of the Annunciation, Rabbi Pinhas Miller from the outlying Jewish community shook hands with the Pope, saying, "Shalom Uvtucha" . . . "Peace and blessing." A carpet led down the center aisle, flanked by railings hung with scarlet cloth. Greek and Latin prelates, Moslems, Israeli officials, and diplomats, including those who had rushed back from Megiddo, filled the bleachers on either side, along with their families—Japanese, Indian, and African, as well as European—about eight hundred of them.

A forty-voice boys' choir sang, "You are the rock," as the Pope walked through the church, pausing along the way for greetings, introductions, to lift his hands benignly. He looked weary, but pleased. At the end of the nave he descended fourteen steps, out of sight, into the rockhewn cavern regarded as the abode of Joseph and his betrothed Mary, the spot where an angelic announcement reached her. "Hail, O favored one, the Lord is with you! . . . Do not be afraid, Mary, for you have found favor with God. . . . You will conceive in your womb and bear a son, and you shall call his name Jesus. He will be great, and will be called the Son of the Most High. . . ." Mary had trembled in wonder. "How can this be, since I have no husband?" . . . "The Holy Spirit will come upon you, and the power of the Most High will overshadow you. . . ." And Mary had said, "I am the handmaid of the Lord; let it be to me according to your word."[5]

Inside the grayish white stone grotto, you can still see the wall ledges, the chiseled bins and niches for domestic uses. An inscription over the altar there says in Latin, "Verbum Caro Hic Factum Est" . . . "Here the Dear Word was made Flesh." The Pope, after celebrating Mass, delivered an address from the cave in French. He said that Nazareth "is the school of initiation into the understanding of the life of Jesus. . . . Here one understands the need of observing the settings of his dealings with us: the places, the time, the customs, the language, the religious atmosphere—all of which Jesus used to reveal himself to the world. Everything speaks to us. Everything has meaning."

The remarks had a relevance for the recent surge of Biblical studies in the Roman Catholic Church, employing linguistic, archaeological, ethnologic, and other scientific tools to gain a fuller, more accurate grasp of Scriptural meanings. Overcoming past objections, both the late Pope John and Pope Paul have encouraged such inquiry, as stimulated by Cardinal Bea and others, paralleling Protestant work in the field.

"At the same time," Pope Paul said, "the influence of the light of the gospel flows from the mysterious, free, and unmerited outpourings of grace. . . ." His stout voice was carried over loudspeakers both in the church and to the crowd outside. "Oh, how we would like to become children again and to return to learn our lessons in this humble and yet sublime school of Nazareth." Understanding the gospel, he added, is a "never-ending education." These words also underlined an ecumenical point—that the church still needs to learn and deepen its comprehension of doctrine. This outlook had been obscured until recently in Catholicism, and its resurgence has opened territory for exploration along with Protestantism and Orthodoxy.

Pope Paul said Nazareth also offers other important lessons—the value of silence, of simple domestic life, human labor, humility, and the greatest of all, love. "We believe, O Lord, in thy word. We will try to follow and live it." Closed-circuit television carried the Pope's image to those in the church. He said that blessedness, as exemplified by Jesus of Nazareth, comes through generosity, forgiveness, loving the poor as brothers, sacrifice, and struggle for justice. "Blessed are we if . . . we learn to pardon and to struggle on, to work and to serve, to suffer and to love. . . ." Being in Nazareth, he said, made that task clear, and gave him a sense of "new wisdom and fresh courage."

After the service, the Pope had a ten-minute breakfast snack of bread, butter, jam, and black coffee in the adjoining Franciscan monastery, Terra Sancta. He ate at an oval table, with a vase of red roses in the center. But time pressed. He spent, altogether, an hour and twenty-three minutes in Nazareth. He left at 12:08 P.M., escorted by nine motorcycle police, to quick-tour the rest of Galilee, that enchanting domain of tranquility and storm, of revolutions and gentle wisdom, of green valleys and buckling, rock-ribbed hills formed by dead volcanoes, of vineyards, date palms, and sabra cacti, of herds of sheep and roaring caterpillar tractors. "And he went about all Galilee, teaching. . . ."[6] An old rabbinical saying calls it the "land enriched only by the waters of heaven."

Along the road, by fields, through villages, and across mountainside

pastures, intermittent little bands of people in rustic dress stood behind stone fences to smile and wave at the passerby. His stops were
intense, touching, and transitory.

So swiftly fled the time that just four miles east of Nazareth at
Cana, the village where Jesus prolonged a wedding party by convert-
ing water to fine wine, the Pope's convoy scarcely paused, although
nearly the whole populace of four thousand had turned out to welcome him. He made a gesture of sympathetic helplessness, and went
on—already more than an hour behind schedule.

Sixteen miles northeast of Nazareth, the winding hilly road topped
a lofty brow, and there below lay the Sea of Galilee, shining in the
sun like a blue-green sapphire set in the cup of the mountains.

On those shores Jesus mustered his band of fishermen. "Follow me."
And there he built his ministry.

Most of the bustling lakeside towns he knew, Magdala, Bethsaida,
Capernaum, are merely ruins now, except for Tiberias, the capital
built by Herod Antipas near the center of the thirteen-mile western
shore. It still is a thriving resort town. But north of there—the principal area of Jesus' activity—is mostly vacant shoreline today, dotted
with trees, the isolated shrines, the white foam breaking on the rocks.

Four times along that stretch of shore, in a space of three miles,
the Pope left his car. Each spot of ground, each path and hill, the
very air, seemed imbued with events which ever since have lifted
hearts, inspired the church, and gripped the minds of men.

He first stopped at the Church of the Loaves and Fishes, situated in
a sloping, grassy draw beside the lake. Tradition marks it as the place
where only five loaves and two fishes, when blessed by Jesus, became
a bountiful meal for a restless, hungry crowd of five thousand. "And
they all ate and were satisfied." [7] The little church's bell rang as the
Pope alighted at 1 P.M. Only eight Arab Christian families live there
now in a little community called Tabgha. One resident asked excited-
ly, "Is it true that the Pope will walk on water?" A prelate shushed
him, apparently irritated at such ingenuous faith. The impulsive Apostle Peter had once tried walking on water, in imitation of Jesus, and
went under, gurgling, "Lord, save me!" [8]

The Pope prayed briefly in the church. Another Arab offered him a
cup of coffee on a tray. Finding it steaming hot, the Pope poured it
into another cup to cool it. "I'm so moved to be here," he told the
Benedictine priest who maintains the church and who had scrubbed it
inside and out for the occasion. As he left, the Pope removed the
stole he wore and draped it on the smiling priest's shoulders as a gift.

A quarter mile to the north, the Pope stopped again, left his car at the road, and walked down a 250-yard dirt trail beside tall pine and eucalyptus trees to the lakeside. Sun, soil, and sea combined to give that spot a quality of quiet, restfulness, and pleasant grace. Shielded from the wind by the encircling hills and trees, a clearing of sun-warmed green grass stretched beside the shore. A little basalt stone structure—called the "Sanctuary of the Primacy of Peter"— stands there.

It memorializes the place where the resurrected Jesus assigned a paramount responsibility to Peter, the apostle of whom Pope Paul is considered by his church to be the 262nd successor. "Feed my lambs," Jesus told the hardy fisherman. Three times Jesus asked Peter about the steadfastness of his love, and three times Peter vowed it. "Yes, Lord; you know that I love you. . . ." Said Jesus, "Feed my sheep." [9]

Pope Paul seemed entranced by the place. After praying inside the church before its rough rock altar, he came out and stepped down to the edge of the lake. He stood there gazing out over it. The water lapped lazily against the jut of rock at his feet, tossing up bright beads in the sunlight. It was a soothing interlude, after the strain of crowds. A rapt wonder shone in his eyes, and his lips moved silently. He stooped down and lifted up a handful of water, watching it trickle away. Then he gazed again out over the blue surface.

In the stillness, in the soft song of the surf, it seemed as if the centuries rolled back and the voice, the strength, the love and wisdom of the Nazarene emanated once again from the mists of those waters. "Why are you afraid, O men of little faith?" [10] It is an odd lake, so serene at times, and again so suddenly violent, rent by gales sweeping out of the mountain gorges and churning the placid water into six-foot waves. "Peace! Be still!" [11] And the waters calmed, and also the fears. The warm springs and sweet water of that lake still swarm with mullet and blenny, the kind Peter, Andrew, James, and John used to catch. A legend says that of all the seas God made, he selected the Lake of Galilee for himself.

Again the Pope bent down and dipped a hand into the water. By this time a platoon of photographers had infiltrated closely around him, even wading knee-deep into the water in front of him to get their shots, and the mood of reverie was interrupted. The Pope smiled genially, raising his arms in blessing. Even then he seemed reluctant to leave. Several times he turned as if to go, only to turn back and stare longer out over the lake. After fifteen minutes there, he left. An associate said the stop was a high point for the Pope in his trip.

A mile and a half further north, he stopped briefly at the ruins of

Capernaum. In Jesus' day it had been a crowded fishing port of fifty thousand people. Today it is a fenced enclave of heaped dark lava rock, crumbling columns, old millstones, and other artifacts beside a Franciscan church. Jesus, after leaving Nazareth, "went and dwelt in Capernaum by the sea." [12] The remains of a synagogue there denote the one where he often taught. The Pope examined some old mosaics, supposedly from the house where the Apostle Peter and his wife had lived, and then led the assembled clergy in a prayer ending "Hallelujah!"

Leaving at 2 p.m., he drove next to the top of the nearby Mount of Beatitudes, crowned by evergreens and feathery olive trees and over-looking the stretch of shoreline he had just visited. From the terrace of the domed convent there, he looked out over the sacred country and beyond, across the lake to Syria, where many border conflicts have erupted.

From this hilltop, Jesus preached his revolutionary and immortal sermon. "Blessed are the poor . . . those who mourn . . . the meek . . . those who hunger and thirst for righteousness . . . the merciful . . . the pure in heart . . . the peacemakers . . . those who are perse-cuted for righteousness' sake. . . ." [13] Love your enemies and pray for those who persecute you. . . . [14] Where your treasure is, there will your heart be also. . . . [15] No one can serve two masters. . . ." [16] Judge not, that you be not judged." [17] At the convent, the Pope had a lunch of soup and fish, like those the apostles used to catch, and for dessert, oranges.

It was midafternoon. Most of the papal cavalcade now headed back toward Jerusalem. But two cars remained to ascend to a place of mys-tery. The Pope and Cardinal Tisserant now occupied one of the cars, Cardinals Cicognani and Testa the other. They drove about fifteen miles southwest, once more to the margin of the Plain of Esdraelon or Jezreel.

There, majestic and alone, soared the awesome Mount Tabor. It rises like a great ethereal hemisphere, 1,843 feet above the level plain, its sides steep, shadowy, and corrugated by time. It has a haunting history. Abraham bivouacked there. The tribes of Israel, in the time of the Prophetess Deborah, fortified themselves there against the Canaanites. Altars to God were raised there, and also heathen idols, denounced by the Prophet Hosea as a "net spread upon Tabor." [18] Galilean insurgents against Rome fought from there. A He-brew legend relates that the mountain itself once spoke in eerie gran-deur: "I am Tabor, and on me rests the divine presence, for I am the loftiest mountain and the waters of the deluge did not cover me."

That dome-like summit also is regarded as the place where one of the most mystifying events of Jesus' career took place.

A narrow, crooked road, curling around hairpin turns, beneath over-hanging branches and along cliffs took Pope Paul to the top. Beyond a stone arch, topped by a cross, an avenue of cypress trees led up to a square before the Franciscan Basilica of the Transfiguration. Flags of the Vatican flew there, and those of the Franciscans, too—five red crosses on a white field. The Pope walked along a path strewn with red roses to the basilica. Its bells tolled. Just inside he knelt, then moved forward to the cylindrical-shaped altar, ascended the fourteen steps, and knelt again. Eight candles burned there. A hush fell over the fifty onlookers, monks, nuns, and others.

Tradition marks this as the high place to which Jesus took his three closest disciples, Peter, James, and John. There, apart from the others and the distractions of the world, a glowing vapor enveloped them and suddenly they recognized Jesus as more than just a great and manly teacher. "The appearance of his countenance was altered, and his raiment became dazzling white. And behold, two men talked with him, Moses and Elijah. . . ." [19] Dazed by the glory, blinking in the bright cloud as if heavy with sleep and fear, the three disciples heard a voice saying, " 'This is my beloved Son, with whom I am well pleased; listen to him.' When the disciples heard this, they fell on their faces, and were filled with awe. But Jesus came and touched them, saying, 'Rise and have no fear.' " [20]

Pope Paul lingered there, watching the sun set in splendor over Galilee. In that last hour of light, it was as if he wanted to absorb to the fullest the mood and message of this unfathomable land. From the mountaintop, he had a sweeping view—the smooth valley below, the tender, rolling hills to the north, the purpling lake, and beyond it, the dark knobs of the mountains of Gilead. After a long pause outside the church, he walked to a large monastery balcony and remained there in thought, gazing at the fading landscape. The sun hung momentarily, like a golden-red ball, silhouetting the coastal hills, then slowly disappeared, unfurling flames of crimson, orange, and violet across the firmament. "Yet I tell you, even Solomon in all his glory was not arrayed like one of these." Simple words, penetrating words, spoken unforgettably in this land, long ago. "Do not be anxious about tomorrow, for tomorrow will be anxious for itself." [21]

As night fell, the Pope rode back to Jerusalem by a different route, traveling west to the coastal corridor linking Galilee and southern Israel, following it southward across the Plains of Sharon by the sea, then slanting east again through the Judean hills. Headlights of his car threw long shadows along the canyon walls. At 7:45 P.M., he reached the Israeli sector of the holy city, where Mayor Mordechai Ish-Shalom greeted him with warm words, token gifts of bread and salt symbolizing welcome, and the traditional Hebrew words, "Blessed be he who comes in the name of the Lord."

Once again, along the festooned and brightly lighted streets of new Jerusalem, enthusiastic throngs acclaimed the passing guest, but with an orderliness quite different from the chaotic scramble the previous day on the other side of the divided city. The smoothly effective policing characterized the day's entire 250-mile looping circuit through Israel. Before leaving, the Pope made yet another stop—on Mount Zion.

Its landscaped contours, walks, and roadways glowed under special illumination, and excited bells chimed as the Pope mounted to the lighted stone monuments at the summit. Situated there are the black-domed tomb of King David, the Dormition Monastery regarded as the place where the Virgin Mary spent her last days before falling into a sleep of death, and the two-story house of the "Upper Room," the cenacle where Christ celebrated Passover with his disciples on the night before his crucifixion—his last supper.

The Pope first visited the Dormition chapel, where he spoke briefly to the assembled clergy about his desire that the various faiths, Christians and Jews, live together in peace and brotherly love. An effigy of the Virgin Mary reposes there. The Pope then moved through an arcade and up an outside stone stairway to the cenacle, a barren, second-floor chamber in grayish white, illuminated by a kind of unreal, semi-light.

It presumably was here that Jesus shared that final dramatic meal with his apostles before his arrest, observing that one of them would betray him. "Is it I, Lord?" Jesus answered, "He who has dipped his hand in the dish with me . . ." And Judas, pale and shaken, fled. Then Jesus blessed bread and wine and passed it to his men. "Take, eat; this is my body. . . . Drink of it all of you; for this is my blood of the covenant, which is poured out for many for the forgiveness of sins." [22] He told believers to continue that meal in his memory. It became a central part of Christian worship.

Inside that chamber, a thick oriental rug had been placed in the middle of the room for the Pope's visit. But he knelt instead on the rough stone floor, remembering perhaps the words which Jesus used on that last night. "A servant is not greater than his master; nor is he who is sent greater than he who sent him." [23]

Meanwhile, in an adjoining shrine, the "Cave of the Holocaust,"

Cardinal Tisserant stood before black marble slabs inscribed with long lists of the dead, and lighted six candles in memory of the six million Jews who died under Nazism. The somber, dark-walled chamber contains grisly mementoes of the Nazi massacres, including parchments of human skin. Pope Paul had offered to meet Chief Rabbi Nissim there, but apparently because of the rushed schedule, neither appeared. As Cardinal Tisserant lighted the candles, Israel's Minister of Religious Affairs, S. Warhaftig, exclaimed, "Six for six million!" The cardinal repeated the phrase, "Six for six million." He added quietly, just above a whisper, "We participate in the sorrow of the Hebrew people." Then he bowed his head briefly in prayer before he turned and went out.

Moments later, in circumstances of courageous candor, Pope Paul spoke to his Jewish well-wishers of what he termed "unjust accusations" that the late Pope Pius XII failed to condemn sufficiently the Nazi murders. This obviously referred to the controversial modern play, "The Deputy," by German writer Rolf Hochhuth, which alleges that Pius remained silent in the face of the death-oven horrors. In a voice heavy with emotion Paul said, "Pope Pius XII did all he could during World War II for all those who were in need, without distinction. Everybody knows what he did for the defense and the rescue of all those who were caught in its tribulations, without distinction." Paul paused, adding: "We nurse only feelings of good will toward all people. The church loves them all equally."

Paul's remarks, praised by Israeli newspapers as a forthright expression of friendship, came as he bade farewell to Israeli leaders at the Mandelbaum Gate, the red-and-white metal bar marking the only regular crossing point between Israel and Jordan. It usually is only one-way, except through special arrangements, since Jordan prohibits entry from Israel. But the normal barriers didn't function on this trip.

Hundreds of Israelis, including many bearded Orthodox Jews, ringed the gate as the Pope stepped from his car, smiling, and shook hands with President Shazar, the second time they met that day. He told the Pope that "the hopes of all who dwell in Zion" are in accord with his work for justice, progress, and peace. "As for us, our hand is stretched out in a gesture of peace towards the neighboring states. . . ." He quoted the Prophet Micah: "Let every nation walk in the name of its God and we in the name of the Lord our God forever."

"May your departure be in peace," he told Pope Paul.

The Pope, who that day had covered almost the proverbial limits of the Holy Land from Dan to Beersheba, said: "It was the most unforgettable day of my life." He added: "We lift our eyes on high and pray that God's blessings may be lavished upon you. . . ." And again: *"Shalom."*

They shook hands once more. The Pope drove back into Jordan at 9:07 P.M. His whirlwind tour of Israel had lasted eleven hours and twenty-two minutes. Rejoined by the Jordanian armed jeeps, he drove directly to the Apostolic Delegation quarters, where he met a half-hour later that night with Orthodox Patriarch Athenagoras, an encounter to be detailed later. The Pope didn't get to bed until late again. He must have been getting tired. But there would be no rest tomorrow.

CHAPTER 7

Monday Morning

The Pope went to Bethlehem, of course. Bright and early on Monday, January 6.

"But you, O Bethlehem, Ephrathah, who are little to be among the clans of Judah, from you shall come forth for me one who is to be ruler in Israel, whose origin is from of old, from ancient days."[1] So wrote the Prophet Micah of old.

In Hebrew, the town's name means "house of bread"—of sustenance for life. It is the city of David, the ancestral town to which Joseph and Mary went from Nazareth to register in a tax census nearly two thousand years ago, the place where Jesus was born.

Perched on an east-west ridge of pink sandrock and limestone, it is six miles south of Jerusalem over the old direct road. But the Pope had to travel a winding new route thirteen miles long since it must skirt the twisting truce line which protrudes between the two cities.

A red-coated lancer riding a black Arabian stallion led the papal motorcade into the banner-bedecked little town at 7:45 A.M. Golden sunlight bathed the rolling Judean countryside roundabout and the shepherd's valley spreading below Bethlehem on the east, regarded as the pasture where the angelic tidings burst upon the fearful herdsmen. "Be not afraid; for behold, I bring you good news of a great joy which will come to all the people; for to you is born this day in the city of David a Savior, who is Christ the Lord."[2]

Once more King Hussein's helicopter kept overhead vigil. And this time barbed-wire rolls and steel barricades, reinforced with troops, kept back the crowds surrounding Manger Square fronting the oldest church on earth, the Church of the Nativity, first erected in the fourth century in the time of the Emperor Constantine.

A triangular blue arch, bearing royal and Vatican colors and portraits, and an umbrella pine Christmas tree, dangling with lights, decorated the square. The Pope's party walked along behind the traditional Moslem kuwasses, wearing gold-embroidered red uniforms and silver swords, beating the pavement with silver-headed canes to announce the approach of an important personage. "Thump, thump, thump . . ." They made a drumbeat that could be heard above the bells, organ music, and the chanting choirs. Another flock of white doves winged upward from opened cages; one of them landed momentarily

110

at the Pope's feet and then took off again. At the church the Pope clasped the hands of two Greek Orthodox prelates, took off his wide-brimmed red hat, and bent low to go through the tiny door, less than four feet high.

He circled along cloisters into the adjoining Church of St. Catherine, filled with worshipers, and prayed briefly there before re-entering the old central basilica and descending the sixteen dark steps into the cave marking the place where "you will find a babe wrapped in swaddling cloths and lying in a manger." [3] The cave is thirty-four feet long and eleven feet wide, draped with blue and gold brocades, lit by fifty-three hanging lamps, their soft glow heightened now by television lights. In one end, a fourteen-pointed silver star embedded in the marble floor commemorates the precise place of the birth, and another chapel nook, the manger. There Pope Paul knelt in worship, in the age-old prayers, repentance, and praise of the Mass. "Behold, the Lord ruler is come and a kingdom is in his hands."

The day marked the feast of the Epiphany, or "manifestation," of Jesus as the Christ. For Western churches, this recalls the visit of the wise men from the East. For Eastern Orthodoxy, it recalls the baptism of Jesus. In both cases, it means his manifestation as Lord.

Like the magi of old, Pope Paul laid gifts of gold (a golden rose), frankincense (incense burning in a thurible), and myrrh (from the Eastern city of Mecca where Mohammed was born) on the altar. Then, with his voice piped outside by loudspeakers, he delivered the major address of his trip—a ringing appeal for peace among men and unity among Christians.

"This is the historic hour in which the church must live her profound and visible unity," he said. "It is the hour in which we must correspond with the wish of Jesus Christ 'that they may be perfectly one, so that the world may know, Father, that it is thou who hast sent me.'" To help bring this about, the Pope added, the Vatican Council must act to "give to the church's life new attitudes of mind, new aims, new standards of conduct"—in thought, prayer, education, law, art, and words. The call for such efforts falls not only on the Roman Catholic fold but on "our Christian brothers who are not in perfect communion with us." His implication was that partial communion among the churches already exists.

"It is now clear to everyone that the problem of unity cannot be put on one side. Today the will of Christ is pressing upon us and obliging us to do all that we can, with love and wisdom, to bring to all Christians the supreme blessing and honor of a united church."

In the meantime, he said, "we are ready to consider every reasonable possibility by which mutual understanding, respect, and charity may be fostered so as to smooth the way to a future—and, please God, not too distant—meeting with our Christian brothers still separated from us." He said, "Our affection goes in advance of the steps to be taken." Like other ecumenical leaders, he said reunion must not involve hollow compromises "which are not the fruit of free conviction." Instead, he said, the valid solutions must come through "the effect of the Spirit of the Lord, who breathes when and where he wills." In that brief phrase the Pope disavowed any rigid advance presumptions about how, and from where or through whom the answers might be found. The Lord's Spirit "breathes when and where he wills. We shall wait for the happy hour to come."

He laid down only one requirement for all: That reunion "is not to be obtained at the expense of the truth of faith. We cannot be false to Christ's heritage. It is not ours, but his." With that, no church would differ.

"For the present, we ask of our separated brothers only that which we set before ourselves as our objective, namely, that every step toward reunion and interchange of views should be inspired by the love of Christ and the church."

Seldom had a pope declared his church's commitment to such an open, unqualified, and reciprocal search for Christian reunion, unhedged by any preconditions or demands on any party except the guidance of the Lord in truth.

In that appeal, made from the lowly cave where the Lord of all Christians came personally to mankind, the Pope pledged:

"We shall take pains to keep alive the desire for understanding and union and we shall put our trust in prayer which, even though it is not yet united prayer, rises up nevertheless simultaneously from ourselves and from Christians separated from us like two parallel columns which meet on high to form an arch in the God of unity."

The Pope not only declared his church's dedicated kinship to other Christians, but its underlying ties to Moslems and Jews and all "those who profess monotheism and who worship, as we do, the one true God, the supreme living God, the God of Abraham, the God all High."

Giving words to another point which his trip dramatized, he also asserted the church's affection for the world itself, for all its people and their accomplishments, a unitary concern beyond theology but drawn from it. "If the world thinks itself to be a stranger from Christianity, Christianity does not consider itself a stranger from the world, no matter what attitude the world adopts toward it." The Pope's words sounded a far different attitude from that in the day when the church seemed to regard withdrawal from others and from society in general as its proper course. "Let the world know that the representative and promoter of the Christian religion esteems and loves it with a great and inexhaustible love. . . . There is no good human quality that he (Christ) has not respected, elevated, and redeemed. There is no suffering that he has not understood, shared, and ennobled."

In the name of the Prince of Peace, he also appealed to the world's chiefs of state for "a new spirit of concord and generosity so as to eliminate at whatever cost the anguish and suffering to the world of a new world war whose consequences would be incalculable. Let them collaborate more efficiently to gain peace and truth in justice, in freedom, and in friendly love."

Pope Paul left Bethlehem at 9:15 A.M. for another meeting with Patriarch Athenagoras on the Mount of Olives, before heading back to Amman to emplane for Rome, at the end of a gruelling two-and-a-half days in which he had covered many miles, and in the history of the Roman Catholic Church, many milestones.

On a ceremonial dais at Amman Airport, surrounded again by government dignitaries, honor guards, bands, and various church leaders, Paul VI told the Moslem king: *"Salaam aleikim"* . . . "Peace be with you."

He thanked Hussein for his kind hospitality and said he would carry "forever in our heart" the memories of the Holy Land and its inhabitants. "May God reward them, may he wipe away their tears and grant them peace, prosperity, and happiness." Then, quoting St. Paul in a passage which seemed aimed at the present Jordan-Israeli conflict, he said:

" 'Let all bitterness and wrath and anger and clamor and slander be put away from you, with all malice, and be kind to one another, tenderhearted, forgiving one another, as God in Christ forgave you.' " [4] And, repeating the apostolic salutation, he added, "Peace be to this land, and to all who dwell herein." It seemed to be an appeal for an end of strife between the two countries. King Hussein, replying, said: "You have asked me, sir, to work with you and with other world leaders for world peace, and my answer is that I will do so with all my heart and strength. While I work for peace I will also work for justice, because there can be no lasting peace without justice to all men." To Arabs, this meant rolling back the Israelis. But the King went on to voice a warm good-by, promising to preserve the sacred shrines for all pilgrims, and calling the Pope the "greatest pilgrim of them all."

"Khatirkum," the Pope said, an Arabic salutation of farewell.

Before the Pope left Jerusalem, he also had dispatched 224 messages to heads of other nations, to United Nations Secretary General U Thant, and to major Protestant and Orthodox church bodies, urging renewed efforts for "welfare and peace among all peoples in justice and brotherly love" and pledging his dedication to those ends. To the various church leaders, he voiced gratitude for the signs of greater "Christian and fraternal collaboration." A stream of appreciative replies from church leaders, queens, presidents, and premiers, including Communist government heads, went back to the Vatican. Among others, W. A. Visser 't Hooft, General Secretary of the World Council of Churches, embracing most major Protestant and Orthodox denominations, voiced "assurance of our prayers for your ministry and for the unity of the people of God."

By his journey Paul VI had demonstrated the new mobility in his church and a new accessibility to others. He had scrapped the policy of papal confinement, self-imposed a century before by Pius IX. He had breached the Vatican wall and gone eastward, a messenger of a new church era which abandoned the aversions, suspicions, and exclusivism of the past, and brought the church into juxtaposition with the sundry ranks of men, with Moslems, Jews, and Christians of all kinds, and shown a readiness to stand with them in mutual respect and friendship on their ground and level without assuming Constantinian pre-eminence or prerogatives.

Any valid pilgrimage to the Holy Land is, first of all, to seek forgiveness and inspiration to do better. Pope Paul sounded that intent.

And his deportment bore it out. If nothing else, his familial entry into the house of Israel and the warm personal exchanges between him and his Israeli hosts amounted to a striking rebuke to any residue of anti-Semitism in the church. Both his itinerary and his words combined to undercut any notion that the origin of this fratricidal distortion could be found in authentic Christianity, whose very life had come through Judaism, through its clime, its culture, and its people.

The Vatican Council moved to make the same point. But something like the Pope's trip, acting out the promptings of conscience in direct, personal terms, could serve to do more than any number of official statements and conferences.

Throughout, his trip added up to a compelling example of tolerance. It demonstrated that Roman Catholicism was willing to go out of its way to enhance contacts with Moslems and Jews, as well as with other Christians. It presented Paul VI as a man unafraid to tread new roads. It showed that he wants to find ways to live with other Christian bodies and other religions and to continue the reforming work started by John XXIII. It symbolized "the sweeping changes taking place in what once seemed to be an unchangeable church," commented *The United Church Herald*, a Protestant weekly. [5]

Some people complained about publicity aspects of the trip, the huge concentration on it of news and broadcasting media. Indeed, these operations may have been distracting, not the least to the Pope himself. But this is a day of a literate world which demands information, a world whose deepening interrelationships confer a right and a responsibility to scrutinize events far and near. It is this obligation which focused such immense news facilities on an unprecedented event in the long history of an institution whose scope and influence touches not only its own members but others. One past criticism of Rome has been church secrecy. But the church, and the exigencies of the times, combine to work a change. And in the story of civilization and religion, Paul's pilgrimage made up a chapter essential to the record.

In other centuries Rome went to the Holy Land with its crusaders intent on conquering, possessing, and driving out the Moslem "infidels." But this time Rome went in comradely trust, received by a Moslem ruler, shielded by Moslem guards. It was a big difference.

The Pope's visit did not dispel the festering animosity between Arabs and Israelis and had no obvious enduring effect on it. Yet, through his influence, the barriers of hate did come down for a moment. Of course, they promptly went back up again, and some say the momentary show of co-operation left no dent in the bitter wall. But who can know or plumb the depth of any fact accomplished, no matter how momentary? Who can gauge for sure the hidden currents it released, the subtle imprints it left, or stay the hand of their continuing effects? That for a single interval the tank traps and barbed wire disappeared between Arabs and Jews, that you could walk back and forth freely through the Mandelbaum Gate without diplomatic dissimulation, that both sides displayed a common interest and cordiality out of kindred motives and toward the same end—these things would not resolve any technicalities of state. But neither could they be erased from the chemistry of time and event nor stricken from the cumulative store of the yesterdays which unfathomably make our tomorrows. They happened.

The trip also served as a harbinger. Pope Paul, and other popes to come, would now do more traveling. Eleven months later, he flew to India and ten months after that to New York, and talk flourished about possible trips to other places. Paul had come out of the Vatican shell, out of the Roman hibernation, out of the contrived realm of ostrich feather fans and superfluous pomp, to mingle face-to-face with the world and its people, with its great and its lowly, its problems, inequalities, and dangers. On foot, knocked around, feeling the pinch and pressures of the public, Paul has cast aside the illusory curtains within which popes so customarily have lived. And in doing so he found exhilaration.

More than anything else, however, the trip was a reminder of the "first things" in Christianity, of the incarnation, the teachings of Christ, his disciples, the cross. The church returned through its chief pastor to basics, to the landmarks of its sources, its directives and its purposes. By treading again the footsteps of Christ in reverent attentiveness, the Pope spotlighted the common ground on which the question for Christian reunion is centered, and called for inner pilgrimage and search by all churches in that nourishing spiritual soil from which they all sprang.

"By going back to the sites that held Christ and saw the birth of the infant church, the Pope calls us all to go back to the mainsprings of our faith," says Monsignor John M. Osterreicher, a Roman Catholic expert on Judeo-Christian relationships. [6] The physical journey was not the end in itself, but the acting out of a summons to an inward journey. "It is the beginning of a profound meditation," Pope Paul told cardinals when he got back to Rome.

Calling the pilgrimage a first step toward church reunification, he also told a general audience that it "was like the turning up by the plough of land hitherto hardened and inert, arousing an awareness of thoughts and divine designs that have laid buried, but not crushed, by centuries of history and experience, which now seems to open up to prophetic voices." He added:

"A return to the gospel must be our continuous exercise of thought, of spiritual fervor, of moral renewal, of religious and human sensitivity. . . . This return to the founts of the gospel does not carry with it a disavowal of what the church has derived from Christ, but an increasingly intense effort in bringing our Christian profession closer to its original conception, a search for greater essential faithfulness to the Lord's thoughts." [7]

In that mutual terrain, with that readiness to listen and learn, church leaders of many denominations saw the foundation and the hope for eventual Christian reunion, through common discovery and accord in a common Lord's undivided truth.

Curiously the pilgrimage had begun at the scenes of the death of Christ and concluded at the scenes of youth and birth. The road had gravitated backward from an end to a beginning. Possibly the church moved on that kind of road, out of the heavy, trudging vale of age into the region of being young again.

Certainly the tang of early life recovered was in the air when a Westerner and an Easterner embraced in Jerusalem, after a long winter of silence and scorn, and suddenly it seemed spring.

PART THREE

The East-West Rendezvous

"And men will come from east and west, and from north and south, and sit at table in the kingdom of God."   *Luke 13:29*

CHAPTER **8**

Assailing the Silence

An abandoned path to find . . . a chasm to cross . . . a darkness to pierce . . .

Athenagoras, a man of large size and sight, had tried it in the past, but found no way. The obstacles overwhelmed the approaches. He had dreamed of it, talked of it, insisted it could be done, and struggled to bring it about. But the path had remained hidden, the chasm had seemed too wide and the night impenetrable. He never gave up, though. It called to him, tugged at him, and urged him on.

Finally it came to pass.

Patriarch Athenagoras I of Constantinople, spiritual leader of all Eastern Orthodoxy, could not have accomplished it alone. Nor could any man. Yet his ardent and astute persistence kindled the cause. It found a like impulse in Paul VI. So it came about that the Patriarch of the East, the 268th successor in a church post which ancient accounts say began with the Apostle Andrew, and the Pope of the West, the 262nd holder of an office which those same traditions say began with the Apostle Peter, broke through the formidable impasse and reclaimed a long-lost heritage.

They embraced as brothers, which is what Andrew and Peter were in their lifetimes. They revived a vanished legacy. Only once before in 1,254 years had the chief pastors of the Orient and Occident met, and that was long ago under military and political pressures. This time, they met freely without reservations or barter, in fraternity of faith.

The event signaled a reversal in the longest cold war in Christian history.

It spanned a yawning divide between churches of the West and East.

And it made January seem like June in Jerusalem.

"My dear brother in Christ," exclaimed Athenagoras. He grasped Paul's frail shoulders.

"Thanks be to God," said Pope Paul.

Only as measured against the past can the truly epochal significance of that present moment be understood. So much antagonism and suspicion, so many bitter centuries had divided Roman Catholicism and

119

Eastern Orthodoxy. It was as if a mammoth glacier had crept between them, swollen by time and hardened by arctic rage, sundering the continents of Christianity. For more than a thousand years— twice as long as the strictly Western conflict between Protestantism and Rome—the barrier had grown. It loomed treacherous and seemingly impassable, a trackless Himalayan icecap bisecting the church. In that midnight zone separating the ancient Eastern and Western sectors of Christianity, a frigid silence reigned. No words were exchanged. No thoughts were shared. No couriers moved.

An iron wall seemed fixed between them.

Athenagoras had sought throughout his regime to find a way to breach it, without apparent results. A huge, affectionate man, with the exuberance of his native East and the practicality of the West where he spent eighteen years as Greek Orthodox Archbishop of the Americas, he saw divisions among Christians as their critical failing in the modern interlinked world. In 1949, shortly after his election as patriarch, he sent a courtesy note to Pope Pius XII. It evoked no reply, nor acknowledgment.

The wall remained impervious.

Around it, however, other tides of Christian reconciliation already had begun to flow, with a momentum destined to surmount not only East-West religious barriers, but political ones as well.

Under the leadership of Athenagoras, the several national branches of Eastern Orthodoxy had become vigorous participants in the Protestant-originated interchurch movement, including the World Council of Churches, founded in 1948, and the various regional co-operative councils. Ever since the sixteenth century breakup in the Western church, when Protestants left Roman Catholicism, there had been irregular communications between Eastern Orthodoxy and West European Protestant theologians—Lutherans, Anglicans, Presbyterians, and others. In 1920, the Patriarch of Constantinople had called for the creation of a "league of churches" to pool their strength in common Christian endeavors. Thus some ground had been laid for Orthodoxy's early entry into the new ecumenical organizations with Protestants. (Long isolated from the others, however, and among the last major Orthodox bodies to join the World Council was the Russian Orthodox Church, in 1961, predating its subsequent contacts with Rome.) But through the years, not even tenuous diplomacy had been maintained between the two principal sees of ancient Christendom, Rome and Constantinople (now Istanbul).

A void had separated them.

Athenagoras I had continued seeking to revive some correspondence across it, along with the growing Eastern bonds with Protestantism. It wasn't easy. A sort of mute paralysis had settled over the intervening distance, on both sides. Athenagoras kept probing.

In 1952, he called on Rome's Apostolic Delegate in Turkey, Archbishop Andrew Cassulo, making an unprecedented overture. In 1954 he wrote a lengthy letter to Francis Cardinal McIntyre of Los Angeles, saying in part: "The powers of Christ, divided and in many respects in evident opposition, are not able to stand impressively together against the contemporary enemy. The cross in hands that are not joined in peace and love fails to impress. The gospel spread and interpreted by opposing groups that seek converts from each other fails to touch hearts and change lives. All these are happening while the forces of the enemy increase. . . . Putting aside all barriers and obstacles, the church must offer her whole strength to help and protect our faltering civilization." [1]

The appeal came from the highest office in the Eastern church, and seemed aimed indirectly at stimulating reciprocal contacts on that level. None developed.

On occasions, Pius XII had urged unity by allegiance to Rome. But this offered no leeway for mutual give-and-take conversation. The prolonged rigid silence went on.

Then suddenly, after John XXIII became pope in late 1958, the inhibitions started slipping away. " 'There was a man sent from God, whose name was John,' " Athenagoras observed, quoting the New Testament description of John the Baptist, forerunner of Christ's mission of unity and peace. [2]

Warm, relaxed notes and tokens of mutual esteem began flowing back and forth between Pope and Patriarch. A hearty candor marked both men, and it showed up in their budding relationship. "I have told the Pope that only in paradise can one live alone," Athenagoras remarked in fond good humor. [3] Particularly on Christmas and Easter, the two exchanged small gifts and greetings of friendship. John had spent twenty years as a papal diplomat in the predominantly Orthodox Middle East—in Bulgaria, Turkey, and Greece—acquiring a firm personal regard for the Eastern churchmen. After becoming pope, the first non-Roman Catholic prelate whom he received was Archbishop Iakovos, head of the Greek Orthodox Church in North and South America, as emissary for Athenagoras. Thereafter, deputations between Rome and Constantinople began circulating for the first time since the late Middle Ages.

Nevertheless, they still moved through an intermediate zone brittle with the distrust and scars of centuries.

Even the subtleties of ecclesiastical etiquette, with their implications of relative authority, served to impede closer associations.

Extolling Pope John, Athenagoras told me in a 1961 interview at the patriarchate in Istanbul: "I would like to visit him on condition that he would return the visit." In other words, Orthodox sensitivities on the matter precluded any arrangement that might imply one-sided capitulation. On the other hand, by Vatican custom, the pope only received; he was not received. Connotations of gesture tended to anchor both sides. "So far, we have only been able to send messengers," Athenagoras said. But his voice brimmed with confidence about the possibilities opened up by John. "I love him. He is a fine man, a broad-minded, goodhearted, and great man." A hand at his heart, the Patriarch leaned forward, eyes bright, his vast beard brushing the desk. "He realizes the conditions under which Christians are now living, that we can do nothing divided, that we cannot preach peace when divided among ourselves."

Yet East was East and West was West. Against the long-entrenched background of hostility, some Orthodox leaders, particularly Archbishop Chrysostomos of Athens and all Greece, frowned on any dealings with Rome whatever. Athenagoras, whose leadership hinged on persuasion rather than arbitrary rule, could not ignore the deep-seated qualms. At the same time he asserted readiness for concourse on a reciprocal basis. "We Orthodox have opened our doors to all other churches, to all other Christians." He spread his arms, and with them, the black wings of his robe. "We have also opened our eyes, our hearts, and minds."

It was this dawning disposition, both in the East and the West, which finally overcame the encumbering formalities and enabled the "twain to meet" in the most extraordinary encounter of modern times.

Before it happened, or could happen, however, there had to be some specific, bold initiatives—and these came from Paul VI and Athenagoras I. An odd meshing of intuitions and timing figured in it.

To a striking degree Athenagoras personifies the Eastern Orthodox churches—warm, buoyant, optimistic, majestic, even awesome. A towering, six-foot-four man of seventy-nine, hairy-visaged as an Old Testament prophet, and garbed in voluminous black, he exudes zeal and beneficence. But his energies are not random; they burn with purpose; he has marshaled them to it—the healing and strengthening of broken Christianity in a faith-threatening age.

"It is suicide to be divided," he told me. He stared through a window at the sky, gray over the Bosporus' Golden Horn. "We say that Christ is the light of the world, the hope of the world. But how can we transmit this idea to humanity if we are divided and opposing each other?" He clasped his hands, and his head tilted upward, his eyes igniting above the white tumble of beard. "We are all Christians, all baptized in the name of the same Holy Trinity—we have the same Lord, the same gospel, the same history, the same destiny here and hereafter." In this identity, and in the gathering surge toward Christian reunion, he found high hope. "We have lived for centuries without this dialogue, without this happiness, this beauty of the human heart and soul. We have lived in estrangement, even in hatred. But now we are moving. After centuries of division, it is not so easy. But we are moving, by the force of destiny, by the force of the gospel, by the force of the blood of Christ."

In Athenagoras the movement has behind it an adroit church diplomat—a man of unusual breadth and learning, as well as fervor. In his quarter century as patriarch, he has brought Orthodoxy to the forefront of world Christian attention; it had been little known in the West before. He speaks a half dozen languages—Greek, Turkish, English, French, Russian, Spanish. Under strained circumstances in predominantly Moslem Turkey, he has gained respect and popularity, precariously holding it even under stress of the recent Turkish-Greek conflict over Cyprus. (Back in 1822, Patriarch Gregorius V of Constantinople was hanged under orders of Sultan Mahmoud II on charges of plotting with Greeks against the government.)

Athenagoras also has managed to weld the autonomous, national segments of Eastern Orthodoxy into a systematically co-ordinated federation, after centuries of virtual detachment. A series of all-Orthodox conferences, launched in 1961 in Rhodes, has shaped the new cohesive pattern, for action as a whole church, rather than in fragments. From his former service in the United States, he drew his passion for intergroup harmony and unity in diversity. "America is a miracle of unity," he said. Impulsively, he sang a few phrases of "America the Beautiful." Signed photographs of Presidents of the United States dot the wall of his sparely furnished office.

He maintains that, as a varied nation stands united on mutual principles, the varied churches should stand together in mutual faith—and action. In his view a reunited Christianity must accept and appreciate variety, not suppress it. "Every church must preserve and contribute the treasures it has, united with others in mutual respect and dignity." Athenagoras is no sentimentalist who would gloss over basic doctrine for the sake of agreement, but beyond the essentials, he contends there must be great flexibility and freedom in practice—a characteristic of the Eastern churches. While holding the same basic doctrines, they have taken on wide geographical differences in rite, language, and methods.

Like other ecumenical exponents, Athenagoras recognizes that full reunion will require accord on primary doctrines, within the broad latitude of practice, and that this will take much time and cross-pollination of insights, understandings, and terms. But meanwhile, he says the urgencies of the world demand that the churches form a "common front" for co-operative action and service. "We must work side by side always more closely and in greater brotherhood in the field of practical action," he says. "In this way unity will fall one day into our hands like ripe fruit. This is why we wish to visit the Pope, so that we may embrace each other, weep over our long separation, express our pain about the past and our happiness for the future."

As to how doctrinal consensus will come, he once observed jokingly: "The theologians should be locked up on an island for a few years and we should come to an agreement. We should ask them to solve the doctrinal problems and then let us know the conclusions they have reached. The speed of world events and the recession of Christianity do not permit us to wait for their decisions." [4]

However, personal good will, expectancy, and urgent purpose could not alone dislodge the time-encrusted complications which kept patriarch and pope in official isolation from one another.

Only a fortuitous chain of incidents and curiously interlocking steps served to override the deadlock. So closely geared did the sequence become that in the end there was uncertainty as to just where, or through whom, it originated. This ambiguity itself may have been necessary. Indirect and sometimes vague factors make up much of the tangled, abrasive barrier between Roman Catholicism and Eastern Orthodoxy.

The long, sad history of that division is as much emotional, political, and administrative as it is doctrinal—probably more so.

In many ways the two ancient blocs of Christendom share the same beliefs and heritage. Unlike most Protestant bodies, other than Anglicans (Episcopalians) and Swedish Lutherans, both Orthodoxy and Roman Catholicism maintain the apostolic succession, tracing their lines of bishops back to the apostles. Each recognizes the priesthood and sacraments of the other as valid. For the first thousand years of the Christian era, both participated in the same church councils, evolved the same doctrinal creeds, and accepted each other as parts of the same holy, catholic, and apostolic church, sometimes differing, sometimes not quite understanding each other's viewpoints, but co-existing in loyal tension as one church, one people of God.

Then came the rupture over papal authority, the Great Schism of 1054. The heavy curtain fell between East and West. Both sides claim the other split from the true church and went into schism.

It was not, however, an instant affair. The minute seeds of irritation had appeared far back in the fourth century. Time sprouted them; harsh acts magnified them into the open break; the long separation extended and solidified them into total alienation.

What lay behind a conflict of such dominating and enduring dimensions?

In a sense, undertones of the problem may go back to the very beginning of Christianity, when two of the apostles of Jesus asked that they be granted special seats of prestige in his reign. He rebuked them. "Whoever would be great among you must be your servant, and whoever would be first among you must be slave of all." [5]

It had been a mundane request for dominion.

To an extent, a mundane struggle for dominion also severed Rome and Constantinople. Scholars of both sides recognize this.

Yet it was a fiercely jealous struggle, of devastating consequences.

"There are few sadder pages in the history of the church than those that record the lack of love, the suspicion, the pettiness, and the stifling narrowness that both sides revealed," writes Orthodox historian Alexander Schmemann.[6] It was a matter of "mutual ignorance and contempt," wrote Pope Pius XI in *Rerum Orientalium.*

Underneath, it involved the relative rights of the two Christian centers, although it scarcely was discussed in those terms. Outwardly, it usually concerned quarrels over subsidiary points and maneuvering for advantage. Looking back, however, historians capsule the basic conflict as one of authority: Rome's assertion of the primacy of the pope as ruler of the church versus Constantinople's insistence on regional jurisdiction under general church government by councils, with the pope holding only a presiding primacy of honor. Other matters, of usage and culture, brought that difference to a head, and subsequent events sharply intensified it.

At the time, a single word produced the main outward dispute of doctrine. That word—*Filioque*—flared as the shibboleth of battle.

It had to do with the Nicene Creed, the classic statement of Christian faith common to Eastern Orthodoxy, Roman Catholicism, and most of Protestantism. In its original form, as drawn up by the Council of Nicaea in 325 and the First Council of Constantinople in 381, it described the Holy Spirit as proceeding *ex Patre*—"from the Father." Western churches, beginning in the ninth century, added the word *Filioque*—"and the Son." Both Roman Catholics and other Western Christians, including Protestants, use the expanded version. Orthodoxy sticks to the original. Interestingly, however, the East-West break was already headed toward its climax before the *Filioque* gained currency in Rome itself in 1014, although it previously was used in Spain and other Western church provinces.

The trouble started before that. Its political framework was set when the Emperor Constantine in A.D. 330 made Constantinople the capital of the empire—the "new Rome." The two Christian centers became almost equal in strength and influence.

Friction over prerogatives arose periodically between them, occasionally bringing dramatic confrontations between pope and patriarch and forceful interventions by emperors. Eastern churches from the first had accorded special recognition to Rome, as the church of the apostles Peter and Paul, but its developing concept of supreme rule aroused resistance. Papal control was openly challenged in the ninth century by a newly named Patriarch of Constantinople, Photius, after Pope Nicholas I refused to approve his installation in office. He thereupon accused the Pope of heresy in allowing the *Filioque*, forbidding marriage of priests, and observing fasts on Saturday. The two engaged in a long struggle of mutual excommunications, bargains, and fallings out. For one interlude, Photius was ousted from office by the Emperor, and later reinstated with papal approval. But there never was much understanding afterward.

After the division of the Empire (when the Frankish conqueror Charlemagne set up a separate Western throne in Rome in 800) and through the troubled and stormy period of the Dark Ages, the chief pastors of Rome and Byzantium drifted further and further apart in attitudes and customs.

The decisive break, however, is dated in the eleventh century.

The crux of the issue still lay in respective jurisdictional rights, but in the circuitous rivalry of those times, it remained couched in arguments over ceremonial matters that have long since faded into unimportance. Patriarch Cerularius of Constantinople had issued a tract condemning the infiltration of Western practices, namely fasting on Saturdays and the use of unleavened bread for communion. (Orthodox and most Protestants use leavened bread.) The move, recognized in Rome as a rebuff to its oversight, drew a blast from Pope Leo IX, who called Constantinople sinful, scandalous, even ruled by women. In 1054 papal legates led by Cardinal Humbert arrived in Constantinople to try to settle the wrangling. The patriarch refused to see them. After five weeks of waiting, they lost patience. On July 16, 1054, in front of worshipers assembled in the patriarchal Cathedral of St. Sophia, they strode up to the high altar and laid on it a bull of excommunication against Cerularius. Then they stalked out, symbolically shaking the dust off their heels. The patriarch promptly had the bull burned, and summoned a patriarchal council which excommunicated those responsible for the insult.

One church had become two, and so it has remained. But the real hardening of antagonism came afterward.

Estrangement turned into hate with the Rome-sponsored Crusades and the bloody sacking of Constantinople in 1204. Although the West sometimes romanticizes the Crusades as purely religious expeditions to reclaim the holy places, Eastern Christians remember them as power plays against their Turk-threatened domain. The men of the Fourth Crusade, mustered by Pope Innocent III, turned aside from their Palestinian objective to pillage Constantinople, killing thousands, desecrating the Orthodox sanctuaries, and carrying off church relics and treasures as spoils. The Latin invaders took over the city and ruled it for fifty-seven years until the Greeks recovered it in 1261. The East came to regard the West as barbarous, land-grabbing, uncivilized. The West looked on the East as treacherous, shifty.

The moldering bitterness of that far-distant period still lent some strength to the hindrances through which Athenagoras and Paul had to work to prepare for their meeting.

Other burdening alluvia of time and geography and the lack of any living communion had deepened the barrier.

Theological thought had taken different tangents. The East was Hellenized, contemplative, concerned with worship, stressing God's love, grace, and glory. The West was Latinized, administratively oriented and activated, with its emphasis on moral law and discipline. To a degree, Rome's tendencies carried over into Western Protestantism. However, Protestantism developed collective church governments akin to that of Eastern Orthodoxy, with both laymen and clergy having roles in church tribunals.

On the issue of authority, Rome and Constantinople had moved steadily further apart as the Western church concentrated increasing control in the Vatican. Rome's 1870 declaration of papal infallibility in serious doctrinal pronouncements drove the wedge deeper. The issue, with its ancient roots, has grown into the overshadowing obstruction between Rome and other churches. Actions bearing on it by the Vatican Council, coupled with unifying trends in other churches, may temper it somewhat. But it remains the imposing roadblock.

Other doctrinal disparities have developed through the years.

Orthodoxy rejects Rome's 1854 definition of the immaculate conception of Christ's mother, the Virgin Mary (that she was born free of sin), and also Pope Pius XII's 1950 declaration of Mary's bodily assumption into heaven. (The nature of the "body" was not specified, however, as is sometimes assumed.) Although Orthodoxy nurtures deep veneration for Mary, it objects to Rome's unilateral fixing of dogmas about her apart from the rest of the church. Some Orthodox theologians disapproved not so much of the teachings as of Rome's independent action to make them absolutes of faith.

Orthodoxy also takes exception to Roman Catholic specifications on purgatory and indulgences (the asserted allaying by good works of temporal suffering for sin). Also, Rome has a chiefly celibate priesthood while Orthodoxy allows for married priests, although its bishops must be celibate. (Roman Catholicism also includes some married priests, particularly in its Eastern Rites, and a few in West Europe in the Latin Rite.) This, however, is a matter of system, not theology. Orthodox, like Protestants, receive communion in both bread and wine, while Roman Catholics generally receive only bread (on the theory that either element includes the wholeness of the other). Again, Rome's usage is for practical reasons, not doctrinal. In fact, the Second Vatican Council urged more occasions for communion in both kinds. (This had been a demand of the Protestant Reformation.)

Some of these differences present scant difficulty. But running through them is that galling old question: the location of authority over the church.

It is an elusive, tortuous issue. All of the churches, Roman Catholic, Orthodox, and Protestant, are agreed that the book of Holy Scripture, the Bible, sets forth the unalterable Christian rudiments. But the problem lies in just who is empowered to determine the church's interpretation and application of Scripture. Again, all of the churches, Roman Catholic, Orthodox, and Protestant, consider the Holy Spirit to be the source of this commanding guidance, in accordance with Christ's promise that the "Spirit of truth . . ." would remain with his followers and "will teach you all things . . ." [7] But through whom is that guiding force transmitted?

Rome holds that it comes through the church's teaching *magisterium,* the bishops, and acts to safeguard the chief bishop who heads the church, the pope, from error in serious doctrinal pronouncements. This (and not the pope's wisdom or righteousness) is the general basis of the "papal infallibility" definition. The underlying dependence is not on the pope and hierarchy themselves, but on Christ's guiding presence and the trust that he will make sure the leaders of the church express that guidance, particularly the chief leader, the pope.

In contrast, Eastern Orthodoxy declines to pinpoint the human channel of divine guidance, or specify its outlet, maintaining that it comes both through the leavening of time, reflection, and all the faithful. (Rome's theologians also recognize that truth may come through lay people; ascertaining the truth is up to the hierarchy.) Although Orthodoxy implants deep respect for its clergy and their guidance, it does not deem them an infallible vehicle of truth at any one point in time. Bishops head local churches, but only Christ is considered the "shepherd" of the whole church. In operational procedure, Orthodoxy holds that only general church councils can make doctrinal decisions, and that the decisions themselves remain subject to the judgment of the Holy Spirit working in history and in the consensus of the entire church.

Orthodoxy uniformly upholds the Christian doctrines as worked out by the first seven ecumenical councils, before the East-West split, considering this the "pure, unadded-to" faith of all Christians, but does not accept the conclusions of the fourteen subsequent Roman Catholic councils. The seven councils of undivided Christianity all were held in the East, at the call of the Emperor. For the most part, Protestantism also affirms the interpretations of the early councils.

By Roman Catholic reckoning, which counts the councils before and since the split, Vatican II is Number twenty-one.

In its moves to broaden church authority, to augment regional direction, to balance out papal powers with the rights of the entire episcopate, and to increase the role of the laity, the council is lessening the breach with Orthodoxy, as well as with Protestantism. But keen differences persist over the focal point of church rule.

Patriarch Athenagoras has said: "We are ready to recognize the pope as 'first among equals' as he was in the history of the West and of the East for a millennium." [8] But in the Orthodox view, the title is a badge of honor and dignity, rather than command, with its holder supposed to lead rather than decree, to advise rather than direct, to call church leaders together for joint action whenever major decisions are necessary. Athenagoras puts it simply: "If the pope and I are approaching a door so narrow that only one can pass at a time, then of course he goes first."

A gracious word, lightly spoken. Nevertheless, it illustrates the weight of the sensitivities to be dealt with. While such things may seem picayune in the present atmosphere, they had plagued the past of Rome and Constantinople.

Yet, in one stroke, the aloofness would disappear once the two met in the humanity of two men, in the new style that was set in Jerusalem.

The Eastern Orthodox churches today comprise a loosely knit federation of four ancient patriarchates—Constantinople, Jerusalem, Alexandria, and Antioch (now Damascus)—and fourteen other autocephalous or independent jurisdictions, including churches of Greece, Russia, Cyprus, Poland, Estonia, Latvia, Finland, Bulgaria, Yugoslavia, Albania, Rumania, Ethiopia, Australia, and the Americas. Most of them are headed by metropolitans or archbishops. Besides the four senior patriarchates, however, there are four others of later origin, in Russia, Bulgaria, Yugoslavia, and Rumania. Moscow was given patriarchal status in 1582 by the Patriarch of Constantinople, and became known as "the third Rome." Its patriarchate was eliminated in 1721 by the czar, who took direct control, but restored in 1917; it is now held by Patriarch Alexis.

Diverse in language and culture, but unified in doctrine, the Eastern composite of self-governing churches is held together by the Patriarch of Constantinople, who is acknowledged as the "elder brother" or "first among equals" of the Eastern patriarchs. His authority, however, depends on the skill and vigor of his own leadership, rather than any binding powers. Joint policies and programs, like local ones, are determined in council. Variety and persuasion are the key to interaction among the several jurisdictions.

Calculations of the number of Eastern Orthodox Christians vary widely, from 140 million to 300 million. The lower figure, cited in some references, derived from a period when membership behind the Iron Curtain was presumed virtually nil. But recent figures from churches in Russia and its satellites change that picture. Athenagoras and his American exarch, Archbishop Iakovos, put the overall total at more than 200 million.

Roman Catholics number more than 550 million.

Protestants total close to 250 million.

In the Orthodox view, Rome is simply one of the five ancient patriarchates (along with the principal Eastern sees of Constantinople, Alexandria, Antioch, and Jerusalem). To achieve full reunion, Athenagoras says it would have to be "on the basis of the ancient church order, when the prelates of the five patriarchs were equal, the pope being *primus inter pares* (first among equals)."[9] Patriarch Athenagoras believes that Orthodoxy "can be a bridge" between Rome and Protestantism, with which Orthodoxy has long-standing ties in the World Council. "Both Orthodoxy and Rome preserve features of the early church despite Roman accretions which the Reformation sought to eliminate," he says. "But we cannot come without our Protestant brothers. The union of all is what God demands, not bilateral fronts."

However, in his view, much could be done in advance of any full solution, by way of extensive collaboration in study and action. The first requirement: to reopen the lines between pope and patriarch.

So long as these remained closed, not even the attempt could be made to reach understandings with Rome; much less could Orthodoxy become an intermediary between Rome and Protestantism.

But breaking the ice was skittish going. It didn't take hold in Rome until the pontificate of John XXIII. From then onward, it became an exploratory, testing operation on both sides.

In late 1958 John made his inaugural appeal for Christian brotherhood. Athenagoras responded appreciatively in a 1959 New Year's encyclical, adding: "Every appeal for unity must be accompanied by such concrete deeds as are necessary" on a basis of "equality, justice, spiritual freedom, and mutual respect." He expressed hope that Rome would in "brotherly spirit turn toward the East" to hasten the "dawn of a really new year in Christ." Shortly thereafter, in January, 1959, John startled his own church and others by announcing a world-wide Roman Catholic council to seek renewal and unity. Quickly then, in March, 1959, Athenagoras' top representative, Archbishop Iakovos, the able head of Greek Orthodoxy in America and a World Council of Churches president, met with the Pope, the first such personal contact in the modern era. Afterward, Athenagoras said in a 1959 Easter message: "The barriers which the ages have raised between Christian confessions do not make impossible their mutual understanding, rapprochement, and reunion."

Pope John began sending out feelers, personal envoys, messages to other Christian centers, including Constantinople. In the spring of 1960 Athenagoras hailed the apparent ending of Rome's "ecclesiastical seclusion" and said: "We are on the threshold of the Christian evolution. . . . We have a great mission to fulfill. We must either do it in unity or risk failure." In mid-1960 John created the Vatican's Secretariat for Christian Unity to maintain official, continuing liaison with Orthodoxy and Protestantism. Roman Catholic observers began attending Protestant and Orthodox assemblies, including the World Council general assembly in India and the pan-Orthodox conference on the island of Rhodes in 1961. Through early 1962, as the start of the Vatican Council neared, teams of the Vatican's Christian Unity Secretariat, usually led by its Dutch secretary, Monsignor Jan Willebrands, roved Protestant and Orthodox headquarters, arranging invitations to council observers.

At this point a temporary snarl developed.

Handling the invitations was a ticklish business, considering the background of edgy psychology and fears of compromise in the various camps. Rome took care not to announce invitations publicly until acceptance had been assured, so as not to embarrass anv group. Past experience had shown the pitfalls. At the last Vatican Council, in 1869, after news of an invitation to the Patriarch of Constantinople leaked out before he received it, he returned it unopened to the Vatican's messenger, considering it an insult to the avowed equality of pope and patriarch.

This time Rome attempted discretion. But a disrupting note arose.

Instead of dealing with all Orthodoxy through Constantinople, the Vatican's envoys had negotiated separately with the different Orthodox jurisdictions. This caused some offense. Archbishop Iakovos said it seemed "aimed at disrupting Orthodox unity and undermining the authority of the ecumenical Patriarch (Athenagoras)." As a result most major Orthodox sees, including Constantinople, sent no observers to the Vatican council's first two sessions in 1962 and 1963. However, the Russian Orthodox Church did send observers. Archbishop Chrysostomos, of Athens, called the upshot a "serious blow to the unity of Orthodoxy."

While it momentarily complicated the fragile, new Rome-Constantinople diplomacy, it pointed up a relaxation of the Vatican's relationship with Communist-ruled areas.

This additional "opening to the East" also had begun under Pope John, whose pleas for peace impressed even former Soviet Premier Nikita Khrushchev. Without any slackening of opposition to atheistic materialism and infringements on human rights, Pope John had moved to find some accommodation for the church's survival under Marxist governments. Following his 1961 encyclical, *Mater et Magistra*, in which he said socialization was not necessarily in conflict with Christianity, Khrushchev sent greetings to the Pope on his eightieth birthday, the first direct contact between the Soviet government and the Vatican since the 1917 Communist revolution. Spurning counsel to ignore the message, John replied: "I thank you for the thought. And I will pray for the people of Russia."

Austria's Franz Cardinal Koenig of Vienna, a scholar of comparative religions, became the Pope's ambassador on missions to Poland, Hungary, and Czechoslovakia, seeking to ease tensions between church and state.

In February, 1963, Archbishop Josef Slipyi of the Ukraine was released after eighteen years in Siberian imprisonment, and returned to Rome. On March 7, 1963, Khrushchev's son-in-law, Aleksei I. Adzhubei, editor of the Soviet newspaper *Izvestia*, and his wife, Rada, visited Pope John. "We talked about advancing peace," Adzhubei said afterward. "The Pope is a great and good man. When you open your eyes and look at him closely, you feel profound respect for him and immediate confidence." Khrushchev's daughter, Mrs. Adzhubei, observed that the Pope has "big and good peasant's hands just like my father." [10] (The Vatican newspaper, L'Osservatore Romano, did not mention the audience.)

That same spring, Khrushchev sent congratulations to Pope John on the award to him of the Italian-Swiss Balzan peace prize, as did Moscow's Orthodox Patriarch Alexis, who called the award "a testimony to the untiring efforts of Your Holiness for blessed peace on earth and good will among men." Pope John replied that he was deeply moved and "we pray from the bottom of our soul for your person, the clergy, and the faithful" of the Russian Orthodox Church. In April, 1963, Cardinal Koenig had met a second time with Joszef Cardinal Mindszenty, Roman Catholic primate of Hungary, laying the groundwork for his possible release, although Mindszenty has been inclined to stay put pending further concessions by the Hungarian government regarding church rights. The next month, the government released five bishops who had been under house arrest. Mindszenty, imprisoned on anti-state charges in 1949, has been in asylum in the United States legation in Budapest since being momentarily freed by the 1956 Hungarian freedom uprising.

John's new Eastern policy drew attacks from some quarters. An Italian weekly, L'Espresso, charged he had gone too far "to the left" and seemed "soft on Communism." In the United States, radio-preacher Carl McIntire, who has made similar charges against Protestant and Orthodox leaders for admitting the Russian Church into the World Council, said the Pope apparently "anticipates a Communist victory" and is "laying the groundwork" for the Roman Catholic Church in a socialist world. [11] Concerning the soft-on-Communism charges against the Pope, Boston's blunt Richard Cardinal Cushing offered a terse rejoinder: "A colossal lie!" [12]

After Pope Paul succeeded John in June, 1963, he continued the same low-key approach to the Soviet bloc. Khrushchev sent congratulations and good wishes on the Pope's election, and Paul replied, expressing "real and sincere gratitude" and prayerful hopes that the Russian people "in prosperity and organized social life, may make an important contribution to the real progress of humanity and to a just peace in the world." Poland's primate, Stefan Cardinal Wyszynski, said he had been assured that Paul intended to continue John's policy of improving relations with Iron Curtain countries. [13] Cardinal Koenig said that the doors opened by John "not only remain open, but are being opened even more widely," and that conditions for Christians in Communist zones may slowly improve "if we maintain contacts." [14]

In July, 1963, Pope Paul sent a delegation headed by Bishop Francois Charriere of Switzerland to Moscow to the golden jubilee celebrations marking the fiftieth anniversary of the consecration of Russian Orthodox Patriarch Alexis. In September, 1963, the head of the Russian Patriarch's external affairs department, Metropolitan Nikodim, visited Pope Paul, prayed beside the crypt of Pope John, and placed a bouquet on it. In October, 1963, Roman Catholic Archbishop Josef Beran, primate of Czechoslovakia, was freed after fourteen years' confinement. In December, 1963, in another Russian Orthodox gesture of friendship toward Roman Catholicism, Metropolitan Nikodim attended Christmas Mass at Moscow's only Catholic church, staying through the entire fifty-minute service. On his Holy Land trip, Paul sent a message of good will and hope for peace to Khrushchev, among other world leaders. In February, 1964, Paul sent a further note to the Soviet Premier, expressing gratitude for his year-end appeal for negotiations instead of arms to resolve international disputes. In March, 1964, French Roman Catholics, Protestants, and Orthodox formed a committee to "throw light on the position of Christians" in the Soviet Union. Committee Chairman Francois Mauriac, noted Roman Catholic writer, said the aim was not ideological struggle but the "disarmament of minds" so genuine converse could take place.

After Premier Aleksei Kosygin, along with new Communist Chairman Brezhnev, succeeded Khrushchev in mid-1964, the reopening of church lines in the Soviet sphere continued. A pact was signed with Communist Hungary, restoring the church's right to form the hierarchy and communicate freely with it. Negotiations for a similar accord went on with Communist Poland. The Yugoslavian Communist party rescinded a long-standing rule that party members must not practice religion. In December, 1964, the Roman Catholic Archbishop of Westminster, John Heenan (now a Cardinal), visited Russian Orthodox Patriarch Alexis in Moscow, and said later: "It is quite obvious that the ecumenical movement is working for better relations between the Russians and ourselves." In January, 1965, Pope Paul named twenty-seven new cardinals, two of them in the Soviet zone. In his encyclical, *Ecclesiam Suam* (Paths of the Church), he said the church's dialogue must include even atheists, who are often "spurred on by noble sentiments and by impatience" with self-seeking mediocrity in society, borrowing ideas "from our gospel modes." Echoing Pope John, Pope Paul said Communist "movements themselves cannot help but evolve and undergo changes, even of a profound nature. We do not despair that they may one day be able to enter into a more positive dialogue with the church."

Thus the efforts went on for a modus vivendi for the church, even across the political borders of East and West.

Although Rome's developing contacts with Eastern Orthodoxy had hit a temporary snag (except in the case of the Russian Orthodox Church), they soon regained momentum. Since the Patriarch of Constantinople had no representatives at the Vatican Council's opening session, Pope John had full documentation on it sent to him. John's death had thwarted tentative feelers about a meeting between him and Athenagoras. Then came Paul's election, and Athenagoras sent a friendly greeting, once more voicing hopes for definite steps toward unity.

Back flew a papal messenger, Pierre Duprey, a French priest-specialist on Eastern Orthodoxy, with an enthusiastic letter from Pope Paul echoing the Patriarch's hopes, and saying he wanted to do "everything which may help to restore perfect concord among Christians. . . . Let us leave the past to the mercy of God, and listen to the council of the apostle: 'Forgetting what lies behind and straining forward to what lies ahead, I press on toward the goal for the prize of the upward call of God in Christ Jesus.' " [15] The Pope said that Catholics and Orthodox have the same baptism, the same priesthood, and celebrate the same Eucharist. He recalled Jesus' prayer "that all may be one," and added: "May the Lord open our hearts to the inspiration of his spirit and guide us towards the full realization of his will." [16]

It was the most positive and sanguine exchange to that date between pope and patriarch. And it augured the phenomenon ahead.

When less than two months in office, Paul declared in an address on August 11, 1963, that the barriers between Rome and Orthodoxy "are not based on real differences" and should "fall without delay." [17] Soon afterward, in September, 1963, a pan-Orthodox conference at Rhodes voted unanimously to accept "the proposal of Ecumenical Patriarch Athenagoras" that "our venerable Eastern Orthodox Church should propose to the venerable Roman Catholic Church that we start a dialogue between the two churches on a basis of equality." This action laid the foundation for a fuller contingent of Orthodox observers at the fourth and fifth Vatican Council sessions in 1964 and 1965, and also for Athenagoras (who dispatched emissaries to both sessions) to meet with the Pope personally, without overstepping the Orthodox consensus. Nevertheless, sticky hurdles remained to be overcome.

Archbishop Chrysostomos, primate of the Church of Greece, deplored any dealings whatsoever with Rome. He had refused to send representatives to the Rhodes meeting, declaring that unity discussions with Rome were pointless. "The Orthodox Church breathes always with democratic principles, while the papal church is centralist and absolutist," he said. [18] After the conference decision, he insinuated it had failed to act to protect the faith. An immediate subject of bitterness, aside from the corrosions of history, has to do with Rome's Eastern Rite Churches, which maintain parallel institutions, liturgy, and offices similar to those of Orthodoxy in predominantly Orthodox territory. This is regarded by Orthodoxy as an unwarranted and unfriendly invasion. The 1961 pan-Orthodox conference had protested Roman Catholic proselytism and said its Eastern Rites are "a real impediment and obstacle to any genuine attempts by the churches to achieve real unity." The Eastern Rite Churches, sometimes called Uniates, make up a comparatively small proportion of Christians in Orthodox areas.

Aside from this general problem, however, the Rhodes decision faced prickly opposition in high echelons of the Greek Church. The Pan-Hellenic Union said the move could split Orthodoxy and warned that "papists . . . are treacherously working for the enslavement of the Orthodox Church." [19] The crucial spotlight fixed on Athenagoras.

On his way home from Rhodes, he stopped at Athens and engaged in an assiduous round of conferences with bishops and theologians there. Within a week, the Greek synod had ratified the Rhodes decision, so long as any dialogue with Rome was "on equal terms." Athenagoras returned to Istanbul, commenting, "Isolation is a disgrace, and aloneness is isolation." Then he added a remark that was particularly intriguing in the light of later events: Differing Christians should meet, listen to one another, and "see one another with our own eyes." [20]

Exactly what transpired in the next few weeks is uncertain. The results are known; the precision process that led to them is somewhat unclear.

Yet it unfolded like a finely executed ballet, each succeeding movement not quite expected yet developing the theme and building harmoniously into its completion.

Publicly, the next consequential step came when Pope Paul at the close of the Vatican Council's second session on December 4, 1963, announced his plan to visit the Holy Land. Immediately afterward, Athenagoras responded with his proposal that the trip be made the occasion for a meeting of leaders of all churches, East and West, in the "holy city of Zion." Thus, the idea appeared to come from him. Yet, at a stopover in Rhodes on the way to Jerusalem, he said, "The idea of a meeting originally came from the Pope." In that case Paul must have had in mind that Jerusalem would afford the necessary neutral setting for a meeting when he announced his trip. However, for him to have declared that purpose publicly could have aroused inner Vatican protests against any gestures implying equality of Rome and Constantinople. On the other hand, if Athenagoras had limited his public proposal specifically to a pope-patriarch meeting, it might have cast Orthodoxy in the role of supplicant, or indicated bipartisanship.

In any case, the overt series of moves, from both sides, fitted together neatly, progressively, and with finesse, almost as if they had been honed and readied in advance.

Pierre Duprey, Undersecretary of the Vatican's Christian Unity Secretariat, a former theology professor in Jerusalem, and a friend of Orthodox churchmen, served as the Pope's interlocutor in the preliminaries. He promptly appeared in Constantinople to consult with Athenagoras. Then, on December 28, only a week before the Pope's flight to Jerusalem, the Patriarch's Metropolitan for England, also named Athenagoras, conferred in Rome with the Pope. As disclosed later, the text of his formal message said in part concerning the possible meeting of pope and patriarch: "It seems that you are called to climb the same mountain, the mountain of the Lord. Your Holiness climbs from one side and the Ecumenical Patriarch from the other. Those who understand the significance of this daring climbing pray that you both may meet on the top, in the land sanctified by our common Redeemer, near his cross, near the empty tomb, and from then on you may walk together, trying under the cross to reconstruct in Christian solidarity the broken bridges and build the abandoned roads, knowing that Christ has nothing else to teach but one, old lesson of love, that we may be one as he is one with the Father." [21]

Still, however, there was no firm announcement that the meeting would take place. Some Curia members were said to oppose it, and to have misgivings about the whole venture. The Orthodox Synod of Greece also had reservations, suggesting that the Pope should first give up the claim of supremacy. Abbots of three major Greek monasteries declared any meeting must be on "equal terms" and the Pope must agree to abolish all "proselytizing Byzantine Rites" in Orthodox countries. [22] Some Protestants worried that Rome might be trying to woo Orthodoxy away from its working ties with Protestantism. Old anxieties, old sensitivities, and old wounds rose to the surface.

Finally, almost at the last moment, amid pro-and-con speculation, word came from an unexpected and previously uninvolved source, Orthodox Patriarch Benedictos of Jerusalem, that the Bishop of Rome and the Bishop of Constantinople would, indeed, meet in the Holy

Land. Sometime, somewhere in the coming, going, and conferring, the project had been sealed; perhaps innately it had happened long before in the minds and dispositions of two men.

It presaged what Greek Orthodox Iakovos of America called "the greatest moment of modern church history." [23]

Just what the circumstances of their encounter would be remained for events to reveal.

CHAPTER 9

An Embrace

On the evening of January 5, 1964, the smell of smoky, fat-soaked torches blended with the snap in the night air on the side of the Mount of Olives. Along its winding, gravel roads, several hundred people had deployed, with sputtering flares.

Leaders of the two historically hostile hemispheres of Christianity had lodgings on the mountainside that night—Pope Paul at the Apostolic Delegation quarters, and Patriarch Athenagoras at the Villa Galilea, the residence of Jerusalem's Orthodox Patriarch Benedictos. The two stone edifices are about five hundred yards apart.

Both overlook the Garden of Gethsemane, the wooded bower where Jesus implored peace and unity among his followers on the last night before his crucifixion. "This is my commandment, that you love one another as I have loved you." [1]

At 9:30 P.M., a black sedan bearing Athenagoras pulled out of the courtyard of the Orthodox villa and, its headlights lancing above the pale fingers of the torches, rolled down the short, curving road to the Apostolic Delegation quarters. Beside the Patriarch rode his American colleague, Archbishop Iakovos. As the gate swung open, about one hundred newsmen, priests, cameramen, and others surged forward, struggling to gain admission along with the car. Soldiers held them back.

Athenagoras bent low, sliding out of the car, and then drew himself erect, majestic as the tall cypresses around him, the black profusion of his mantle and the flowing black veil from the flat, round *kalymmafhion* on his head enfolding him as abundantly and darkly as the foliage on the trees. Another bearded man, Cardinal Tisserant, greeted the Patriarch in the yard and escorted him up the steps to the lighted doorway where a thin figure in red mozetta and white cassock and skullcap, Pope Paul, waited. He took a step forward.

It was 9:35 P.M.

Their hands spread, the two caught each other's shoulders, the old, bewhiskered Patriarch's six-foot-four frame bulking above that of the five-foot-eight, clean-shaven Pope as they leaned forward in early Christianity's customary "kiss of peace," first on one cheek and then on the other, a symbol of community in faith and devotion to each other as brothers in the Lord.

139

"May Jesus Christ be praised!" the Pope said, those first words tremulous, yet exultant on his lips.

"Thoxa si Kyrie! Thoxa si Kyrie!" the expansive Patriarch repeated in Greek. "Glory to the Lord!"

The two clasped hands, holding them together for a drawn-out moment, their gazes locked like glinting magnets. At long last, across the miles, across the bulging range of the centuries, across the bogs of silence, distrust, and atavistic antipathies, the chief bishop of the West had met the chief bishop of the East.

Arm in arm, their hands still clasped, the Pope led the Patriarch into the ground-floor reception room.

It was a simply furnished room. There had been some last-minute changes in it. Some time before, attendants had prepared a small throne-like chair for the Pope, its seat and back scarlet-covered and trimmed in gold. At its right, a plain easy chair had been placed for the Patriarch. However, before the Patriarch's arrival, Pope Paul had noticed the arrangement and asked that chairs of the same kind be provided, directly facing each other.

Now, with his guest in tow, the Pope gestured with one arm, inviting him to be seated. Both sat down. Only a half-hour before, the Pope had seemed almost worn out on his return from his day-long tour of Israel. But now, at this hard-won, pregnant juncture of church history, he got a second wind. Close acquaintances of Paul say that he has a strange quality of actually appearing to lose weight and become almost gaunt under exhausting circumstances, and then within a matter of hours, fleshing out to his normal bloom. Observers present said that kind of reanimation occurred that night. In company of the fervent seventy-eight-year-old Patriarch, whose lined, grizzled face fairly twinkled with pleasure, a fatigued Pope, an ordinarily more reserved, yet comparatively young man of sixty-six, suddenly recovered spark and elan.

Only once before, in more than twelve centuries, had a pope and patriarch met, and that had been in sharply contrasting circumstances dictated to a large extent by military, financial, and political pressures.

It had taken place 525 years before at the Council of Ferrara-Florence from 1438 to 1439 in an abortive attempt at reunion. The Eastern Emperor, John VIII, seeking support from Rome against the Moslem push toward Constantinople, had sailed to Ferrara with an Orthodox delegation of seven hundred, including Patriarch Joseph II. They had been so short of funds that they had traveled at papal expense. In the strained atmosphere at that time, the initial encounter between the Patriarch and Pope Eugene IV was delayed a whole day while their aides argued over whether the Patriarch should be required to kiss the Pope's foot.

The council, however, shifted to Florence after a plague broke out in Ferrara, and ended with the Orthodox prelates subscribing to Rome's terms. These included accepting the *Filioque*—that the Holy Spirit proceeds "from the Father and the Son"—and the granting of primacy to the pope among Eastern patriarchs along lines existing before the 1054 split. Among factors weighing on the Orthodox were their dependence on Rome for transportation home and their fears that, without Rome's help, the Eastern Empire would be destroyed by Islam. Patriarch Joseph, a man almost ninety, died in the later stages of the council and was buried at Florence. The other Orthodox insisted that their agreement remained subject to their church synods. However, on July 6, 1439, the Pope proclaimed a reunion decree entitled *Laetentur Coeli* (Let the Heavens Rejoice).

It turned out to be a paper reunion only. On their return home, Orthodox leaders found sentiment strongly opposed to the agreement; they speedily renounced it as forced on them. It stirred such outrage in Russian Orthodoxy that its leader, Isidore, who had been made a cardinal and papal legate while in Rome, was imprisoned on his return to Moscow, but escaped back to Rome. The futile political-military objectives of the mission—to secure Rome's help—became academic fourteen years later with the fall of Constantinople to the Turks in 1453 after a stirring siege. It was nine years later before Patriarch Dionysius I officially repudiated the ephemeral reunion accord. The age-old schism had continued, with added resentments.

There had been an earlier misfired reunion attempt at the Council of Lyons in 1273, only two decades after the Greeks recovered Constantinople from the conquering Latins. The Eastern Emperor, Michael VIII, seeking to forestall a threatened new Western attack, sent ecclesiastical delegates to Rome. An "accord" was reached. But it, too, was generally rejected by Orthodoxy and came to naught, with the church conflict further exacerbated by the failure of the sought-after political entente. During this affair, however, the patriarch remained in Constantinople and never met the pope.

Other than the uneasy confrontations between Pope Eugene and Patriarch Joseph in 1438-39, no pope and patriarch had faced each other since 710 when Pope Constantine I went to Constantinople at the call of the emperor to explain his resistance to certain conciliar canons. He met with Patriarch Kyros. Three times before between 536 and 653, popes and patriarchs had met, each time in Constantinople, twice when the pope was brought there under arrest by the emperor. But for a period of 1,254 years, the only meeting had been at that tangled and thorny encounter five centuries before in Florence.

But now they sat face-to-face, having come together at their own volition, in a glad, friendly atmosphere far different from the rankled settings of long ago. Both of them displayed keenly animated emotions.

"This moment, Your Holiness, is one of the most significant for mankind," Athenagoras said. "Humanity at its highest spiritual level has the opportunity at last to guide the world toward peace."

Gesturing spiritedly, often clasping his hands, Paul answered, "Your Holiness, we must bring our churches closer together. It will not be easy, but we are already on the right road. Nothing is insurmountable in our striving to unite mankind, but we must unite beforehand."

For twenty minutes, the Pope and Patriarch talked in private, and other than a few early snatches of remarks reported overheard, only they know the exact content of that conversation. But its gist and its warm, hopeful tenor showed in their subsequent public statements and in their elated manner when it was concluded.

At that point, in a mood of pleased amiability, they summoned their retinues into the room—the three cardinals who had accompanied the Pope from Rome, and four theologians and Archbishop Iakovos who had accompanied the Patriarch. Athenagoras then read a five-minute formal discourse. Stately in his black garb, an emblem of office dangling on a golden chain at his chest, he addressed the Pope as "my dear brother in Christ" and voiced gratitude to God "for having led us from the West and the East to meet in his Holy Name. Truly this is a reason for great joy. . . .

"For centuries the Christian world has lived in the night of separation. Its eyes are tired from staring into the dark. May this meeting be the dawn of an enlightened and blessed day in which future generations, communing in the same chalice of the precious blood and body of the Lord, will praise and glorify in love, peace, and unity the only Lord and Savior. My dear brother in Christ, you see by searching for unity with each other, we find together the Lord. Let us proceed on the road which opens before us and he will join us on our way as he joined the two disciples on the way to Emmaus. He will show us the way to follow and he will hasten our steps toward the goal which we are seeking."

He spoke in French, a lilt of poetry in the words, and the resonance of feeling vibrated through that room. When he finished, he and the Pope, along with their associates, joined in chanting the

Lord's Prayer. "Our Father . . . thy kingdom come, thy will be done, on earth as it is in heaven . . ." The Pope escorted the Patriarch to the doorstep. Again they embraced. The Pope stood silhouetted against the light as the Patriarch crossed the yard and entered his car.

It was 10:12 P.M. They had spent thirty-seven minutes together. Their second meeting, twelve hours hence, would prove even more dramatic. Nevertheless, that first introductory interlude, when ancestral foes exchanged the accolade of brotherhood on the side of the Mount of Olives, lifted the curtain on a new road of reconciliation between the poles of the Christian world.

Even in the immediate environment in which it took place, it ran directly counter to the long record of hostile rivalry between Jerusalem's "Latins" and "Greeks," whose jealousies over precedence at the holy places often turned pious processions into unholy brawls. But the Pope and Patriarch, by their large-hearted example, broke with that grievous pattern and raised a new standard of relationships.

As a prelude to the meeting, Pope Paul had met the night before with Jerusalem's Greek Patriarch Benedictos and also with Armenian Patriarch Derderian. Following the Pope's grueling ordeal in the streets of the old city, he had received the two separately, first Benedictos and then Derderian, at the Apostolic Delegation. Later that night, en route to the church beside the Garden of Gethsemane, he had paid a return call on Benedictos at the Villa Galilea where the slender, bearded Orthodox Patriarch served him a glass of Benedictine wine and called his visit "a landmark in the history of the Holy Land."

As a pilgrim and a guest, the Pope had willingly entered a domain in which he was not in a position merely to receive as the sole host, but in which he also accepted the hospitality of others. He told Benedictos that he looked forward to the time when the different churches showed the same unfeigned mutual love which caused ancient pagan Romans to write of early Christians, "See how they love one another." He added, "We realize the part taken personally by Your Beatitude in this change of climate."

Athenagoras had arrived the next afternoon, Sunday, welcomed at Jerusalem's airport by King Hussein and an applauding throng of Orthodox and Roman Catholic dignitaries. Among those accompanying him was a metropolitan of the Church of Greece, Veroias Kallinikon. He had accepted the Patriarch's invitation to go along despite objections from his superior, Archbishop Chrysostomos of Athens, who had denounced the planned meeting and encouraged prayer vigils for the protection of Orthodoxy against the "dangerous tactics" of the Patriarch.

At the time of Athenagoras' arrival in Jerusalem, Paul was touring Israel. After he returned to Jerusalem that night and was paid a call by Athenagoras, the delicately balanced scales of protocol provided for Paul then to call on the Patriarch the next day. Everything was to be on an equal footing in this land where Jesus summoned masters to be as servants.

At Bethlehem the Pope had declared himself "profoundly pleased" with the previous night's initial meeting with the Patriarch, saying it had been "realized in a most amiable way and revealed itself full of the best hopes. We thank our Lord for it with all our hearts and we pray him that he himself who started us in this good way of peace and unity wishes to carry it to a good end."

From Bethlehem, he drove directly to the Villa Galilea, again on the sacred mountain, arriving there about 9:30 A.M. The tall, old Patriarch in black waited outdoors in the garden where he and the Pope again embraced. Bright sunlight, filtering through the acacia trees, dappled the flagstone walk with light and shadows as Athenagoras led the Pope into the house. In the reception room, relaxed and smiling, they sat down together in identical armchairs. Others withdrew, and for nearly ten minutes they again conversed alone, sipping Turkish coffee.

At one point, Athenagoras reportedly remarked, "What do we do now?"

"I don't know," the Pope answered. "When I get back, I will consult the cardinals and see." [2]

A scramble at the door, as cameramen pressed to get through, interrupted the private talk, and both men looked up startled. However, as the clamor subsided, they invited their entourages inside. The Pope introduced two of the Vatican's Christian unity experts, the Dutch Jan Willebrands and the French Pierre Duprey, both of whom Athenagoras already knew. "He greeted me as his son, and that is the relationship between us," Duprey said later. The Pope, facing the Patriarch, then delivered a short, formal address matching that of Athenagoras at the first meeting.

"Great is our emotion and profound our joy in this truly historic hour, when after centuries of silence and expectation, the Catholic Church and the Patriarchate of Constantinople meet once again in the persons of their highest representatives." He thanked the Patriarch for fostering the occasion. Quoting Scripture, he said it was fitting that the meeting should be near the place of the cross where

Christ said, "I, when I am lifted up from the earth, will draw all men to myself." [3]

"Doubtless on one side and on the other, the roads which lead to union may be long and sown with difficulties. But these two paths converge toward one another and eventually reach the sources of the gospel." He said a new surge of good will, "thanks be to God, animates ever more all Christians truly worthy of that name" to "surmount disunity, to break down barriers," and to "engage resolutely upon the path which leads to reconciliation."

Divergencies of doctrine, liturgy, and discipline remain to be examined "in a spirit of fidelity to truth and of understanding in charity," he said, adding that this must be done in a fraternal spirit of mutual pardon and love, under the transforming power of the Lord. "We raise toward God a grateful prayer and beg him to help us follow along this path, and to bestow upon you and upon us, who have undertaken it with faith and confidence, that blessing which will ensure happy results. With these feelings, it is not a good-by that we say to you, but, if you allow us, an *au revoir,* based upon the hope of other fruitful meetings in the name of the Lord."

Athenagoras nodded his head approvingly. Again they joined in the Lord's Prayer. As they finished and their gazes met directly again in warm esteem, the Patriarch suggested, "Let us read together from the Holy Book."

They opened their Bibles to the place and alternately, the Pope reading a verse in Latin, then the Patriarch reading one in Greek, they recited aloud a passage from the seventeenth chapter of the Gospel of John. Both men trembled with emotion as they read. The verses, relating the prayer of Jesus given on the very mountain not far from where the two now stood, reads in part:

"Yet not for these only (the apostles) do I pray, but for those also who through their word are to believe in me, that all may be one, even as thou, Father, in me and I in thee; that they also may be one in us, that the world may believe that thou hast sent me. And the glory that thou has given me, I have given to them, that they may be one, even as we are one: I in them and thou in me; that they may be perfected in unity, and that the world may know that thou has sent me, and that thou hast loved them as thou hast loved me."

After the reading, they looked about at the assembled onlookers, smiling. *"Nous sommes en accord,"* the old Patriarch said in French. "We are in agreement." Paul added, also in French, "We have come together in peace and love."

The Patriarch presented the Pope with a golden cross and a gold chain bearing an *engolpion*, worked in diamonds and rubies.

Over his red mozetta, the Pope slipped on the emblem of Orthodox bishops, as the dignitaries of the two confessions watched.

Paul then gave Athenagoras a commemorative medal and a golden chalice.

The Patriarch thanked him, adding, "I ardently hope that one day we will mix water and wine in this chalice."

The Pope said, "A day will come when all Christians of the world will drink from the same chalice."

Athenagoras, putting a hand on the Pope's shoulders, said, "If Rome is no longer only in Rome, it can become the real center of Christianity."

The second meeting had lasted forty minutes. Altogether, the two men had spent an hour and seventeen minutes together.

The Patriarch escorted the Pope back outside to the garden where they parted, again with an embrace. Describing that farewell, Athenagoras said later, "We both wished for a new meeting, when at the same moment, as though from a single mouth, we said good-by."[4] They later issued a joint communique saying that they "pray God that this meeting may be the sign and prelude of things to come for the glory of God and the illumination of his faithful people."

Of "what things to come" had that epochal tryst been a prelude?

The casual bystander may assume it was merely a display, a passing performance, like diplomats of rival governments indulging in public amenities without modifying their essential opposition. But this is to misconstrue the nature of the Rome-Constantinople stalemate. One of its toughest, knottiest difficulties was its glum silence, its numbing decline into total non-communication, with the festering fruits of that condition mounting through the centuries—the mutual ignorance of one another, the inevitable aversion for the remote, alien, and unknown, the unalloyed partisanship. Once estranged, they had become ever more distantly strangers.

But Paul VI and Athenagoras I had broken through that wordless, isolating barrier. And they had discarded the immobilizing ramparts of status on both sides which had erected it. Their reciprocal undemanding styles had set aside the very restraints which kept their offices apart in the past.

This was no mere ritual courtesy, but the progenitor of a sweepingly different and revitalizing relationship between the two largest blocs of Christianity in the East and the West.

The restoration of communication between them "may well go down in history as a major turning point in Christian history," commented the interdenominational Protestant weekly, *The Christian Century*.[5] Pope Paul, in a subsequent letter in April, 1964, to Athenagoras, whom he addressed as "Most beloved brother in Christ," said their meeting "marked the beginning of a new era in the relations" of their churches and created prospects "for a strengthening of the bonds already tied."[6] Athenagoras said he and the Pope had agreed to the formation of a common front for the good of all mankind. He also foresaw early launching of "concerted undertakings."[7]

Plans germinated for setting up commissions to engage in theological exchanges.

To lay plans, a succession of papal and patriarchal delegations circulated back and forth between Rome and Constantinople, including a 1965 call on the Orthodox primate by Cardinal Bea.

What had been a closed line between the two Christian centers became a "hot line."

Other concrete results appeared. In the United States, Greek Orthodox Archbishop Iakovos met with various Roman Catholic prelates, including Francis Cardinal Spellman of New York and Richard Cardinal Cushing of Boston, to discuss machinery for starting theological dialogues. Iakovos said the Jerusalem meeting had sparked a "communion of love" and constituted a "definite commitment for unity of the two churches."[8] He also said it "promises beyond any doubt a conference of all Christian churches" in the near future aimed at joining their forces in dealing with modern social ills.[9]

Something decisively new had been started there on Mount Olivet, not immediately in resolving specific issues, but in the whole psychological and tactical disposition of leaders of the two Christian bodies toward each other. The change had even wider implications. Since Orthodoxy is a major force in the World Council of Churches, which also includes most of Protestantism, any strengthening of ties between Rome and Orthodoxy also tends to bring Protestantism into the new frame of relationships, with Orthodoxy as the church in the middle.

Augustin Cardinal Bea, president of the Vatican Christian Unity Secretariat, said there is no basis for any fears that Rome wishes to draw Orthodoxy away from the World Council. "Any friend of Christian unity is grateful to the World Council of Churches for what it has done and is doing to advance the great cause of union," he said. He added that Orthodox-Roman Catholic meetings "did not mean that Rome intended to forget the Lutheran and Reformed Churches of the West."[10] Warming ties with them already had developed before the East-West breakthrough.

That encounter, however, epitomized in the most far-reaching terms of men, time, and geography the vast dimensions and powerful impact of the ecumenical tide.

It not only had toppled the glowering, millennium-old blockade between two poles of the church, but it also had cut through international political barricades between East and West. Christian tribulations were not over in the Communist orbit, but a new concerned element was at work in the church voices now flowing across the Iron Curtain. Patriarch Alexis of Moscow sent his personal endorsement of the Jerusalem meeting, expressing hopes for "further development of contacts" with Roman Catholicism in the quest of a reunified Christianity.

Perhaps the churches, so long divided and scrapping among themselves, may yet be the force which will forge a peaceful and just unity among the members of the human family.

At least a step was taken in that direction in Jerusalem by a pope and a patriarch in the mid-twentieth century, a pair who plainly manifested their intent to walk together in the path of reconciliation.

Before leaving, Pope Paul had planted at the Apostolic Delegation the young shoot of an olive tree which he had brought from Italy. And on his departure for Rome, he took with him an olive sprout from the mountain where he and Athenagoras prayed the prayer that Jesus prayed there. The tree symbolizes peace. That was the thing the Pope sought to bring with him, and to take back with him to the center of his church.

It seemed to be an ingredient at work there in the vast overhaul going on at that prodigious parliament, Vatican II.

PART FOUR

In Council

"What is the road we should follow? And what is the goal toward which our journey leads? The journey is made within the framework of human history, bearing all the marks of time, and is conditioned by all the limitations of our present life. Yet at every moment we must be guided by the ultimate and decisive goal which we know awaits us at the journey's end. The answer is Christ: Christ from whom we begin; Christ who is both the road we travel and our guide on the way; Christ, our hope and our final end."

—POPE PAUL VI,
Second Vatican Council, September 29, 1963.

CHAPTER *10*

Five Crossroads

A bishop walked slowly to the center of the great hall of St. Peter's, carrying a beautiful New Testament which had been hand-printed in illuminated letters in 1472. He placed it, open, on the altar table there while a choir sang, "Christ conquers, Christ rules, Christ commands."

The music ended. A moment's hush, and Eugene Cardinal Tisserant, dean of the College of Cardinals, led the 2,300 assembled prelates in a prayer of contrition, dependence, and hope.

"We are here, O Lord, Spirit of God, we are here, conscious indeed of the burden of sin, but gathered together especially in your name. Come to us, and remain with us. Deign to purify our hearts. Teach us what to do and how to proceed; and show us what we should accomplish, so that with your help we may be able to please you in all things. . . . May you be the sole initiator and guide of our decisions. . . ."

Each weekday morning during sessions of the Second Vatican Council, this "enthronement" of the gospels as the sovereign Word (by a different bishop each day), and this hearkening to divine guidance opened deliberations which in sum charted a transformation in the Roman Catholic Church.

Through the four years of 1962, 1963, 1964, and 1965, the work went on with general sessions held from fall into winter and subsidiary commissions laboring during the recesses. Catholic lay auditors were included during the 1964 and 1965 sessions, with women present at a council for the first time in church history. Through week after week of trenchant analysis, of proposing, listening, urging, learning, debating, voting, through about 2,500 formal addresses in the annual sessions, through more than two thousand additional written interventions and petitions, through floor clashes and off-stage conferences, through consultation with the theological experts—the *periti*— and with Protestant and Orthodox observers, through the toil of minds and hearts, the magistrates of the church set its new directions.

And the task continued, not only in Rome, but in Christian communities around the world.

Its nerve center, however, resided in that vast gray-white basilica where the "council fathers" met day after day, striving to give a clearer meaning, fuller performance, and broader relevance to their faith.

At a long desk at the front of the *aula* sat the four cardinal-moderators: the brisk, dynamic Julius Doepfner of Munich; the sociable, scholarly Leon-Joseph Suenens of Malines-Brussels, Belgium; the moderate Giacomo Lecaro of Bologna, the only Italian of the four; and the bearded Eastern Rite cardinal, Gregory Agagianian, an Armenian.

Tiers of seats on either side of the nave, 615 feet long, held the assembled bishops, the church overseers from around the earth considered "successors of the apostles," white men, black men, yellow men, clad in long purple soutanes with white rochets and purple capes over their shoulders. In a front section on the left sat the scarlet-robed cardinals, and across from them on the right, the Protestant and Orthodox observer-delegates, garbed variously in clerical collars, business suits, and robes, occupied a special tribune of honor—convivially termed the "best seats in the house."

Out of that arena, suffused by floodlights and the unleashed currents of discussion, stemmed the lightnings which galvanized the ancient ecclesiastical edifice.

The phenomenon, its force surprising both those inside and outside the church, began with the burst of intuition in the late Pope John. His call for a council—shocking to those who thought the pope now ruled alone—struck fertile ground, and through the sessions of husbanding and harvest, spread like new greenery through the Christian landscape. Surveying the young but hardy growth, that prescient, old German Biblical sage, Augustin Cardinal Bea, said:

"From the mustard seed of the first idea of the council a tree is about to spring to life, the size of which we cannot now even imagine." [1]

Its sap and tendrils penetrated virtually every part of the church and reached beyond there, impinging vitally on connections with other Christians, on the flexibility of doctrinal expression, on religious liberty, on relationship with Jews, on diversity in ways of worship, on the rights and responsibilities of laymen, on checks and balances in church government, on the conjunction of papal authority with that of other bishops, on the ruling writ, the Bible.

And each day, that book was set out as the key text.

"La Biblie Torne a Roma," headlined an Italian newspaper over a full-page analysis near the close of the council's first session. "The Bible Returns to Rome." [2]

A pricking label perhaps, yet in an affirmative sense, it sounded a note pervading the whole undertaking. An emphasis on Scriptural underpinnings, a re-examination of the prime Christian directives—this accent ran through the measures passed, the redraftings voted, the trends set in motion. Both Popes John and Paul had called for a resubmission to basic sources; Paul had dramatized the point with his Holy Land trip. Spiritual reanimation, he says, derives from going to the "origins of faith," not necessarily by travel, but in ever closer adherence to the Lord's teachings. [3]

This was the declared yardstick as the council worked to discard the extraneous and to reinforce the authentic. This did not mean taking the church back to the first century or jettisoning its valid understandings gained since then, but rather revamping its usages and attitudes, in the light of the founding principles, to meet the needs of the present age.

It also called forth efforts to deepen ties with others who affirmed those same principles, in order that the Christian voice might ring more intelligibly in a clangorous world.

That objective, too, rested on the primary one.

"Whatever truly unites us to Christ," said the late Albert Cardinal Meyer, Archbishop of Chicago, "must unite us also to those who are in Christ, and in his heavenly Father." [4]

In its sweeping quest, exploring its original constitution, weighing the demands of the present hour, and seeking to allay the divisiveness of the past, the church probed itself to its very depths. Not unnaturally in such deep-going reassessment, keen differences of opinion developed on the extent and kind of action needed.

Roughly speaking, a traditionalist, centralist, or "closed-door" wing sought generally to preserve the status quo, while the progressive, autonomist, or "open-door" school advocated extensive reforms. Such classifications aren't intended to lump individuals since their positions may shift from issue to issue, but the two opposing tendencies plainly asserted themselves and brought the council's crucial tests. "There was a real cleavage, not just a question of semantics," says Bishop Ernest J. Primeau of Manchester, New Hampshire. [5]

It punctuated the floor debate, created questions about the handling of the agenda, threaded the talk at the coffee bars in St. Peter's and outside at the little cafes along the Via Della Conciliazione and in the press panel briefings given by the *periti* and individual bishops. It crackled in petitions circulated for signatures, echoed in the side meetings at hotels and religious houses, and steeped the running commentaries in church journals nearly everywhere.

At stake in that vying of minds, unitedly dedicated to one cause but disagreeing on how to enhance it, was the future course of the church, its relationship with other communities of faith and beyond that, with society at large. It was an historic crossroads.

The outcome?

The full results still are being formulated, and the job of translating them into canon laws, educational curricula, mission work, and the conduct of parishes will go on for years beyond the council's adjournment, but the council already has set the bearings. Out of its free and lively ferment of viewpoints, its strains and temporary stalemates, its halts, starts, progress, and suspenseful air, it has generated a headway which delineated its ultimate handiwork. It has proclaimed a transition. It has launched an airing out, an opening up, an immense renovation.

As the Vatican Council moved through its fourth and final session of 1965, Protestant observer Douglas Horton said the church had lifted the curtain on "a new dawn" for Christianity. Cardinal Suenens, primate of Belgium, summarized earlier: "The council has opened all the doors and closed none." [6]

As in any major institutional overhaul, however, there were kinks of resistance, apprehension, and foot-dragging along the way. In "certain quarters of the Roman Curia," says French Jesuit theologian Robert Rouquette, "there is hot-blooded disagreement with the majority of the council, shock at the freedom of the bishops and at the rediscovery of the episcopal collegiality (corporate church government)." [7] The Vatican officials, the executive-administrative cabinet of the church, "have been carrying on for many years without change," comments Joseph Cardinal Ritter of St. Louis. "Naturally they're hesitant and suspicious." [8] This was not the prevailing disposition, however.

Yet some commentators, inside and outside the church, surmised after both the 1963 and 1964 sessions that their failure to reach a final vote on relationships with Jews and on religious liberty represented a resurgence of old-guard strength. Despite a rash of such speculation at the end of the 1963 session, an ensuing 1964 session ballot gave overwhelming preliminary approval to the document affirming innate ties with Judaism and repudiating the old "Christ-killers" canard.

Furthermore, although a procedural ruling by council presidents delayed a vote on an endorsement of religious liberty at the close of the 1964 session, a vast majority of bishops—seventeen hundred of them—demonstrated their fervent support for it by signing petitions in its behalf. Even the sharpest critics of the delay conceded that the ruling for it was technically correct—since the finished draft had not been in hand the prescribed length of time for a vote before adjournment. Afterward, Bishop Leo C. Byrne of Wichita, Kansas, noted perceptively, "We lost a battle, but we shall win the war." The outcome was inevitable. And quickly, in the 1965 session, the council overwhelmingly approved the religious liberty document, declaring the right of all men to worship as their conscience leads them, publicly and privately, and the duty of government to protect that freedom.

Beforehand, however there were repeated rounds of published theories about palace intrigue and inferences that Curial pressure had put the Pope in a Hamlet-like "to-be-or-not-to-be" state which kept him from intervening decisively. Paradoxically, such criticism involved deploring the absence of the very thing which, from past indications, would be the most likely to stir criticism—"papal domination." The Council's wide-open liberty, untrammeled by orders or interventions from the top, was its especially refreshing quality, sweeping away widespread impressions of autocratic rule. "This is an assembly of free men," Pope Paul said at the close of the 1964 session.

He not only asked that religious liberty be made the first item on the 1965 agenda, but reaffirmed his own support for it. Earlier he had literally rescued the declarations both on the Jews and on religious liberty from oblivion, by countermanding a move by Curia officials in October, 1963, to cut both documents sharply and bury them in other larger pronouncements. Indeed, a small but determined council minority keenly opposed both declarations and sought by various means to scuttle them, but without avail. The Jewish statement already had express sanction. And in perspective, the delay in the religious liberty vote became quite academic—a mediating gesture, perhaps, but without any effect whatever on the result.

The pronouncement was given approval in the 1965 session—to "crown the work of the council," as Pope Paul put it.

In short, the procedural snags and stresses did not necessarily reduce or essentially even deflect the running tide, already released and ratified. American Protestant theologian Elmer J. F. Arndt, a Congregationalist observer-delegate at the Council, said it had shown unmistakably the Roman Catholic Church's determination "to be renewed and reformed." [9]

Five capital events stamped the seal on the new order.

Many lesser ones added to its magnitude, but the five provided the decisive early landmarks. Two of them came in the 1962 session, two in the 1963 session. They laid the framework for the unfolding series of further steps in the 1964 and 1965 sessions.

The first large pointer appeared at the opening of the council on October 11, 1962, when the late Pope John declared a far-reaching and provocatively fresh approach to church doctrine. Doctrine is the core of beliefs, the fundamental affirmations, on which Christianity is built, and over which the churches broke apart. The traditional Roman Catholic position that dogma is unchangeable has implied that nothing could be done so far as doctrine is concerned to alleviate conflicts with other churches.

In actuality, ecumenical scholars recognized that much of the trouble stems from mutual misconceptions of unfamiliar terminology used by others. This is a result of the long breakdown in communications, ever more crippling the ability to understand the "foreign" terms of one another, particularly in the subtle science of theology. Nevertheless, at bottom, beneath all the prejudice and external misassumptions, the basic rupture lies in doctrine.

If Rome's statement of it were fixed and static, Rome could not budge at the basic level toward Christian reunion. Pope John shook the unshakable.

To the 2,540 bishops, cardinals, heads of religious orders, Eastern Rite patriarchs and metropolitans, brought together for the first time in ninety-two years, he said: "The substance of the ancient doctrine of the deposit of faith is one thing, and the way in which it is presented is another. And it is the latter that must be taken into great consideration, with patience if necessary, everything being measured in the forms and proportions of a magisterium which is predominantly pastoral in character." No pope had ever made that distinction; none had ever formally declared a difference between truth and its clothing in the limited and variable formulations of men. Heretofore Rome has provided for evolution of new doctrines, but except in the upper theological strata, it has not called for improved renditions of the old. And that, not new dogmas, is what Pope John urged. "The whole world expects a step forward towards a doctrinal penetration," he said. Something then could be done about the root difficulties.

A field of incalculable possibilities was opened.

This did not rescind or minimize Rome's teaching that the integral content of doctrine remains unalterable, a given treasury of truth, to be perpetuated among men. The striking recognition, however, was that inadequate definitions and partial human understandings could becloud that content, that language itself is an imperfect, historically conditioned medium, variously grasped according to the mentality of every age, and that the church should be opened to clearer insights into doctrine and better expressions of it.

Protestantism and Orthodoxy take a similar position. Like Rome, they hold that divine truth is permanently abiding. Yet they, particularly Protestants, concede their faulty human comprehension and words for it, and leave latitude for truer explanations of it. They could move on that level. The past implication has been that in any reconciliation with Rome they would have to do all the moving—a one-way "return."

But Pope John made clear that Rome also could move in seeking that goal and intended to do so, as part of the mutual progress toward it. Although the "living substance" of apostolic and evangelical truth remains the same, "it is very natural that innovations of times and of circumstances suggest different forms and attitudes of exterior transmission of doctrine itself," he said in a later address to the council. For that reason, he added, the church often applies the maxim, "one art, a thousand styles." [10] That is, the heart of it remains steady, but it could be reflected in countlessly varied and more apt ways.

"The Pope sees that we can advance toward unity in doctrine through different formulations," says noted Catholic theologian Hans Küng of Germany. "For instance the Latin Church and the Greek Church always had differing formulations of the same faith and today we have observed that different Protestant and Catholic formulations often have fundamentally the same basic faith." [11]

Many church scholars took up the theme and its potentialities. A Dutch Catholic theologian, Edward Schillebeeck, says that by sealing off doctrine in static terms and language disassociated from current thought modes and circumstances, "truth which was formerly discovered and still remains true, is now placed in a false light." Men can never "contemplate the 'naked' truth," he says, but only glimpse living insights into it. [12] As St. Paul said, we see in a glass darkly. "We have this treasure in earthen vessels" [13]—human vessels which never match up to the full reality. Archbishop Edward D. Howard of Portland, Oregon, comments: "Safeguarding the integrity of dogma does not mean that nothing can be done regarding existing difficulties in the field of doctrine. Too often the difficulties arise from the fact that the sense of dogma is not well understood or is even perverted." [14] Adds the vigorous and genial Archbishop of Atlanta, Georgia, Paul J. Hallinan: "For the twentieth century nothing less than accurate 20-20 vision will do. The old truths do not change, but the teaching of them needs revision." [15]

Pope Paul elaborated on the theme repeatedly. He told the opening of the council's second session on September 29, 1963: "Theological doctrine has the possibility of magnificent developments which merit the attentive consideration of our separated brethren also and which, as we ardently hope, may make the path toward common agreement easier." At the close of the second session, on December 5, 1963, he reiterated that in "our search for profession of the truth," the church is determined "to find means and expressions capable of closing the gap between our separated brethren and ourselves."

The second vivid signal of the council's temper involved a climactic reappraisal of an age-engrained doctrine—one lying at the very crux of the Protestant dispute with Rome and the sixteenth-century breakup in the Western church.

An overwhelming council majority, on November 22, 1962, made clear that it wanted a new, more sensitive approach to the torment-ing, old issue—the relation of church traditions to the Bible.

The decision that day, as evaluated by numerous Catholic scholars, signaled an end to Counter-Reformation theology, the hard, defensive line taken against the Protestant revolt, and may well be seen in ret-rospect as a "turning point" in the history of the church.[16]

Simultaneously, Protestantism also is taking a new, amplified view toward the question. Both sides are thus reassessing their intransigent, fighting positions on it which split the church.

In the rise of Protestantism 450 years ago, it drew its challenge to Rome from the premise that the Bible constituted the only source of divine truth. Back as far as Italy's Peter Waldo in the twelfth century, England's John Wycliffe and the Czech Jan Huss in the fourteenth century, this tenet fired the anti-Rome defiance, as it did in the six-teenth century with Germany's Martin Luther, Britain's Thomas Cran-mer, Switzerland's Ulrich Zwingli, and the French John Calvin, who fled to Geneva. *"Sola Scriptura!"* became the driving credo of the ref-ormation wave which spawned the host of new churches, Lutheran, Presbyterian, Baptist, Congregationalist, and others. "Only the Scripture!"

Rome sternly countered at the Council of Trent on April 8, 1546, with its declaration that Christian "truth and teachings are contained in Sacred Scripture and in the unwritten traditions" handed down oral-ly through the church. On this basis, Roman Catholic teaching manuals and catechisms ever since have generally maintained that divine revelation comes from "two sources"—Scripture and church tradition—implying they are separate.

A flat reiteration of this thesis, accompanied with negative admoni-tions about scientific Biblical research, was presented to the Vatican Council by a theological commission headed by Cardinal Ottaviani, prefect of the powerful Holy Office, the Vatican's supreme court on doctrine. The two-sources schema on revelation ignited a fuse at the Council which flamed into an eye-opening light.

Not that the bishops ignored the Council of Trent, but in the past decade, with the upsurge of Roman Catholic Biblical studies and the ecumenical movement, much rethinking had gone on, and the routine formulas didn't suit the "open-door" council fathers, aware of the developing new concepts.

These modifying trends have arisen among both Catholics and Protestants. Curiously, approaching from opposite poles of the issue, both groups have moved toward a middle ground.

Protestants have increasingly recognized that tradition plays a part in conveying God's revelation; that the *sola scriptura* slogan itself is a tradition, just as are the other particular heritages of Luther, Calvin, John Wesley, and Roger Williams; that tradition includes the accumulated church insights of the ages, of the great Augustine, and other church fathers, East and West, as well as continuing discoveries about Scripture; that tradition contributed the great confessions of the faith, the Apostles', Nicene, and Athanasian creeds, widely accepted in Protestantism, and also the articles of faith of the reformers, the Augsburg and Westminster confessions, among others; that corporate church decisions (traditions), under the guidance of the Holy Spirit, even formed the Bible itself by winnowing apocryphal material out of canonical Scriptures in the third and fourth centuries. Protestants have not abandoned their premise that the Bible is the primary, ruling guide of faith, and the authoritative revelation in the light of which all tradition must be judged. But they have acquired a growing respect for the church's historical dimensions and the value of its traditions, along with the continuing role of scholarship in contributing to them.

Lutheran historian Jaroslav J. Pelikan says there is a "growing awareness of Protestants that they cannot apprehend the message of the Bible without the church and its tradition. Before there was a New Testament there was a church confessing, teaching, remembering, celebrating, and handing on the sacred mysteries of the faith. Out of this process of 'handing on' came our Bible, as the historical and critical scholarship of the past two generations has shown. If this is so, then the Bible cannot be read outside the context of tradition. I think I would be safe in saying that some such declaration—I am tempted to call it an 'admission'—would come from a very large percentage of Protestant theologians today, and that very few of them would say 'Scripture alone' in the sense in which the slogan has sometimes been used." [17]

At the same time, many Roman Catholic theologians have increasingly stressed the interdependence of tradition and Scripture, pointing out that the two cannot be disconnected as separate "sources" of divine revelation under the dualistic views emanating from the Council of Trent. They maintain that Scripture and tradition together constitute but "one source" of God's self-disclosure, and that tradition must be rooted implicitly or explicitly in Scripture. They maintain that "all revelation is somehow contained in Scripture," says American Catholic theologian James Brady, and that "tradition is the guide accompanying Scripture, the key of understanding to those who read the word of God." [18] Thus, says American Jesuit Avery Dulles, "they can agree with Protestants that in some genuine sense all revelation is contained in Scripture, while insisting at the same time that Scripture never discloses its full meaning unless read in the atmosphere of authentic tradition." [19]

These theologians contend that the Council of Trent, in saying God's truth is contained in the Bible "and" tradition, used the conjunction simply to mean that Scriptural truth is "also" expressed and clarified through tradition. They point out the unvarying Roman Catholic doctrine that all teachings of the Bible are decisive, that they cannot be played down, altered, or contradicted by any tradition, and that Christian revelation was objectively completed in the lifetime of Christ and the apostles. Tradition is then regarded as supplementing that basic revelation, containing it, cohering in it, and leading to fuller understanding of it. "They are interconnected so that the one supplements and complements the other," says Swiss Jesuit Mario Von Galli. "They must therefore be seen as a totality, and only thus can they be correctly understood." [20]

If tradition were regarded as independent of the Scriptures, then "we have no principle by which to purify Catholic life, to distinguish what is healthy from what is unhealthy in it," says Canadian theologian Gregory Baum, a consultant to the Vatican Secretariat on Christian Unity. He says that it is through deepening knowledge of Scripture "that the tradition of the church is constantly purified and made more authentic. It is through this return to the Word of God that we can distinguish within the life of the church the elements which are authentic and those which represent unwholesome developments." [21] This, too, parallels current Protestant thinking.

Thus, harmonizing tendencies sprang from the growing Catholic stress on the Bible and the maturing Protestant sense of the essential role of church study and tradition in interpreting Scripture.

However, the older, conventional Catholic view separates tradition and Scripture. And it was this "double source" theory which was put before the Vatican Council—the schema entitled De Duplici Fonte Revelationis. "The theology embodied in this document did not rise above the banalities of outmoded theological textbooks," says noted American Biblical scholar George H. Tavard, one of the council *periti* —expert advisers. [22] And it touched off a slow burn.

Since the document was presented in an aura of highest official sanction, the bishops at first reacted hesitantly. They were accustomed to being told by the Holy Office, not telling it. However, the outspoken Joseph Cardinal Frings of Cologne, Germany, and Achille Cardinal Lienart of Lille, France, rose to protest the omission of the newer concepts. This drew rejoinders from Ernesto Cardinal Ruffini of Palermo and Ottaviani, both of whom have decried modern Catholic Biblical trends. They said the schema represented the authoritative viewpoint.

But the lid was off, and the debate rolled on for more than a week, a tellingly significant one in the annals of the church.

A succession of progressive-minded cardinals, including Bernard Jan Alfrink of Utrecht and Paul-Emile Léger of Montreal, argued that the schema would be a setback to relationships with other Christians and put a cloud over the freedom of Catholic Biblical investigations. Some traditionalist church leaders fear that the new research may cast doubt on the historical accuracy of Scripture. On the contrary, the Biblical scholars insist that it brings the real meaning of Scripture into clearer light. This intricate work, utilizing the tools of literary, historical, and ethnic inquiry, developed early in Protestantism, and lately has burgeoned in Catholicism. Scholars of both branches now collaborate extensively in the field. Progressive bishops saw the future of this enterprise threatened by the proposed revelation schema.

As the forensics spiraled toward a peak, Bishop Emile Joseph De Smedt of Bruges, Belgium, made a memorable appeal for recognition that Christian truth comes from "that which has been communicated by the Lord himself" and that "all of us, Catholics and non-Catholics alike, have recourse to this one same source." He said the ordinary terminology used on each side has been misinterpreted by the other, with resultant "prejudices, suspicions, quarrels." He urged revised theological manners and methods so "Christians of various denominations may help each other arrive at a clear and more exact understanding" of each other's doctrines. "We must have a clear idea of the present-day teaching of the Orthodox and Protestant churches," he said. "We must know what non-Catholics feel is missing or not sufficiently explained in Catholic doctrine."

His address, in its full details, has come to be regarded as a sort of guide to ecumenical dialogue. As for the revelation schema, he said its "substantial deficiencies could have been avoided if these commissions had taken the trouble to collaborate among themselves." This may have been an indirect reference to the fact that Cardinal Bea, head of the Unity Secretariat, and a key figure in sparking the new Biblical studies in the church, had offered to work with Cardinal Ottaviani's theological commission in preparing the schema, but had been turned down.

In the midst of the drawn-out fluctuating discussion, with traditionalists arguing that the church must stand firm in its formulations to guard the stability of doctrine and ward off unfamiliar theories disturbing to the faithful, a plain-spoken, unpretentious prelate from Missouri, Joseph Cardinal Ritter, injected a definite word that brought the whole matter to a head. *"Rejiciendum est!"* he declared, his Latin ringing with incisive certainty. "This draft must be rejected!"

He called it "out of date, ambiguous, pessimistic, negative, calculated not to inspire love for the Bible but rather servile fear." As he sat down to an approving murmur, the stooped, old Cardinal Bea took the microphone, gently thanking the compilers of the schema for their work, but saying the results would take the church backward, not forward. He said the whole thing ought to be reworked.

When the question came to a vote on November 21, an overwhelming 1,368 voted to discard the draft. Only 822 favored retaining it even as a general basis for continued discussion. Pope John ordered the schema withdrawn and the subject turned over to a new joint commission, including Bea as its co-chairman along with Ottaviani. The title of the rewritten schema was simply "On Divine Revelation," without the double-source implications and with the way left open for the unitary viewpoint.

It was discussed and strongly supported in the 1964 council session, prior to final action on it in 1965. Voicing the new understanding, the late Cardinal Meyer of Chicago told the council that church tradition does not stand alone, but is constantly tested and purified through an unchanging God-given norm, the Scriptures. Jesuit theologian R. A. F. Mackenzie, an expert advisor at the council, said that Protestant reformers used the Bible to criticize the church for avarice and worldliness in the sixteenth century, and that "such a measurement of the church against the standards of Scripture is just as valid today. . . . It is a much-needed function." [23]

The prime point, however, was that the bishops said "no" to the old-style doctrinal sharpshooting. They "demonstrated that they did not want a traditionalist theology which simply repeated the formulas of the manuals, but that the time had come when theology must be open, creative, and forward looking, in sympathy with new spiritual movements among Catholics and the world," says Baum, an Augustinian priest-specialist on interchurch relationships. [24]

The action on revelation itself offered a revelation, namely, that the centuries-old Bible battle that flared in the Protestant Reformation has turned into a program of peace.

Pope Paul strengthened that program by pointedly commending the Pontifical Biblical Institute, the pioneering institution which Cardinal Bea headed and enlivened for nineteen years and whose stimulus to Scriptural studies often in the past ran into restrictions from the Holy Office. On April 21, 1964, a Biblical commission issued an instruction, ratified by Pope Paul, urging Catholic scholars to use all the "new means" of linguistics, history, and form criticism to analyze Scriptural texts so as to "throw full light on the perennial truth and authority of the gospels" and to "penetrate more deeply the nature" of their testimony.

The case for the Catholic Biblical movement, once frowned on in high circles, had achieved sturdy standing.

The third illuminating beacon of Vatican II, which was followed a year later by final approval of the monumental constitution, De Ecclesia (Concerning the Church), first appeared midway in the second session, on October 30, 1963. The "turning point," Bishop Wright of Pittsburg called it. [25]

On that day a six-to-one council majority endorsed for the first time a broadened concept of church government to integrate the authority of the pope with that of the rest of the bishops. As later spelled out in the thirty-thousand-word constitution, De Ecclesia, formally approved November 21, 1964, by a vote of 2,251 to 5, the church asserted its collective or fraternal rule. The principle has taken on a familiar tag, "episcopal collegiality." It means that the world-wide college of bishops in unity with the head of that college, the pope, governs the church in partnership.

"The monarchical concept of the church is abandoned, and the church again has established its original structure," wrote Catholic theologian Joseph Ratzinger of Germany's Muenster University. [26]

The idea, keenly resisted by traditionalists, could go far toward reconciling differences with Eastern Orthodoxy about church authority and greatly reduce differences with Protestantism.

It also blasts the old myth of papal "dictatorship," which has been rather thoroughly exploded by the very character of the council anyhow.

"It clearly dispels some of the stereotypes most Protestants and many Catholics have had about papal monarchialism and one-man rule," [27] says American Presbyterian observer-delegate Robert McAfee Brown.

The new constitution is the council's weightiest theological treatise and basic to all the other actions. Its name, *De Ecclesia*, comes from the original Greek of the New Testament, meaning "the assembly" of God, those "called out" to serve him, or in short, the church. Laden with Biblical citations, the constitution takes a new look at the twenty-century-old ecclesiastical institution, seeing it primarily as a supernatural entity uniting the "People of God," and secondarily, as a visible, juridical structure.

This is a vital shift in emphasis. It veers away from the past tendency to lay down exacting specifications according to the Aristotelian method, and instead recognizes that in men's eyes much about the church is mystery. Rather than focusing on the outward hierarchical organization as stressed in the Counter-Reformation, the emphasis is on the intangible realities of the church permeating all members, clergy and laymen, and extending also beyond Roman Catholic jurisdiction. "The head of this body is Christ," the constitution states. It clarifies the distinctions between the divine organism of the church and its fallible human instrumentalities, and also recognizes a mysterious churchly breadth which encompasses all Christians among whom Christ "is operative . . . with his sanctifying power."

What caught the world's main attention, however, was the new, corporate approach to the church's earthly governance.

The constitution declares that the world-wide company of bishops are successors of the apostles, as the pope is successor to the chief apostle, Peter, and in like manner they share authority and responsibility with him. By virtue of Christ's commission to all his apostles, the bishops as their successors have "supreme and full power over the universal church, provided we understand this body together with its head, the Roman Pontiff, and never without this head," the constitution says. It specifies that bishops and pope are "joined together." While papal primacy is clearly maintained, and the pope's office still recognized as a complementary organ of "full, supreme" authority, it is linked parallel to that of the entire body of bishops, and beyond that to the collective conscience of the whole church community.

Only the unfolding developments of the future can reveal just how this mutually balanced and joint rule is to be applied in actual practice. There were strong prospects for an internationally representative "small council" or synod sitting regularly with the pope after the conclusion of Vatican II. And at the start of the 1965 session Pope

Paul announced establishment of such a continuing body, with most of its members elected by national conferences of bishops. A tremendous departure from the idea of arbitrary papal rule to one of shared prerogatives was evident in the fresh initiatives sweeping the church as well as in the precepts laid down in the new constitution.

It points out that the co-responsibility for the church includes, in varying ways and degrees, the "common priesthood of the faithful"— the lay members of the church. "Each individual part contributes through its special gifts to the good of the other parts and of the whole church. Through the common sharing of gifts and through the common effort to attain to fullness in unity, the whole and each part receives increase."

In short, this asserted a corporate type of church government, with both body and head essential to the functioning of the whole. It doesn't lessen the primacy of the head but correlates it inseparably with the total body.

For the sake of "our separated brethren" and the cause of Christian unity, it must be clearly shown that "definitions of the pope are never to be understood against or without the consent of the church," Archbishop (now Cardinal) Lawrence J. Shehan of Baltimore, Maryland, told the council. [28]

The move aims at balancing out the dogma of "papal infallibility" on doctrine so as to place it in the context of the whole church's teaching office. The First Vatican Council in 1870 fixed the "infallibility" dogma and had plans to relate it to the total episcopate presided over by the pope. But that council, interrupted by the seizure of Rome by Italian nationalist troops, did not finish its work. As a result, the sheer "papal infallibility" dogma has loomed ever since as a major issue of disagreement with Protestantism and Orthodoxy. They hold that the church should be jointly governed with dispersed authority. The "collegiality" view is closer to this.

Pope Paul, at the opening of the second session, told the bishops that "you have banished the fear wrongly deduced" from the First Vatican Council that "the supreme powers conferred by Christ on the Roman pontiff to govern and vivify the church were sufficient without the assistance of ecumenical councils." He said he looked forward to the development of ways for "more effective and responsible collaboration with our beloved and venerable brothers in the episcopate."

On promulgating the new constitution, at the close of the 1964 session, Pope Paul told the bishops that "the assistance of your authority" is essential, and he eagerly embraced their prerogatives "so as to integrate them with our own." He said, "We feel more trustful in the help of Christ because we are and want to be all gathered together more closely in his name." The Pope added: "Collective action is more complicated than individual action, but . . . we shall be able to overcome with prudence and charity the obstacles inherent in a more complex organization of ecclesiastical government."

In practical terms, the plan represented a reversal in the centralizing trend built up in reaction to the Protestant break-away. "The highly centralized government, however, is not really in harmony with Catholic ideals," says Father Baum. With the present-day shift back to a family-like structure, "greater freedom will exist for the initiative of men whom the Spirit inspires. Until now, so many good ideas, so many ways of pastoral renewal, could not be translated into action because the church was so completely centralized. [29]

Bishop Wright said there were grounds for hope that, in the amplified view of the pope's undiminished teaching office, it "will be seen in the perspective of the total infallibility of the church."

One of the most crisp, concise statements of the expanded concept came in the period of preparation for the council, in a joint pastoral letter by the Dutch hierarchy, on December 24, 1960. It said:

"The infallibility of the papal office cannot be separated from the totality of the faith into which God has placed it. Because of the premature adjournment of the First Vatican Council, the separate definition of papal infallibility gives the impression of being completely unrelated. Actually this personal infallibility lies embedded in the infallibility belonging to the world's bishops by virtue of their office, and they in turn rest on the infallible faith of the whole believing community."

In use, "papal infallibility" has been an extremely rare thing. It is considered operative only when the pope specifies a solemn doctrinal pronouncement *ex cathedra* ("from the chair"). It has been exercised definitely only once since being defined—in Pius XII's 1950 declaration that the Virgin Mary was assumed "body and soul" into heaven. And this was only after a world-wide poll of bishops, with a majority approving and about a fourth disapproving. "Infallibility" does not imply that the pope is particularly virtuous, informed, or intelligent, but only that as the earthly head of the church, he will be safeguarded by the Holy Spirit from basically or seriously misrepresenting the faith, in accordance with Christ's special mandate to Peter and broad promise of continued guidance.

"And I will pray the Father, and he will give you another Counselor, to be with you forever, even the Spirit of truth . . . he will teach you all things, and bring to your remembrance all that I have said to you." [30]

That assurance, however, was made to all the apostles, of whom the bishops are considered successors. The "collegiality" view thus sees them as active participants in overall church government—a role derived not from the pope but directly from Christ.

Before passage of the weighty and widely encompassing new constitution, there had been prolonged, sometimes peppery, debate about it. The discussion had continued at intervals through the 1963 and 1964 sessions.

Archbishop Joseph Descuffi of Smyrna, Turkey, said the twin infallibilities of the pope and the whole church "must be joined together in one and the same infallibility." [31] Francis Cardinal Spellman of New York cautioned against collegiality. "The theology we all learned in the seminary teaches us that the pope alone has full power over the entire church," he said. "He does not need the help of others." [32] Bishop Aurelio del Pino Gomez of Lerida, Spain, gave an interview, saying it would be "suffocating of the power of the Roman pontiff" to fasten it to the whole college of bishops.

On the other side, there was sharp criticism of the Roman Curia and insistence that it should serve as an instrumentality of both bishops and pope, rather than stand as an intermediary between them. Archbishop Eugene D'Souza of Bhopal, India, said Curial practices had become detrimental when writers are suppressed with no explanations given, "when general regulations are issued which are not suited to local conditions, when a suggestion proposed after mature reflection by bishops of a certain province, even of a nation, is rejected with a laconic *non expedit*—'better not'. . . ." He said the Curia must be "thoroughly reformed." [33] Pope Paul has plans for that in preparation.

Eastern Rite Patriarch Maximos IV of Antioch said collegiality also should include a continuing international synod, made up of rotating members from regional episcopates, to sit with the pope as a supreme executive and judicial council. "Since it will not be isolated in a center closed in on itself, the idea will not even occur to it of wanting to monopolize everything, regulate everything, lord it over everything, acting with exaggerated uniformity and, at times, meddlesomeness. It will understand that the problems of peoples must be settled by these peoples, and with them, but never without them." [34]

Several others, including Franz Cardinal Koenig of Vienna, envisioned a representative "senate" of bishops, meeting regularly as an interim governing body between full-scale councils. These proposals later took concrete form in Pope Paul's action in setting up a permanent senate. As part of the decentralizing shift, wider prerogatives also were being accorded to regional and national episcopal conferences.

Some theologians described this as a sort of "states' rights" system, allowing greater initiative and freedom to meet local needs. This, too, encountered resistance. "It would introduce a radical change in the structure of the church and could easily develop into a genuine threat to the unity of the church," said James Francis Cardinal McIntyre of Los Angeles. [35]

In the course of the 1963 debate, Paul Cardinal Richaud of Bordeaux, France, and Giuseppe Cardinal Gargitter of Bressanone, Italy, implied that there had been Curial tampering with the schema. It seems "somewhat out of harmony with the intentions of those who prepared it" and does not sufficiently develop the collegiality concept, Richaud said. Gargitter said the test apparently had undergone "several surgical operations" and "expounds its doctrine under the one-sided light of insistence on the rights and the central organs of the Roman Curia. . . . The original text drawn up by the preparatory commission was much more complete and well balanced." [36]

A behind-the-scenes struggle went on about bringing the issue to a test. Opponents sought to avert a vote. Council presidents conferred with the Pope. Four days later came the sweeping, preliminary vote of October 30, 1963, heralding the final decision of the following session, and revealing clearly for the first time that the council wanted the collegiality principle included in *De Ecclesia*.

Afterward Cardinal Ottaviani insisted the vote was not binding and "only an indication of the thinking of the Council Fathers." [37] Ernesto Cardinal Ruffini also discounted it. But they were mistaken. The decisive step had been taken. At the close of that session on December 4, 1963, Pope Paul declared that the "collaboration of the episcopacy in new ways required by the needs and organic nature of the church will be very precious to us." He ordered the document redrafted "in accordance with the minds of the fathers as expressed specifically in the general congregations." This was done, culminating in the formal adoption of the constitution in November, 1964, as the new charter of collective church government. It "opens up a new era for the government of the church," said Cardinal Valerian Gracias of Bombay. [38] It had not been easy. The cause of the friction, Cardinal Ritter related later, was that for many years, the habit of the Curia "has been more and more that of telling the bishops what to do, and the council is trying to tell the Curia that it is subject to the bishops." [39] It is a matter of sorrow, says Bishop Francois Charriere of Geneva, Switzerland, that a minority "attempts to defend the pope against the pope." [40]

In big and little ways, however, Paul VI let his own feelings be known.

Soon after he took office, he notified bishops that during the council

in Rome they could wear their mozettas, a short button-up cape symbolizing episcopal jurisdiction and which previously could not be
worn outside their own areas. Then on December 3, 1963, the Pope
took control over forty technical matters away from the Vatican, and
placed them in the hands of local bishops. An incident described by
Bishop Endre Hamvas, head of the Hungarian bishops' conference, indicated Paul's attitude toward episcopal relationships.

Hamvas, in his first audience with the new pope, took off his
skullcap in accordance with custom and held it in his hands.

"Put on your cap," Paul told him. "You are a bishop yourself."

A closer working fellowship was in the making among the far-flung
pillars of the church.

In the name of that fellowship, "Paul, bishop, servant of the servants of God, together with the fathers of the council," proclaimed
with them, and not by himself, the decree which marked the fourth
determinative stride of Vatican II—perhaps the most widely felt and
momentous of them all.

Culminating weeks of work by the council, both in the first and
second sessions, a new *Constitution on the Liturgy,* promulgated December 4, 1963, set in motion a vast reform in Roman Catholic
worship practices.

It is the "Magna Carta of Christian renewal," says Godfrey Diekman, an American Benedictine and specialist on liturgics. "A mighty
shaking of the foundations." [41]

It implements a substantial degree of decentralization or "collegiality" itself by giving regional episcopal conferences more autonomy in
determining worship forms appropriate to their own regions. It allows
for wider diversity. It permits use of present-day national languages
instead of Latin in baptism, marriage, confirmation, and other rituals,
including much of the mass—English, for instance, in the United States.
It calls for more active involvement of laymen, including congregational responses and hymn-singing. It recognizes the laity's share in
the "royal priesthood." It urges simplicity and elimination of pretentious display. It encourages special occasions for communion under
the form of both bread and wine (instead of only bread). It specifies
greater emphasis on pulpit preaching and on the Bible by parish pastors.

It "releases worship from its chains," says Archbishop Robert E.
Lucey of San Antonio. [42]

It breathes "reform in almost every line," says Robert McAfee
Brown, a Presbyterian observer-delegate at the council. "A quiet but
deep revolution." [43]

Besides its internal effects, however, the changes foretokened swiftly mounting similarities between Roman Catholic worship and worship in other churches. In many ways, the revisions parallel those espoused by the early Protestant reformers—more attention to the Bible, worship in living languages, communion in both kinds, intensified preaching, simplicity, and flexibility. "All these points were among the principal greivances of non-Catholics and accordingly barriers to ecumenism," says C. J. McNaspy, an American Jesuit. "They are now irrevocably removed." [44] What contributes even further to the closer congruity, however, is that Protestantism itself is in the midst of a strong movement to recapture order and symbolism in its liturgy, qualities which had been thrown out in the stress on preaching and congregational spontaneity.

In effect, Roman Catholicism now moved to combine the congregational activism of Protestantism with its own sacramental drama, while Protestantism moved toward recovering sacramental richness along with its pulpit evangelism. The two paths, again from opposite directions, pointed toward convergence.

Frederick McManus, a thoughtful, energetic monsignor who teaches at Catholic University, Washington, D.C., and one of a vanguard of liturgical experts who led the drive for reform in Catholic worship and who served as a Vatican II consultant, says the new constitution "exceeds the wildest expectations" of just five years ago and will serve an "ecumenical purpose" as well as Catholicism itself.

"It has providential parallels, more or less extensive among other Christians," he says, in that it recovers "the people's part in worship and out of worship" and provides a "new simplicity and intelligibility of rites" through "praying and singing in the mother tongue" and "especially by the new emphasis upon Scripture and preaching." Protestants may have been "quite literally scandalized by the cursory manner in which God's word is proclaimed to the people in the usual Catholic liturgy, a brief passage hurriedly recited to the wall, not even translated into the people's language at weekday Mass. In the future reform all this will change" and jolt the proclamation of the gospel "out of its present mechanical, routine performance" so that "our brothers in Christ may see in us a not unfamiliar devotion to the Scriptures." Also prescribed is a "real revolution in preaching." [45]

The extensive change-over will take time, heavy re-education work in local parishes, and readjustments of set habits to new ones. Under plans worked out jointly by the bishops of the United States, dioceses across the country initiated the change-over at the start of the ecclesiastical year on the first Sunday of Advent, November 29, 1964.

"The Lord be with you," the priest says in English, instead of the usual Latin *Dominus vobiscum.*

"And with thy spirit," comes back the congregation, instead of an acolyte at the altar murmuring *Et cum spiritu tuo.*

"Let us pray."

The priest may face the congregation instead of having his back to it. Scripture readings, the Confession, Introit, Gradual, Offertory, and Communion verses are in English, as are prayers which priest and congregation recite together, the Kyrie eleison ("Lord have mercy on us"), the Gloria, the Creed, the Sanctus just before the canon of consecration ("Holy, Holy, Holy, Lord God of hosts! . . ."). There are special joint prayers and congregational hymn-singing interspersing Scripture lessons, sermon, and the Ordinary of the Mass. Further changes were initiated in March, 1965, and many Catholic scholars foresaw eventual transition to worship entirely in the vernacular.

In Chicago, the Catholic adult-education center and local parishes joined in sponsoring a demonstration of the new Roman Catholic English Mass, incorporating changes sanctioned by Vatican II, for a group of twenty Protestant seminaries and churches, including Baptists, Methodists, Presbyterians, Lutherans, Episcopalians, Disciples of Christ, and United Church of Christ. Afterward Howard Schomer, president of Chicago Theological Seminary, a Protestant institution, commented:

"Many traditional Protestant misunderstandings of the intent of Roman Catholic worship were dissolved in surprise and joy at this ecumenical event." [46]

Since 1570, when Pope Pius V ordered a single, codified liturgy for the Western church, little had changed in Roman Catholic worship. Ecclesiastical legislation, set in 1917, reserved control of the liturgy "to the Apostolic See alone"—to the Vatican.

But the new constitution empowers the "competent territorial bodies of bishops," such as national episcopal conferences, "to decide whether, and to what extent, the vernacular language is to be used"; to initiate "variations and adaptations" in ritual and music and art, suitable to "different groups, regions, and peoples"; to direct experimental forms of worship; to draw up their own marriage rites appropriate to various places and peoples; to permit the use of various musical instruments besides the organ in church services and other innovations—all to be in accord with general church norms and with papal confirmation.

The new accent is on freedom and diversity.

The church "has no wish to impose a rigid uniformity" in its liturgy, the constitution says. It also puts a constant emphasis on the "full and active participation by all the people" as the "aim to be considered before all else"—a distinct departure from the commonly alleged picture of Roman Catholic worshipers as "passive spectators," while the priest goes through a liturgy that is soothing in familiarity but generally incomprehensible to those in the pews.

Worshipers are not to be present "as strangers or silent spectators," the constitution says, but "to take part in sacred actions, conscious of what they are doing, with devotion and full collaboration," joining in "acclamations, responses, psalmody, antiphons, and songs as well as by other actions," taking part as a "royal priesthood, holy nation, redeemed people."

The emphasis is on worship as a communal, interpersonal affair both of minister and laymen, instead of the individualistic or "quasi-private" approach to it.

In chapter after chapter, the constitution insists on more stress on the Bible, extended and varied readings from it, more instruction on it and study of it, including special Bible vigils. "The treasures of the Bible are to be opened up more lavishly, so that richer fare may be provided for the faithful at the table of God's word," the decree says. "It is essential to promote . . . warm and living love for Scriptures."

Sermons, often omitted or only perfunctory at many Catholic Masses heretofore, are made mandatory at all services on Sunday and other religious holidays. The general demand is for more diligent, vital preaching. "The ministry of preaching is to be fulfilled with exactitude and fidelity. The sermon, moreover, should draw its content mainly from Scriptural and liturgical sources, and its character should be that of a proclamation of God's wonderful works in the history of salvation. . . ."

Another plea is for naturalness and a "noble simplicity." Rites should be "short, clear, and unencumbered by useless repetitions." The people "should be enabled to understand them with ease and to take part in them fully, actively, and as befits a community." Churches should get rid of cluttering statuary and artworks which "offend true religious sense either by depraved forms or by lack of artistic worth, mediocrity, and pretense." The number of sacred images in churches "should be moderate and their relative positions should reflect right order. For otherwise they may create confusion among the Christian people and foster devotion of doubtful orthodoxy."

All in all, the 130-chapter constitution invoked an immense renovation both in form and content, affecting the religious lives of Catholics everywhere, sloughing off the superfluous and concentrating on basics, freeing initiatives and creativity, stimulating closer mutuality of clergy and people in worship, and producing new grounds for concord between Roman Catholicism, Eastern Orthodoxy, and Protestantism. Liturgical scholar Diekman calls it "the most important spiritual document ever issued by the Catholic Church." [47]

Like the other major turning points, it did not come automatically. It aroused stout resistance from some Curia officials at the council, particularly because of its concession of greater liberties to regional church leaders and its provisions for use of the vernacular instead of Latin. The voices of Asia and Africa, however, injected a powerful demand for local adaptations and variety. Patriarch Maximos IV made one of the ringing pleas for getting rid of a "dead language" in a "living church."

"After all, Christ spoke in the language of his contemporaries. . . . The Apostles and disciples did likewise. . . . St. Paul explicitly says, 'For if I pray in an unknown tongue, my spirit prayeth, but my understanding is unfruitful.' " [48]

At the outset of Christianity believers used Aramaic, the language of Christ. This soon changed to Greek, since that was the most common spoken tongue in the area of Christian expansion around the Mediterranean. When Latin became the common Western language in the fourth to sixth centuries, the church shifted to it without hesitation. But when Latin faded from popular usage, the church stuck with it through the centuries until Vatican II directed that worship be released from its tightly preserved clerical mold and be recommitted into terms of the people—not only into their speech but their full function in it.

The church was willing to go back fifteen hundred years to "change something overdue all that time," says Archbishop Guilford Young, of Hobart, Australia. [49]

When the liturgical schema originally came to a tentative vote in the council's first session, in which the debate on it took place, 2,186 votes favored it, 46 were opposed. But by the close of the second session, with the outcome a foregone conclusion, it went through with a tidal 2,147 to 4. As with the other pivotal issues, the preliminary show of intent presaged the final result.

The fifth historic turning point was the final approval, on November 20, 1964, of the unprecedented mandate for inter-Christian alliance—*De Ecumenismo*—the Decree of Ecumenism.

It summons the churches to a "change of heart" toward one another. It recognizes that faults and offenses have occurred on all sides, splitting Christianity apart, and urges mutual forgiveness. It views other churches as genuine channels of salvation, and refers to them specifically as "churches." It calls for a halt, in seminaries and elsewhere, to the prejudiced and misleading claims which churches have made about one another, and pleads for accurate, sympathetic understanding. It urges meetings, discussions, and studies among the different churches on "equal footing," and also common prayer. It says that all can learn and improve through such efforts. It also recommends practical co-operation among the churches on causes serving local communities and the world. As a whole, it proclaims an immense and epochal transformation in the character of Roman Catholicism's relationship with the sister churches of Protestantism and Eastern Orthodoxy.

The document "creates a new situation" for all churches, the Rev. Dr. W. A. Visser 't Hooft told the Central Committee of the World Council of Churches, meeting in Enugu, Nigeria, in January, 1965, He is the long-time administrator of this global Protestant-Orthodox body.

The new ecumenism decree, in complete contrast to the anathemas flung at non-Roman Catholics by the Council of Trent, declares that "all who have been justified by faith in baptism are members of Christ's body and have a right to be called Christian, and so are with solid reasons accepted as brothers by the children of the Catholic Church." This has been a constant theme of Cardinal Bea's Christian Unity Secretariat—that all persons validly baptized, whether by priests or ministers, are bound to Christ in his mystical body and thus are part of his church.

Although Roman Catholicism has customarily maintained it is the "one true church," the exclusivist view is avoided in the new decree. It recognizes that "the riches of Christ and virtuous works" exist in other churches, and that such values "can be a help to our own edification. Whatever is truly Christian is never contrary to what genuinely belongs to the faith; indeed, it can always bring a deeper realization of the mystery of Christ and the Church." To a degree, this simply expands the view of the authentic churchly perimeters to embrace others in it, at least marginally.

The worship of other churches "can truly engender a life of grace in ways that vary according to the condition of each church or community," the decree states. " . . . for the Holy Spirit has not refrained from using them as means of salvation. . . ." There is no imperious demand for a "return to Rome," as often voiced in the past, but for dedicated mutual study in search for means of unity. Declaring that "both sides were to blame" in dividing the church, the decree adds: "So we humbly beg pardon of God and of our separated brethren, just as we forgive them that trespass against us."

The document first won tentative approval in the 1963 session on November 21, by a vote of 1,996. Between then and the 1964 session, the statement was revised to make it "even bolder" than the original. "We had somewhat underestimated the growth of the ecumenical movement in the church," explained Thomas Stransky, an American Paulist and member of the Christian Unity Secretariat. [50] The changes incorporated suggestions made by Cardinal Koenig of Vienna, Cardinal Ritter of St. Louis, and Bishop Helmsing of Kansas City that Protestant denominations, as well as the Orthodox, be referred to as "churches" rather than only as "Christian communities." This had been a sensitive point in Protestant quarters, which maintain that for equitable dialogue, both sides must recognize one another as "churches," even though each may consider the others lacking in some respects. "It is only on the basis of such mutual recognition that a fellowship can gradually grow up in which the churches realize their responsibility for one another, and work for one another's sanctification," says Lukas Vischer, a World Council of Churches observer at the Vatican Council. [51]

When the revised and reinforced decree came to a final vote late in 1964, it received even fuller support than before, passing by 2,054 votes to only 64 against. It urges interchurch conversations and meetings, and joint theological study, along with common prayer, to generate understanding among the different churches, more accurate knowledge of one another, and "co-operation between them in the duties of the common good of humanity. . . . Such co-operation, which has already begun in many countries, should be developed more and more. . . ." By mutual dialogue, study, work, and prayer, all will gain "a clearer awareness and deeper realization of the unfathomable riches of Christ," and be led "to undertake with vigor the task of renewal and reform." This, the decree adds, "is the way that, when the obstacles to perfect ecclesiastical communion have been gradually overcome, all Christians will at last, in a common celebration of the Eucharist, be gathered into a single church in that unity which Christ bestowed on his Church in the beginning."

Although reunification demands "unity in essentials," the decree declares that "all, according to the gifts they have received, enjoy a proper freedom, in their various forms of spiritual life and discipline, in their different liturgical rites, and even in their theological elaboration of revealed truth."

The decree brought swift steps to implement it in various countries, including the United States where the bishops set up a new ecumenical committee, headed by Baltimore's Archbishop (now Cardinal)

Lawrence J. Shehan, and a permanent Ecumenical Office in Washington, D.C., to supply guidance and encouragement to the movement throughout the nation. A noted Kansas City theologian, Monsignor William W. Baum, was named executive secretary of the new office. Official theological talks were started in 1965 with representatives of various other communions in the United States—Episcopalian, Lutheran, Presbyterian, and Eastern Orthodox, as well as with the National Council of Churches, embracing most major Protestant and Orthodox bodies in the country. These new conferences paralleled similar sessions initiated on the international level in 1965, including talks with the World Council of Churches. The decree had repercussions in seminaries as well as in parishes. Theology professors and pastors were admonished to avoid the old polemics, and stress the "ecumenical point of view" in teaching and preaching.

Father Stransky, a quick-minded and amiable young priest from Milwaukee and one of Cardinal Bea's ablest English-speaking aides, summed up the church's new attitude in an interview: "We don't like the fact of separation. God doesn't like it. It is an evil. Its origin and its continuance are a sin or the result of sin on both sides. In any case, it is a scandal to the non-Christian world. It would be far better if we all were one, as the Father and Son are one, in order that the world may believe." To accomplish that goal, he said, "our approach is a willingness to accept criticism from non-Catholic Christians," realizing that "there are many things they can teach us which perhaps we have failed to learn from the church."

In the quest of unity, the decree says the church should "daily be more purified and renewed. . . . Every renewal of the church is essentially grounded in an increase of fidelity to her own calling. Undoubtedly this is the basis of the movement toward unity. Christ summons the church to continual reformation as she goes her pilgrim way. The church is always in need of this, insofar as she is an institution of men here on earth. Thus, if in various times and circumstances, there have been deficiencies in moral conduct or in church discipline, or even in the way that church teaching has been formulated . . . these can and should be set right at the opportune moment."

In special circumstances, particularly at ecumenical gatherings, "it is allowable, indeed desirable, that Catholics should join in prayer with their separated brethren," the decree states. "Such prayers in common are certainly an effective means of obtaining the grace of unity, and they are a true expression of the ties which still bind Catholics to their separated brethren." Hundreds of such joint services were held in the 1965 annual "Week of Prayer for Christian Unity," dramatizing the impact of the decree and hinting at its potentials in the future. It says that joint partaking of the Lord's Supper in communion *(communicatio in sacris)* "is not considered as a means to be used indiscriminately for the restoration of Christian unity." This, however, seems to leave the door open, at least partly, to intercommunion under special circumstances which may be considered to justify it—an interpretation expressed by some theologians. Such joint worship was strictly banned under old canon laws, still to be revised in the years ahead. The restrictions were widely applied in the past to include joint prayer as well. But that rule is specifically out. The newly formed United States Bishops' Commission for Ecumenical Affairs, in laying down "interim guidelines for common worship and prayer" in June, 1965, advised generally against intercommunion for the present, but otherwise urged participation in joint services of prayer, preaching, Scripture reading, litanies, and song.

The decree applauds the ecumenical movement developed in recent years "among our separated brethren . . . by the grace of the Holy Spirit" for the restoration of Christian unity. By collaborating with them in theological inquiry, prayer, and service to mankind, the decree asserts, "the road is made smooth" leading to the goal.

French Catholic theologian Jean Danielou says the decree opens "a decisive stage in the movement for bringing Christians together." [52]

It was the fifth pre-eminent landmark of Vatican II, along with the recognition that doctrinal expression and interpretation may be improved, the reappraisal of the ties between tradition and Scripture, the swing away from closely centralized church government and toward communal rule, and the massive reforms in ways of worship. All of these were key steps in the church's rejuvenating journey, and in deepening the kinship among all Christians.

The five milestones also laid a roadbed into an area where other conciliar fruits abounded.

CHAPTER *11*

Further Strides

It used to be that a town, a nation, or a church could rope off its particular corner of the earth and allow only "our kind" of people and ideas in it, with any deviation outlawed or ostracized.

Churches, of various types, have sometimes imposed that policy. So have states, with shadows of it lingering even in America.

But scarcely can one group or church exert exclusive sway any more, anywhere; the world is no longer like that; thought and cultures have interpenetrated, and differences live together.

This has awakened the churches, of all sorts, to an oft-ignored rudiment of their faith—that man from the beginning was endowed by God with freedom of conscience, an inborn option of spiritual choice, and thus should have the right to exercise it without interference by others.

That inward human property—religious liberty—gathered heightened practical potentialities at the Second Vatican Council. Powerful Roman Catholic voices, including those of Pope John and Pope Paul, propelled the cause and reinforced it.

"Every human being has the right to honor God according to the dictates of an upright conscience, and therefore the right to worship God privately and publicly," John declared in *Pacem in Terris*.

Paul termed the council's projected declaration on religious freedom "of far-reaching importance not only for the church" but for all men interested in that standard. [1]

Commended by him for action at the top of the 1965 agenda, and approved overwhelmingly, it held especial drama and significance, since authoritative Roman Catholic pronouncements in the past—until John XXIII—never clearly affirmed the principle. Some seemed to reject it. Moreover, the church's position on it has been a target of steady criticism and has clouded its relationships with other religious bodies. The conciliar schema augured an air-clearing change:

"Religious liberty . . . requires that man must be free from coercion, either by individuals or by social groups, or by any human power. In religious matters no one should be forced to act, or be prevented from acting, according to his conscience, in private or in public . . ."

The document urges such liberty for the whole human family, for

178

all religious groups, and for each human person. It contrasts distinctly with the delimiting papal pronouncements before John.

Expanded and strengthened for adoption in 1965, the declaration's original presentation to the council's second session by Bishop Emile De Smedt of Bruges, Belgium, drew loud applause.

"From God's side," he said in describing the paper's contents, "faith is a supernatural gift which the Holy Spirit freely confers on whom and when he pleases and from man's side it is and must be an assent which he freely proffers to God." The bishop, whose presentation was incorporated in the expanded draft, added:

"Neither any man nor any human institution can take the place of the free judgment of man's conscience. . . . When religious liberty is violated, the very freedom of the human person is violated in its principal matter. . . . The greatest injury is to prevent a man from worshiping God and from obeying God according to the dictates of his own conscience." [2]

This differed markedly from the negative condemnations by Pius IX in the nineteenth century. Some traditionalists opposed the readjustment.

Historically, religious liberty is a relatively new ideal in practice—for churches or societies. Through most of the human record, dominant classes, races, or religions have sought to fortify their own privileges, while handicapping those who differ. Traces of that pattern have long lingered. The United States itself was "for more than half its history, officially Protestant," says Methodist historian Franklin H. Littell, with others subject to various disabilities in fact if not in law. "Coercion is an old tradition, among both Catholics and Protestants. . . . We are all of us—whether Catholic, Protestant, or Jew—just beginning to learn how to function in this kind of a society, in which the political covenant is distinct from the religious covenants." [3]

More than three hundred years ago, in the Treaty of Westphalia of 1648, ending Europe's Thirty Years' War, an old formula was included: *Cuius regio, eius religio* ("Whose rule, his religion"). It meant that the religion of the ruler would be the religion of the country. Aimed at preventing further religious battles, the device prescribed a religious uniformity in each state, with dissenters suppressed and persecuted.

In Protestant countries, Roman Catholics were harassed, hanged, or driven out. In Roman Catholic countries, the same happened to Protestants. In both, Jews were victimized. Scientist Albert Einstein once observed: "I thank God that I belong to a people which has been too weak to do much harm in the world."

In fact Jews waged history's first armed revolt against religious oppression, 160 years before Christ. The Maccabees, with their daring guerrilla tactics, beat off the attempts of mighty Syria to impose idolatry. Had it not been for that original fight for liberty of worship, Hebrew Scriptures and Judaism which gave birth to Christianity might have been stamped out, eliminating the Judeo-Christian heritage from the stream of civilization.

Yet men's ancient tendency to try to dominate the will of others did not stop there, nor since. The pagan Caesars slaughtered Christians and Jews, and "Christian" emperors turned on pagans.

From medieval times and increasingly into the period of inter-Christian strife in Europe, Rome laid on the heavy hand of the inquisition to root out and eliminate heretics. It was a common method of the time—for princes and prelates. Protestantism had its counterparts. Martin Luther's colleagues at Wittenberg once advised the state to execute or imprison Anabaptists. The original Westminster Confession, of Presbyterian note, said the civil magistrate has the duty to suppress "all blasphemies and heresies." In the first five years of John Calvin's sway over the town council of Geneva, a comparatively small town, thirteen persons were hanged, ten decapitated, thirty-five burned, and seventy-six driven out for assorted "crimes," including heresy. Michael Servetus, a Christian iconoclast, was burned at the stake there; Sir Thomas More was executed in England for refusing to recognize the king, instead of the pope, as head of the church. Rome claimed its line of Protestant heretics, going back to Jan Huss, burned at the Council of Constance; Thomas Cranmer, burned in a temporary Roman Catholic restoration in England. A royal reversal there, and mass executions hit Roman Catholics in England; Protestant Huguenots suffered massacre in France.

Whether inflicted by church or state, closely allied in those times, or by public passions, harsh pressures were widely applied to men's religion if it differed from the dominant one. Tolerance for minorities came slowly into civil law, and more slowly into public attitudes. Vestiges of the religious-conformity formula continued into the modern era, both in the old world and the new.

American colonists, pursuing religious liberty for themselves but not immediately for others, set up partisan, separatist systems, generally disenfranchising Roman Catholics, Jews, and non-believers. Nonconformity was sometimes punished by confiscation of property or worse penalties, including the hanging of Quakers and "witches" in Puritan (Congregationalist) New England. Only Maryland, settled by Roman Catholics, and Rhode Island, settled by Roger Williams' Baptists, origi-

nally offered a haven to diverse religious elements, but both soon dis-
enfranchised Roman Catholics and Jews—Maryland doing so after a
Protestant party gained control.

The founding of the United States brought guarantees of no federal
religious "establishment" and equal rights for all, but states and locali-
ties continued limitations on officeholding, in some cases, and taxation
for Protestant-run schools up to the mid-nineteenth century. Chilling
outbursts of anti-Catholicism occurred through those years. In New
England, an unforgotten fireside game was called "Break the pope's
neck." Even into the 1920's, in the uproar surrounding the Scopes
trial in Tennessee, eight predominantly Protestant southwestern and
southern states passed laws to ban the teaching of what they considered a heretical denial of "the divine creation of man as taught in the
Bible"—Darwin's theory of evolution. It was an old story. Rome once
forced Galileo to cease teaching and recant, as dangerous to the faith,
his theory that the earth moves around the sun. "But it does move,"
he murmured as he rose from his knees to be led off to prison.

Coercion could crush the man but not the conscience. While earthly power might make the body bow, belief stayed liege to an inward
voice, owned by no other man.

"Judge not, and you will not be judged," Jesus told his men. "Condemn not, and you will not be condemned." [4]

Inexorable tides of events, unforeseen, unplanned, and often resisted, were driving that lesson home—to realms and religions—even as
tensions over it continued.

In the Vatican Council's document, religious liberty is seen as a
divine law, written into the nature of man by his creation in God's
image, a personal spiritual relationship transcending the jurisdiction of
any other man, state, or institution. That inner spark, that "living
soul," was given freely by God, and it is up to each man to respond
freely, either in acceptance or rejection. It is his personal responsibility; no man may abdicate that responsibility, and no man may assume that responsibility for another, but only for himself. Therefore,
no kind of coercion, physical, legal, or otherwise, may be used against
that divinely implanted franchise, which allows each person to accept
God's grace freely, or not at all.

Even if that person is considered wrong, confused, or in error about
truth, no other man, nor social, political, or human institution may in-
fringe "upon the religious liberty of the individual person," Bishop De
Smedt said in outlining the council draft. This applies whether the
person's "conscience be sincere and true or sincere and false concerning faith, provided only that he sincerely follow the dictate of his

conscience." Furthermore, religious liberty demands that men be free to "carry out the dictate of their conscience in external acts" in "private life, in social life, or in public life," forming religious groups for worship and other activity, immune from coercion of any kind.

The document contemplates a major development in official Roman Catholic teachings—and a clear departure from some old ones.

Church leaders frankly recognize that the advance has come, not only through theological reconsideration, but through the powerful proddings of history and experience in recent times.

In Europe, as in America, irresistible forces had worked to shake off the old Westphalia pattern of state-established religious favoritism. Populations and influences had flowed together in a shrinking, one-neighborhood world, and the old, insular walls could not stand. Germany, Holland, and Belgium, once Protestant dominions, now had large Roman Catholic populations, and had ceased to behave like monopolies. In Scandinavian countries with state Lutheran churches, various restrictions against Roman Catholics have been eliminated only since World War II under the impact of the new coalescing movement of mankind. Protestants had assumed an important place among Roman Catholics of France, with bygone barriers gone; and in Latin America, a swelling proportion of Protestants gradually melted the one-church, Roman Catholic boundaries there. The United States had become a thorough-going composite, and while perplexities still arose about state-school religious practices, the old preferential shadings dissolved, the Protestant-inclined *McGuffey's Reader* had mostly disappeared, and the nation had elected its first Roman Catholic president in the changing style in which citizens of various religions became a community of fair play and mutual trust.

This had figured in the new premises laid before Vatican II.

"We are living in the age of the religiously pluralist society," says American Jesuit John Courtney Murray, who has played a leading part in the drive for a clear Roman Catholic stand on religious liberty. "Men of all religions and men of no religions must live together in conditions of justice, peace, and civic friendship, under equitable laws that protect the whole range of human rights, notably including the right to religious freedom." [5]

Something else had also shaken the old assumptions and shaken them severely—the modern totalitarianisms trampling over all religions. Nazism, murdering millions of Jews, and Communism, throttling both Christianity and Judaism in an aggressive pall of atheism, had thrown into stabbing clarity the evil born of state compulsions or pressure regarding religion. Said Pope Paul:

"What sadness we feel in the face of such sufferings, and how deeply we are grieved to see that in certain countries religious liberty, together with other fundamental rights of man, is crushed by principles and methods of those who do not tolerate opinions different than theirs on politics, on race, or religion. We are sorrowed also by the many injustices which are done against those who would like to profess their religion honestly and freely."[6]

Strangely, and perhaps shockingly, churches which had once sought to force their religious will on minorities through the power of the state had discovered that Judeo-Christianity itself had become a minority, victimized by that very same power when applied to religion. An old device had boomeranged. State enforcement in religious matters had proved itself a treacherous tool.

As to Rome's present attitude about coupling the arm of the state with the church, the fourth-century Constantinian arrangement which filtered down through the centuries, a revealing incident occurred before the Vatican Council began.

Newsmen asked the late Domenico Cardinal Tardini, then Vatican Secretary of State, if government representatives would be invited to take part in the council, as in the past.

"No!" snapped Tardini. "Times have changed."

Religion, it seems, was not considered the governments' business.

However, invitations did go to Protestant and other churches, once the object of Rome's temporal interdictions. Curiously, the alliances had become reversed. The old restrictive church-and-state coalitions had turned into open church-and-church coalitions. Far from finding warrant for legislated state disabilities against each other, the churches increasingly recognized their urgent interdependence in a generation swept by non-religion—and with nearly half of it living under Communism. Rather than clouting each other on the head with discriminatory laws, they found their minority estate to be a joint one, their purposes and strengths intimately and crucially connected.

The hammerings of history had helped forge this deepening bond, and given force to the ecumenical movement for Christian unity.

This movement, too, had prodded Rome's reassessment of its position on religious liberty. For at its very basis, interchurch collaboration depended on mutual respect among those who differ, and on working terms of equality. Many Protestants, disturbed by past papal pronouncements derogating the religious rights of others, have questioned whether Rome could meet on a par with them, on a genuinely even, reciprocal, and unpredetermined footing.

"Both Protestant and Catholic ecumenists are convinced that the

ecumenical movement cannot be securely founded until a clear statement on the subject of religious liberty is fully developed," Chicago's
Albert Cardinal Meyer said prior to the opening of the third council
session. [7]

Without such a statement, said Boston's brusque, old Richard Cardinal Cushing, the council would "fall on its face." Without it, "we
cannot be considered sincere." [8] He told the 1964 session: "The church
must become the champion of religious freedom." [9] There were assaults on this view. Cardinal Ottaviani, the aged administrator of the
Holy Office, argued that the state is competent to choose a religion
for its citizens. "Only truth has rights," insisted Cardinal Ruffini of
Palermo. [10] But this idea that men, states, or groups could determine
truth for any person was being swept from the church's prevailing
outlook. Genuine religious freedom includes not only the right of individuals to differ in faith but "to profess no religion at all," declared
Cardinal Léger of Montreal. [11] And despite the so-called "Day of
Wrath" at the close of the third session, when a majority of prelates
protested postponement of action on the historic declaration, it had
the backing to win overwhelming approval early in the 1965 session.

Yet it had demanded some painful reappraisals of past papal
injunctions.

"It is evident that certain quotations from the popes, because of a
difference of words, can be put in opposition to our schema," Bishop
De Smedt told the council. "But I beseech you, venerable fathers, not
to force the text to speak outside of its historical and doctrinal context, not, in other words, to make the fish swim out of water."

Among the past strictures, some of the sharpest came from Pius IX.
In his "Syllabus of Errors" in 1864, he condemned separation of
church and state, and declared "error has no rights" against truth. In
his encyclical *Quanta Cura* in 1867, he denounced as madness the idea
that "the freedom of conscience of cults is the proper right of each
man."

Roman Catholic scholars today point out that he spoke in the context of a spiraling rationalism which held that conscience is devoid of
any connection with the law of God and free of responsibility to any
divine norm. His censure is interpreted as aimed only at such a view
of an "outlaw conscience." Scholars see his condemnation of the
separation of church and state as directed against a then-current view
that the state was omnicompetent in all matters of life and that the
church should be set apart as having no relevance to society. As for
the old loosely quoted dictum about error having no rights, a clear
distinction is made between abstract error and persons.

While error, in itself, has no rights, says Cardinal Bea, persons do have rights, even to err. "He who errs is always and above all a human being and he retains in every case his dignity as a human person." [12]

Furthermore, Pope John says in *Pacem in Terris* that meetings and discussions with those considered in error and even with those without religious belief "can be occasions for discovering truth and paying homage to it." He also drew a clear line between the claims of abstract error and the rights of persons, prone to err. He said every person "has the right to the free exercise of religion in society according to the dictates of a sincere conscience, whether the conscience be true or the captive either of error or of inadequate knowledge of truth and of sacred things." And he added that other men and the public authority have the duty to "recognize and respect that right."

As for the present status of the Syllabus, long the arsenal for assaults on Roman Catholicism, Jesuit Edward Duff suggests that it "may reasonably be banished as an obsolete bugaboo." [13] However, another old bugaboo haunts the church's past: the so-called "thesis" and "hypothesis" teaching. It held the "thesis" that the predominantly Roman Catholic state should suppress "false religion," but when Catholics were in a minority, the "hypothesis" would apply whereby they claimed religious liberty for themselves and tolerated other religions until Catholics could become predominant. While some few rigid traditionalists may cling to the idea, it has no general standing in the church—and authoritative papal statements contradict it. It "was little short of Machiavellianism," says Paulist scholar John B. Sheerin. "That doctrine has now been abandoned." [14]

In the midst of the church's review of its stand on religious liberty, conditions eased greatly for Protestants in heavily Roman Catholic countries restricting other churches, notably Spain and Colombia. They have been scenes of friction for years. Roman Catholic leaders attribute the difficulties mainly to political and temperamental factors beyond the church's control or approval. Nevertheless, the winds of Vatican II have mellowed the situations. Many once-closed Protestant chapels in Spain have reopened, and more liberal legislation and policies regarding them is developing. In Colombia, ecumenical dialogues between Protestants and Roman Catholics started in 1964 in the gentling climate there.

No matter what the country or its policies, however, religious liberty remains a naggingly delicate issue.

Absolute religious liberty is an illusion. No civilized nation permits human sacrifice, cannibalism, or public mutilation, all of which have been associated with some religions. The United States banned polygamy, formerly practiced by Mormons, and courts have ruled that children may not be denied vaccinations or blood transfusions on religious grounds.

The Vatican Council document recognizes that there are justifiable limits to religious freedom if it harms public good. But otherwise, the conclusion is that the government should keep hands off.

Strong council approval of that principle came in the 1965 session, despite some old-guard backing and blocking efforts. Even before then, the office of the pope had put Rome definitely on the record for each man's right to believe as his conscience leads him, and publicly proclaim his belief without interference—which rather roundly deflates anything any previous pope might have said to the contrary.

The first Roman Catholic bishop in America, John Carroll of Baltimore, said it back in 1784: "We have all smarted heretofore under the lash of an established church and shall therefore be on our guard against every approach toward it. . . . Freedom and independence acquired by the united efforts and cemented by the mingled blood of Protestant and Catholic fellow citizens, should be equally enjoyed by all."

The message finally got to the top of the church.

Another word, akin to it, also percolated to the summit of Roman Catholicism—a forceful affirmation of the church's foundation in Judaism, of the life-giving resources emanating from that mother religion, and of the deep bonds of brotherhood between Christians and Jews.

First presented to the council's second session by Cardinal Bea, and subsequently expanded and given preliminary approval before adoption in the 1965 session, the document also sharply repudiates the old and twisted hate image of Jews as guilty of deicide, of killing Christ. The specific reference, abjuring the terms " 'deicide,' 'Christ-killer,' and 'God-slayer,' " was put into a footnote in the finally approved version, on the ground that these words were both too vicious and illogical to include in the text itself. The footnote says they "are ugly words and must completely disappear from the human vocabulary."

All mankind was, and is, responsible for the death of Christ, the document emphasizes, reiterating a basic Christian tenet, yet one which has often been violated in the long, ugly track of popular and ecclesiastical anti-Semitism left through the centuries.

For a Christian to deny his part in the crucifixion, or to point an accusing finger at others, is to reject "his part in the redemption," says John M. Oesterreicher, an American monsignor who directs the

Institute of Judaeo-Christian Studies. He points out that "God in his sovereign wisdom tied the spiritual destinies of the Jews" to "the salvation of the world." [15]

And this is a keynote of the council declaration.

"Christ underwent his passion and death freely, because of the sins of all men and out of infinite love," the document declares. It points out that Christianity was founded in Judaism, that the original pillars of the church were Jews, and that the "spiritual patrimony common to Christians and Jews is so great" that the church should engage in joint studies and dialogues with Judaism to increase mutual knowledge and respect. Church teachers and preachers are admonished to guard against derogatory teachings about Judaism.

The document came under veiled attack of a politico-religious character in the intervals between council sessions. Pressure by Arab states, hammering the "Christ-killers" charge, was involved. Syria's government newspaper, *Al Thawra*, called the declaration "a crime." In closely closeted meetings, some Curia traditionalists and Eastern Rite prelates sought cuts in the document on the ground that it would bring about disabilities for the church in Moslem countries. However, despite the textual rearrangement, the gist of the original document was preserved, and its condemnation of anti-Semiticism was made more explicit. The document was also strengthened and expanded to include friendly references to other non-Christian religions as well, including Hinduism, Buddhism, and Islam.

These religions "counter the restlessness of the human heart, each in its own manner," the document asserts, adding that the church respects all that is "true and holy" in them. "The church, therefore, admonishes her sons that they converse and collaborate with the followers of other religions in order to serve, indeed advance, those spiritual and moral goods as well as those sociological values that have a home among men of other religious traditions." This echoes Pope Paul's first encyclical, *Ecclesiam Suam*, of August, 1964, and also found expression in his conversations with Eastern religious leaders in India. "We . . . recognize and respect the moral and spiritual values of the various non-Christian religions and we desire to join with them in promoting and defending common ideals of religious liberty, human brotherhood, good culture, social welfare, and civil order," he said in his encyclical.

However, it was the affirmation of basic ties to Judaism that formed the main theme of the statement on non-Christian religions—*De Ecclesiae Habitudine Ad Religiones Non Christianas*. "A special place in this all-encompassing document is given to the Jews, for the church is locked to them by chains of God's making," Monsignor Oesterreicher told a Christian unity service on January 24, 1965, at the National Shrine, Washington, D.C.

The declaration points out that Jesus, his mother, his apostles and the founding membership of the church were Jewish, and that the church developed in the synagogue. It cites "the bond that spiritually ties the people of the New Testament with Abraham's stock." This is from St. Paul's teaching that Christians are all spiritual Israelites, "sons of Abraham," a branch dependent for its life on its Jewish stem. Remember, the apostle advised Christians, "it is not you that support the root, but the root that supports you." [16]

In other words, Judaism was God's chosen instrument for transmitting the truth, from Adam on through the prophets, judges, and patriarchs of Israel, culminating with the Jew, Jesus, in whose heritage Christians share and find redemption. Jesuit Thurston Davis, editor of the Catholic weekly, *America*, observes that the stronger a Christian's faith, the "more 'Semitic' he realizes himself to be." As famed Protestant theologian Karl Barth put it: "In order to be chosen, we must, for good or ill, either be Jews or else be heart and soul on the side of the Jews."

The Vatican Council declaration also denounces the slur that Jews are "cursed," noting that this is "inconsistent with the truth of the gospel and with the spirit of Christ." St. Paul declares that "all Israel" will be saved. "Lest you be wise in your own conceits, I want you to understand this mystery. . . ." [17] The declaration also says that the church, "mindful of the common patrimony with Jews, . . . deplores hatred, persecutions, displays of anti-Semiticism, directed against Jews at any time by anyone."

While all this is elemental Christian teaching, it has been repeatedly smothered in social prejudice, murky church volumes, old and late, and in waves of brutal hostility toward Jews in so-called "Christian" crusades and communities, fanned by the hoarse cries of "infidels," "accursed," and "crucifiers." "These myths," notes *The Providence Visitor*, a church diocesan weekly, "may be found in numberless writings in Christian history, including those of the fathers of the church, popes, theologians, and orators." [18]

The action at Vatican II was intended to call an authoritative halt to such distortions and to undercut secular outbreaks of anti-Semitic propaganda, including that which produced the Nazi savagery.

Not that it "drew its inspiration from Christian doctrine, something which is in no way true," Cardinal Bea said, but he added that it is necessary to root out "from the minds of Catholics any ideas which remain fixed there through the influence of that propaganda." [19]

In a sense, the treatise also reflected a piercing current of self-awareness which grew out of that European midnight when rabbis, priests, and ministers together shared persecution, prison cells, and often death. That experience ushered in a swelling movement of Jewish-Christian interchange in sympathy and scholarship, marked by a new church emphasis on its Old Testament roots, and in many cases, by Jewish studies in the New Testament.

"These bonds are what we would like to strengthen," Pope Paul told a visiting Jewish delegation in October, 1963.

A committee of eminent American Jewish scholars, under the chairmanship of Rabbi Abraham Joshua Heschel, worked with Cardinal Bea's Christian Unity Secretariat in drawing up the declaration on Catholic attitudes toward the Jews.

It paralleled a resolution adopted in 1961 by the general assembly of the World Council of Churches, made up of most major Protestant and Orthodox bodies, denouncing anti-Semitism as "absolutely irreconcilable" with the Christian faith and a "sin against God and man." The resolution added:

"In Christian teaching, the historic events which led to the crucifixion should not be so presented as to fasten upon the Jewish people of today responsibilities which belong to our corporate humanity and not to one race or community. The Jews were the first to accept Jesus and the Jews were not the only ones who do not yet recognize him."

In a way, the long story of persecution of Jews has come full circle. In the early years of Christianity both Christians and Jews were victims of pagan Rome. Similarly, in the present age, the church and the synagogue generally have suffered together under oppressors. But during the centuries between, Christians turned on their forebears in a kind of religious patricide committed by offspring against its parent stock.

Under the first Christian emperors, beginning in the fourth century, Jews were branded a "nefarious sect," banned from positions of authority and professions, and segregated from general community life. Discrimination became harassment, with special badges ordered for Jews and the infamous ghettos begun in the Middle Ages with ecclesiastical sanction. Jews were denied citizenship, their work restricted. The Crusade in 1096 carried out the first in a long series of Jewish massacres. Mass slaughters and expulsions turned the period into one long Jewish martyrdom. One country after another expelled them until nearly all of western Europe was closed to them. Russia's czars stirred repeated barbarities and pogroms. For fifteen hundred years, church and state combined to victimize Jews. Not until the nineteenth century did most European countries restore Jewish rights, in the wake of the French Revolution, which started the process in 1789. It was completed with World War I's Treaty of Versailles and the Russian Revolution in 1917. Then, within two decades came Mussolini and Hitler and the horrors of Auschwitz, Dachau, Buchenwald, Bergen-Belsen, and Treblinka.

During that period, a man named Angelo Roncalli, later known as Pope John, carried out what was called "Operation Baptism" from his post in Turkey in conjunction with the Hungarian hierarchy. It involved turning out thousands of Christian baptismal certificates for Jews in Hungary to enable them to flee the extermination program there. That same Angelo Roncalli, as pope, ordered Good Friday liturgical texts purged of references to "perfidious Jews."

Such individual steps multiplied into many in the task of reconsolidating the ancient and often-abused Judeo-Christian kinship.

"The church of Christ acknowledges that, according to God's saving design, the beginnings of her faith and her election are already found among the patriarchs, Moses, and the prophets," says the Vatican Council text. It urges joint Jewish-Christian studies to foster mutual understanding and esteem.

The reconciling work went on elsewhere as well. In England, Roman Catholics again became active participants in the British Council of Christians and Jews, after having withdrawn from it on Vatican orders in years past. In the United States, a Roman Catholic study of church textbooks, completed at St. Louis University in 1964, turned up various negative and distorted statements about Jews and Protestants, with the findings made available for use in correcting future materials. A similar Protestant analysis, completed at Yale University in 1963, was devoted to the same ends in regard to Jews and Catholicism. The project also included a Dropsie College study to improve the Jewish textbook presentation of Christianity.

"Never before in history have Jews and Christians really confronted each other as brothers, each entitled to the dignity of his uniqueness, both of us respectful of the other's freedom of conscience and right to be," says Arthur Gilbert, rabbinical consultant to the National Conference of Christians and Jews in the United States. [20]

There were various obstructive maneuvers against the Vatican Council declaration. Pamphlets circulated among the bishops asserted that the church must "continue to speak out against the errors of the Jews." In Moslem Middle Eastern countries, which ban Jews from entry, opposition seethed, although church leaders repeatedly insisted the document had no bearing on Arab-Israel political questions. But none of this deflected the council.

By a vote of 1,651 to 99, the bishops gave preliminary approval to the declaration on November 20, 1964, prior to final approval in 1965. "An important, historic document," said Rabbi Dr. Heschel, who had worked with Cardinal Bea in drafting the original version. "It is a major, constructive step in better relations between Jews and Christians." [21]

Although the revisions in the final text caused some reservations among Jewish leaders, they generally applauded the document as a major step forward in Jewish-Catholic relations. For the first time in its history, the church "has committed herself to rejecting the invidious tradition of attributing corporate guilt to the Jewish people for the crucifixion," said Rabbi Marc H. Tanenbaum, of the American Jewish Committee. [22] The declaration asserts that Christ's death "cannot be attributed to all Jews without distinction then alive, nor to the Jews of today." Immediately after its adoption, United States Catholic bishops set up a commission headed by Bishop Francis P. Leipzig of Baker, Oregon, for permanent liaison and consultations with Jewish representatives.

Another far-reaching directive assured of approval at the council's 1965 session opens the church to a fuller, more influential role for the laity—the people in the pews.

Basic premises for according them broader rights and prerogatives are set forth in the monumental new constitution, De Ecclesia. It recognizes that laymen, in ways differing from the clergy, also have "ministries and charisms" of insight inspired by the Holy Spirit, and share "in the priestly, prophetical, and kingly functions of Christ . . . in the church and in the world."

In the past there has been a tendency to portray the hierarchy and priests as "the complete and first-degree members of the church, while the laity were merely passive recipients of their administrations, incomplete and second-degree members," writers Irish Catholic theologian Enda McDonagh. But this "unbalanced development" is being corrected. [23] The readjusted view, instead of drawing sharp lines between hierarchical rule and lay obedience, asserts the unity of clergy and laymen, declaring that all the "People of God" are one, with the same baptism, the same call to service, sharing in various ways "the same royal priesthood."

This blunts an old issue of the Protestant Reformation which stressed the "universal priesthood" of believers as against Rome's emphasis at that time on distinctions between priests and people. Of course, Roman Catholicism still asserts differences in functions, as do other churches, but points up the basic lay-clergy partnership, with each component performing interrelated tasks in a shared enterprise. The Protestant perspective is similar, although it does not assign final authority to the clergy's teaching function, as does Rome. Even this demarcation becomes less definite in the commentaries of many Catholic leaders who hold that instructive guidance comes from laymen as well as clergy, and that both stand under God's corrective judgment.

"God has not abdicated from his church in favor of the hierarchy," says noted theologian Karl Rahner. [24] Some traditionalist council fathers, such as Giuseppe Cardinal Siri of Genoa, opposed the "universal priesthood" thesis, calling it dangerous. But an overwhelming majority, including Pope Paul, supported it.

No longer will the layman "put up with being treated as a passive member, submitting blindly to the authority of the church as a 'silent sheep,'" Bishop Ernest Primeau of Manchester, New Hampshire, told the council. They are "aware of their own dignity and ability, not only in temporal affairs but also in those matters which pertain to the interior life of the church." More emphasis should be put on the layman's "individual responsibility, on freedom of initiative," instead of on "obedience, reverence, and submission," as if their sole function was to "believe, pray, obey, and pay." [25]

The story is told that back in the nineteenth century when someone asked Cardinal Gasquet what was the position of the layman in the Church of Rome, he replied that the layman had two positions—he kneels before the altar and sits beneath the pulpit. Recalling this tale during the council, Bishop John Wright of Pittsburgh said that an expanded version added a third lay position—he also stands in order to put his hand in his billfold. Wright said the lay function does, indeed, involve "kneeling to pray and sitting to learn," but that these are only "preludes to rising to speak, to act, to go forth for the church and in the world."

"All, the teachers and the taught, are under the necessity of being taught by God; all, individually and as a body, are subject to God's judgment and dependent on his mercy," he said. Being ordained a priest or consecrated a bishop is "necessarily secondary" to the prime condition of being a Christian. "It is more important to be part of the people of God than to hold a specific post among them." [26]

While the projected 1965 decree on the laity spells out details for their fuller standing in the church, the underlying principles are expressed in the constitution *De Ecclesia*, promulgated in late 1964. It says that priests and people in the church have a "common dignity as members from their regeneration in Christ." Although "some are made teachers, pastors, and dispensers of mysteries on behalf of others, yet all share a true equality with regard to the dignity and to the activity common to all the faithful for the building up of the body of Christ." Besides being instruments of the church's mission in the world, laymen also may take "a more direct form of co-operation in the apostolate of the hierarchy. . . . Further, they have the capacity to assume certain ecclesiastical functions, which are to be performed for a spiritual purpose."

The principle of fraternal or collegial government, as set forth in the constitution, pertains not only to the bishops, but "reaches to the grass roots of the church," says American Catholic theologian Lawrence Landini. "At first it may be a little hard for our American Catholics to realize this. We've had a different attitude in the past. The bishops had been so removed. The people were more or less lumped together in a class that simply had to accept whatever the bishop suggested." [27] But now they are encouraged to speak out, and contribute their insights to the decision-making process.

The constitution points out that Christ does his work "not only through the hierarchy" but "also through the laity whom he made his witnesses and to whom he gave an understanding of the faith." Laymen are urged to "express their opinion on those things which concern the good of the church. . . . Let it always be done in truth, in courage and in prudence. . . . Let pastors recognize and promote the dignity as well as the responsibility of the laity in the church. . . . Let them willingly employ their prudent advice. Let them confidently assign duties to them in the service of the church, allowing them freedom and room for action. . . . Let pastors respectfully acknowledge that just freedom which belongs to everyone in this earthly city."

Not only in the council's considerations, but in working practice, Rome's developing "theology of the laity" has proceeded to knock out the rigid partitions between laymen and clergy. Ten years ago a survey in the United States turned up only four dioceses with lay members on church school boards. By 1964 at least twenty-six dioceses had them, with the number rising rapidly. More than six hundred American laymen serve as Catholic missionaries. In San Francisco trained lay theologians serve as full-time parish catechists. Cardinal Shehan of Baltimore has lay advisers on church administration. Cardinal Cushing of Boston has announced plans for an archdiocesan synod including lay representation.

"This is the age of the Holy Spirit who is given not only to pastors but to all members of the church," says Belgium's Leon Cardinal

Suenens. "It is a fact of history that members of the laity have at times awakened a sleeping church." [28]

Methodist Bishop Fred Pierce Corson of Philadelphia, a council observer-delegate, mused: "I thought that Protestants had a monopoly on this, but I got a surprise at Rome." [29]

At the council, fourteen leading Catholic laymen served as auditors, named to attend by Pope Paul. They said in a statement: "For the first time in history, an ecumenical council has fully faced the question of the laity, endeavoring to situate them in the People of God on pilgrimage. As a result, our entire participation in the life of the church will, little by little, be transformed. The difference will be felt to the ends of the earth, in every community, even to the smallest parish." [30]

On another subject—one of the most volatile, emotion-laden issues between Protestantism and Roman Catholicism—the council made a decision that would tend to minimize the breach, and rejected a course that would have widened it. However, the action was upheld chiefly in the interest of Biblical and theological soundness, rather than of diplomacy.

It involved the Virgin Mary, mother of Jesus, "blessed . . . among women," [31] around whom theological controversy has swirled since ancient times, but particularly in the breakup between Rome and other Western churches.

Some bishops at the council favored retaining a separate schema about Mary, emphasizing her unique place in God's redemptive work. Others wanted the material on her incorporated in *De Ecclesia,* so as to indicate her relationship to the church as a human member of it, rather than independent from it. Cardinal Santos of the Philippines urged the special treatment, saying that to insert it in the general church schema would be interpreted as a diminution of concern for her, and that while she is part of the church, she is in some ways above it and could not be adequately dealt with if subordinate to it. Speaking for the other view, Cardinal Koenig said that doctrines about Mary should not be divorced from doctrines about the entire church. Including material on her in *De Ecclesia,* he maintained, would serve to guide popular devotions properly, and show that Marian teachings are not something independent, but belong integrally to the life of the whole church.

Some Latin American prelates, including Raul Silva Cardinal Henriquez of Santiago, Chile, and Bishop Sergio Mendez Arco of Cuernavaca, Mexico, said "exaggerated and sentimental devotions" to Mary had become a danger in their countries, and urged that the council keep devotion to her in proper proportion.

The mere procedural question took on high-tension implications and a great deal of "campaign" literature on it circulated among bishops in the days before it was decided.

On October 29, 1963, by a narrow 1,114 to 1,075 majority, the council voted to integrate material on Mary into the constitution on the church. Despite the closeness of the result, it was seen as supportive of Christian unity efforts and also as serving to keep Marian piety, which has soared in the last century, in balance with the rest of Christian theology. The chapter about her, placed in the over-all context of the church, stresses what the New Testament says about her.

Protestants have been keenly averse to Roman Catholic devotion to Mary, contending that it detracts from the worship of Christ. Actually, Roman Catholic teachings stress that Mary is not divine and not to be worshiped, that Christ alone is the cause of man's salvation and the source of his blessings. Praying for Mary's intercession with God is considered particularly appropriate, because of her closeness to him, just as a person might solicit the intercessory prayers of any devout friend or clergyman. In view of Rome's ecumenical concern on the subject, numerous Protestant scholars have urged their churches to seek a more serious, dispassionate estimate of Mary's role in Christianity, since Protestantism has tended to disregard her altogether because of its bias against Catholic teachings about her.

Cardinal Heenan of Westminster, England, says that Catholic doctrines, particularly about the Virgin Mary, often are misunderstood by other Christians because they so often are "misrepresented by Catholics themselves." Partly because of the "extravagance of the language of Catholic piety, those outside the church are often given quite a different picture of Catholic belief" than is actually taught. "They do not realize for example that the apparitions of Our Lady at Lourdes and Fatima are not and can never become the object of divine faith. The church has solemnly laid it down that by the time the last of the twelve apostles died, the revelation of Christian truth was complete." [32]

In the modern upsurge of Marian devotion, however, some Mariologists have worked in behalf of new doctrinal definitions about her as co-redemptrix with, and under, Christ (since she co-operated with God in Christ's coming to earth) and as mediatrix of all graces (since Christ, the source of all graces, was mediated through her). However, such moves gained no ground at Vatican II. It appended a section on Mary to the constitution *De Ecclesia*.

Additionally, however, with somewhat perplexing implications, Pope Paul in his discourse at the close of the 1964 session designated Mary "Mother of the Church." This description would seem to put the view of her in a much more earthly framework than that sought by the proponents of the highly exalted titles. Yet oddly, it drew criticism from some Protestants who felt it ran counter to the council's mediating approach and tended to override it. There were, however, tempering factors. The Pope's statement was not made as an *ex cathedra* pronouncement of doctrine. Furthermore, its effect is to bring Mary into human and Scriptural perspective at the origin of the church's earthly history just as she stands in the gospel story, honoring her in that vital role, but at the same time diplomatically offsetting the efforts of Mariologists to have her place defined in supernatural terms as co-redemptrix.

The constitution, *De Ecclesia*, points out that no title used in reference to Mary "takes away from nor adds anything to the dignity of Christ, the one Mediator." Mary's important but clearly "subordinate role" is commended to the faithful "so that, encouraged by this maternal help, they may the more intimately adhere to the Mediator and Redeemer," the constitution states. It says veneration of her is to "call the faithful to her Son and his sacrifice and to the love of the Father." Theologians and preachers are exhorted to "abstain zealously both from all false exaggerations as well as from too great a narrowness of mind" in considering her singular dignity. "Let them rightly illustrate the duties and privileges of the Blessed Virgin, which always look to Christ, the source of all truth, sanctity, and piety."

It was a presentation which other churches could understand, if not wholly accept, as they considered their own veneration, or lack of it, for the mother of their Lord.

The council relayed some troubling matrimonial issues to Pope Paul for assignment to special commissions set up to make investigations and work out solutions.

Birth-control and mixed-marriage regulations were so treated after extensive discussion. The prevailing council sentiment favored modifications.

On the question of birth regulation, Belgium's Cardinal Suenens cited the world's spiraling population and said the church's traditional outlook was at "cross-purposes with science. Let us not have another Galileo case," he urged. Patriarch Maximos IV of Antioch said that unregulated human fecundity condemned "millions of human beings to unworthy and hopeless misery." He said a majority of Roman Catholic couples disagreed with and disobeyed official doctrine banning contraception, and called for courage to "see things as they are." Montreal's Cardinal Léger criticized "theology textbooks" for inculcating "fear of conjugal love" and said it is not enough simply to call procreation the "primary purpose" of marriage as the church has done in the past in opposing measures to prevent fertilization.

At the council's request, Pope Paul assigned the question to a study commission, saying that in the meantime church restrictions would remain unchanged. But around the world, Catholic theologians, prelates, and physicians weighed the propriety of progestin pills and other means of keeping family size in line with economic responsibility, without thwarting the natural relationships of marriage. Heretofore, the rhythm method—avoiding intercourse in periods of female fertility —has been the only approved means of limiting births. Catholic lay leaders of twelve international societies of learned professions appealed to the church for a "far-reaching reappraisal" of teachings on the matter.

In its 1964 session, the council also voted 1,592 to 427 to turn over canon-law proposals for relaxing restrictions on marriages between Roman Catholics and others to a papal commission for revising.

The draft proposals would change church laws requiring both partners in a mixed marriage to sign pledges to rear their children as Catholics. The draft recommended that in the future only the Catholic partner would pledge to do this "to the best of his ability." This apparently would allow for special circumstances in the marriage that would make the pledge inoperative. The draft statement also would end the practice of excommunicating a Catholic whose wedding takes place before a non-Catholic clergyman. Although upholding the present canon that a mixed marriage, in which one of the partners is a Catholic, must be contracted before a Roman Catholic priest, the proposal would permit bishops to dispense with this "canonical form" if there were "grave difficulties"; if this revision is accepted, the marriages of Catholics contracted with true matrimonial consent outside the church would not lack validity.

American bishops took differing positions on the matter. Cardinal Ritter of St. Louis supported the change, saying it proceeds "wisely and prudently" on a middle course in putting "principles of ecumenism into practice." New York City's Cardinal Spellman, however, opposed any change as dangerous to the spiritual welfare of Catholics. Cardinal Dopfner of Munich said that since it will take several years to revise canon law on the matter, the proposal should be sent to Pope Paul for implementation by the commission on canon law. The council agreed by a strong majority.

The full impact of the council's stock-taking and refurbishing still

It had launched the church on a vast expedition under a flag of compassion and unity. It had acted to mend the torn seams between Scripture and tradition, between papal and episcopal jurisdictions, between clergy and people, between activity at the altar and in the pews, between Mary and Christ's church, between Jews and Christians, between law and liberty, between Catholics, Orthodox, and Protestants, between the changeless rock of truth and man's ceaseless march to grasp it.

And space showed up for further moving forward. "God has shown us an open field," says the scholarly Cardinal Koenig, a one-time professor of comparative religions. "We have to till it." [33]

Others also contributed to the task.

PART FIVE

Origins and Process

"In the upheavals of the present hour, Jesus Christ is gathering his people in a true community of faith and obedience without respect for existing divisions."

World Council of Churches General Assembly,
Evanston, Illinois, 1954.

CHAPTER 12

Pathfinders

It began slowly and uncertainly. A quiet affair, at first, and tentative. No one planned it out or had any blueprints for it or could see where it might lead. The early craftsmen of fifty years ago simply felt the pinch of boxed-in, fighting denominations, and sought a gentler frame of conduct. They made no great fuss about it, launched no crusades, blew no rallying trumpets. They themselves could not be sure of precise objectives, or how to proceed. Little attention was paid to them at the outset. They worked in unfamiliar territory, picking their way, questioning, reconnoitering, hacking out the obscuring brush.

And then, as if an expedition had finally traversed a jungle, the ecumenical movement burst out on the plain of the mid-twentieth century like an advancing legion.

"We have been used for purposes larger than we had in mind," says W. A. Visser 't Hooft, the learned, incisive Dutchman who has guided the main body of that thrust for a quarter century.[1]

What started as a remote exploration by a few Protestant leaders, sensitive to the handicaps and incongruities of inter-Christian strife, has spiraled in the last two decades into an almost universal endeavor, encompassing not only the bulk of Protestantism, but also bringing Eastern Orthodoxy out of a thousand years of isolation from the West, and most lately and abruptly, surging strongly in Roman Catholicism.

At its 1964 annual meeting, the policy-making central committee of the World Council of Churches pondered the course of that little spring which had swelled into an immense pan-Christian river, and concluded:

"We have entered upon a new period in the history of the ecumenical movement—that movement through which God is gathering his people into one, according to his will declared in Jesus Christ." Although it had begun meagerly, born of an urgent conviction of need, and had developed only gradually, "Now the time has come when nearly all churches recognize this urgency and are engaging actively in the pursuit of Christian unity."[2]

The dim, probing trail had grown into a busy intercontinental roadway. Its arteries extended into nearly every field of Christian activity —relief work, seminary education, broadcasting, missions, doctrinal and Biblical research, church-school materials, campus centers, race relationships, evangelism, publications, ecumenical institutes, joint Christian stands on national and international issues. It involved not only the expanding activity and increasing number of co-operative interchurch councils—in cities, states, and regions, and globally—but it also gave rise to a wave of full-scale mergers and multiplying negotiations for other mergers, as well as specialized interreligious groups on matters ranging from psychiatry to architecture. Literally thousands of interchurch pacts and organizations have arisen since the turn of the century. Until around that time there were none regularly constituted by the various denominations.

And the most recent growth has been the swiftest.

In the last five years, the progress has been almost breath-taking, says Franklin Clark Fry, the astute, skilled chairman of the World Council's central committee and President of the Lutheran Church in America. In a "time when the unity of all humanity is being forged," he says, "the isolation of churches from one another is hopelessly outdated." He adds: "The fact that life is fluid, frighteningly unhinged, is in God's favor. . . . As the walls of some traditions come down, fewer windbreaks stand in the way to keep his Spirit from blowing where he wills." [3]

The change has not only been rapid, but deep.

At the beginning of the twentieth century, the separate churches kept guardedly to themselves, self-interested, ingrown, sharply assailing others, and competing relentlessly against each other. No mutual commitments existed, much less any talks for reunion. The chain of divisions, beginning with the schism between Rome and Constantinople and intensified with the splintering sixteenth century church explosion in the West, continued with church divisions splitting into still more subdivisions, chiefly because of biases of culture, language, region, race, or social class. Each segment became aloofly withdrawn, distrustful, and mostly uninformed about others, except for self-superior disparagement of them. For half the Christian era, the divisive trend had gone on.

Not until modern times did the turnabout come. Strangely, in a period shattered by two world wars, fierce ideological conflict, an epidemic of revolutions, and "cold war," the tide of church disintegration reversed. The centrifugal forces became centripetal. After a thousand years of breaking up, Christianity began to mend. "A remarkable feature of this drawing together of the churches is that it has taken place during the very time when the world in its political life was falling apart," says Samuel McCrea Cavert, a prime mover in work leading to the formation in 1950 of the National Council of Churches of Christ in the U.S.A., a co-operative agency including most major Protestant, Anglican, and Orthodox communions.[4]

At the start, the movement was sparked by some rather out-of-the-way circumstances and restive Christians. The entrenched church communities edged into it only peripherally at first, and with dubious mutterings—reluctances which still confront it. Habit, denominational pride, and vested interests do not yield easily. "Ethnocentrism," a major interchurch study calls these deterrents to Christian unity, the "drive for institutional self-preservation." [5] Such factors, more than theology, the study found, have often kept churches apart.

Nevertheless, another and different impulse took root in the hinterlands. In a measure, it was born among Protestant missionaries stung by the honest inquiry of Asians and Africans, "Which Christ do you wish us to honor?" The "Methodist Christ"? "Episcopalian Christ"? "Lutheran Christ"? A simple question, in an environment unconditioned by denominational presuppositions, and it laid bare the flaw of the system. Not only did denominational rivalry seem contrary to the nature of one Lord, but it implied that he was a source of human conflict rather than neighborly love and peace. Then there was the old riddle: "How do you ask a man in northern Japan to become a southern Presbyterian?" Or a Nigerian to become an "American Baptist" or "Danish Lutheran"?

It didn't make too much sense to the people there, if anywhere. Besides being confusing, the traditional separations also seemed comparatively irrelevant in the predominantly non-Christian atmospheres of Africa and the Orient.

Under these nudgings, concern for Christian unity awakened and stirred among the missions' forces, resulting in the World Missionary Conference at Edinburgh, Scotland, in 1910. This was an inter-Protestant gathering to plan co-operation aimed at fostering "in each non-Christian nation one undivided Church of Christ." The findings noted that Christians in those areas, vexed by the divisions, may take matters into their own hands and unite anyway, "regardless of the views and wishes of Western missionaries." [6] That proved to be a prophetic note, for these regions have since produced many of the pace-setting church reunions, such as the Church of South India, in 1947, uniting a million Methodists, Presbyterians, Congregationalists, and Anglicans, and other mergers in the Philippines, Japan, and African countries.

The Edinburgh conference led to formation of the International Missionary Council, an agency to co-ordinate work, training, and information for various Protestant mission bodies. It had some regional forerunners, including the Foreign Missions Conference of North America, an annual consultative meeting launched in 1893. None of these actually linked churches together, but rather formed ties only between the various missions' arms.

But it was a beginning. And it had far-reaching consequences.

There had been other antecedents, generally on the fringes of the churches, undertaken by venturesome individual Christians, often by laymen. A number of them, Bible societies, Sunday school associations, and other alliances, with evangelistic intent, arose in the nineteenth century, involving broad cross-sections of co-operating Christians, outside the jurisdictions of their denominations. Among these were the "Y" groups—the Young Men's Christian Association and Young Women's Christian Association—part of a robust inter-Christian student movement in many countries. It has produced numerous top leaders in the cause of church unity. Two of them, the late John R. Mott, an American Methodist layman, and Joseph H. Oldham, a Scottish Presbyterian, both experienced in mission areas and leaders in the student movement, were key figures of the Edinburgh conference.

Meanwhile, the first genuinely multi-church organizations came into being on the national level: the Protestant Federation of France in 1905, and the Federal Council of Churches of Christ in America in 1908, formed to "bring the Christian bodies of America into united service for Christ and the world." Made up of thirty-one officially represented denominations, the latter concentrated chiefly on works of mercy, social service, and the analysis of the gospel's implications regarding contemporary public problems. It steered clear of doctrinal matters, leaving that to the separate churches, and devoted its energies to joint action concerning the complex, massed influences of modern industrial society. These challenges, too, like differing circumstances in the missions field, whetted the unity trend. Just as church divisions had proved a drawback in the rustic, mostly non-Christian regions, so the fractional sections of Christianity found themselves dwarfed and overshadowed in modern technological societies by the collective non-religious forces of mass communications, mass populations, and mass mechanization. The churches faced "impotence in separation," says Henry Pitt Van Dusen, President Emeritus of Union Theological Seminary. They can exert no appreciable impact on contemporary problems "unless they act unitedly with every resource at their pooled command." [7]

This awareness led to another landmark interchurch gathering, the Universal Christian Conference on Life and Work, at Stockholm, Sweden, in 1925, stimulated chiefly by another veteran of the Student

Christian Movement, Nathan Soderblom, who had become Archbishop of Uppsala. Orthodox representatives took part, for the first time, in the wake of the 1920 appeal for a "league of churches" by the Patriarch of Constantinople. The conference set up a continuing committee to focus concerted church attention on practical human concerns—industrial, political, international. But delegates found they could not discuss practical applications of Christianity without considering its rudiments, doctrine. Some of the world's eminent Protestant theologians participated, including Karl Barth, Emil Brunner, Reinhold Niebuhr, and Paul Tillich. The meeting's concluding statement saw unity among Christians as basically a theological imperative: "The nearer we draw to the Crucified, the nearer we come to one another."

Thus, two compulsions toward unity—from the missions field and in applied Christianity—pointed toward the nub of it all, basic belief. Two years later, Orthodox, Protestant, Anglican, and Old Catholic churches sent delegates to the first Conference on Faith and Order, at Lausanne, Switzerland, in 1927, to weigh differences in doctrinal interpretation. Its main organizer, the late Episcopal Bishop Charles H. Brent, was an American who also had worked in the Student Christian Movement, as a missionary in the Philippines, and who had taken a leading role in the conferences at Edinburgh and Stockholm. To the new assembly, he declared:

"In our hearts most of us are devotees of the cult of incomplete sectarianism. The Christian in one church often categorically denies the Christ in a neighboring church. It would be ludicrous were it not so tragic. . . . When Christians accept Christ as supreme, they cannot walk but as companions and friends. . . . Let us keep this purpose of unity firm in our hearts, and look upon all Christians as brothers beloved. It is thus by practicing unity that we shall gain unity."

The pioneering meetings at Lausanne, on doctrine, and at Stockholm, on concerted Christian action, both stemming from the 1910 Edinburgh meeting on missions, engendered processes which led to the formation in 1948 of the World Council of Churches, the most geographically and denominationally comprehensive alliance of churches ever put together. It originally included the "Faith and Order" and "Life and Work" activities initiated at Lausanne and Stockholm. In 1961 it merged with the International Missionary Council derived from Edinburgh.

This combined the three formative strands of the Christian unity movement—doctrine and worship; Christian service; and missions and evangelism.

Thus the three early parallel paths converged, joining a myriad host of once-solitary, scattered churches in the manifold works of a shared faith. The probing, trail-breaking ecumenical search had found tangible substance and wherewithal. It had become, as described in the much-quoted statement of the late Archbishop of Canterbury, William Temple, "the great new fact of our era."

Surprisingly, the "ecumenical movement sprang from Protestantism," the "seemingly most fissiparous branch of Christianity," says Kenneth Scott Latourette of Yale, world-renowned church historian. "Yet by the mid-twentieth century the ecumenical movement brought together a greater variety of Christians than had any other movement in the nearly two thousand years of Christian history." [8]

Eastern Orthodoxy had entered the effort by the 1920's, taking part in subsequent meetings and in the founding of the World Council, as well as national and regional interchurch councils formed around the earth. In 1961 the Russian Orthodox Church, emerging from a millennium of isolation, became a member of the world co-operative organization, following a series of exchanged visits of church delegations across the Iron Curtain. The first, in 1956, was led by Eugene Carson Blake, Chief Administrator of the Presbyterian Church in the U.S.A., and then President of the National Council of Churches in this country.

"Our differences," said Moscow Patriarch Alexis, "do not reach up to heaven."

With the full-scale engagement of Orthodoxy in the movement, Protestant predominance in it gave way. Somewhat as in the United Nations, vigorous Asian and African church leadership also tempered the early European-American preponderance. What had begun as a groping, sporadic undertaking, within comparatively narrow limits, had swept across barriers of politics, culture, and tradition, creating living ligaments in work and thought between Christians of East and West, old nations and new ones, black, yellow, and white men, of every continent, language, and race and nearly every kind of church.

But the task is considered far from finished.

Although the churches are "considerably closer" to a united Christianity than they have been for centuries, "the final stage of organic unity still is far off," says the Archbishop of Canterbury, Arthur M. Ramsey, one of a six-man World Council presidium. In an interview, the tall, bushy-browed prelate added, "But the first stage of charity and co-operation, so that the churches labor together and are aware that they are allies, has increased miraculously."

Roman Catholicism had declined invitations to the early interchurch meetings, as well as to the founding assembly of the World Council in Amsterdam, Holland, under a policy spelled out in the encyclical *Mortalium Animos* (Fostering True Religious Union) by Pope Pius XI in 1928. It said that unity might be furthered only by "the return to the one true Church of Christ," and that Catholics were therefore not allowed "to take part in assemblies of non-Catholics." This injunction followed a series of Anglican-Roman Catholic conversations at Malines, Belgium, in the mid-1920's. Although Pope Pius XII took a more favorable view toward the interchurch movement, not until Pope John came along did Rome openly hail it as a "cause of holy joy in the Lord."

It has done much to stimulate the cause of unity, says Augustin Cardinal Bea, the Vatican's ambassador in the field. He says development of the World Council "is undoubtedly due to a special grace of the Holy Spirit." [9] Under the new policy Roman Catholic envoys regularly attend Protestant-Orthodox gatherings, locally, nationally, and internationally, often taking part on the programs. Numerous Catholic theologians say there is no doctrinal reason preventing their church from joining the World Council, since each member body retains its own concept of the church. However, it is said that such a step may not be considered feasible for practical reasons, since the size of the Roman Catholic Church would give it a representation overwhelming the present balance in the council.

Members accept the following basis, as expanded at the council's general assembly in New Delhi, India, in 1961:

"The World Council of Churches is a fellowship of churches which confess the Lord Jesus Christ as God and Savior according to the Scriptures and therefore seek to fulfill together their common calling to the glory of the one God, Father, Son, and Holy Spirit."

At its 1964 central committee meeting, the council applauded, as it had before, the "new possibilities" for frank discussion, prayer and cooperation among all Christians, and with obvious reference to Rome, said: "We warmly invite those churches outside our membership to consider how they might be able to enter into this kind of fellowship." While membership does not imply acceptance of any specific view of the church or its unity, the committee noted that member churches have repeatedly made clear they "do not seek a unity characterized by uniformity or by a single centralized administrative authority." The statement said the close relationships and understanding developed in the council "has become a new experience in the life of the churches as they have shared in prayer and action," leading to a deepening dialogue on unity. "Although the churches may have reservations concerning one another's ecclesiological position, they are ready to engage in this conversation on equal terms. It is a conversation in which all are expected to listen as well as to speak, to receive as well as to give, and in which existing differences and tensions are frankly faced."

Some Protestant elements, reared on anti-Catholic strictures, doubtlessly would be alarmed to find their denominational leaders fraternizing in council with the old "Babylon" Rome, just as some Roman Catholics, brought up on anti-Protestant polemics, likely would be dismayed at their prelates meeting in common with the "rebels." Yet already, without organizational connections, the all-Christian dialogue had commenced.

Catholic Bishop Walter Kampe, of Limburg, Germany, has proposed that the Vatican and the World Council establish permanent representatives at each other's headquarters, in Rome and Geneva, Switzerland, to facilitate working relationships. Other suggestions have been made that Rome and the World Council join forces in specific fields of activity in which they already engage separately—relief work, international affairs, and theological study. At the January, 1965, meeting of the World Council's policy-making central committee in Enugu, Nigeria, it set up an eight-member delegation to begin regular talks with a Vatican-named group. Thus, for the first time in history, continuing conversations were opened between representatives of various Protestant and Orthodox bodies and Roman Catholicism. A "momentous step," said Franklin Clark Fry, central committee chairman. Says Cardinal Suenens, of Belgium:

"We must make more of certain forms of practical collaboration, notably in the social and humanitarian field—the problems of hunger in the world, sickness and disasters, birth and housing, illiteracy, redistribution of wealth." [10]

When the World Council was formed in 1948, it included 148 member churches in forty-three countries. Although about a score of those original member denominations have since been reduced to a third of that number by mergers, council membership has nevertheless grown to 215 church bodies in eighty-three countries, with a total of about 350 million members. Marc Boegner, the eighty-three-year-old dean of French Protestantism, the man who banged down the gavel at the 1948 assembly in Amsterdam, declaring the council in existence, says Rome's new attitude is "a miracle of the Holy Spirit." The "former unconditional and merciless rejection of the ecumenical movement" has changed into "a fraternal exchange between mutual observers," he said. He described the present situation as "a time for theologians" to go to work to clear up outstanding divisive questions among the various churches.[11]

Doing that has been a fundamental part of the surge toward Christian partnership.

The movement has taken on many forms besides the interchurch councils. It has resulted in more than eighty multi-denominational mergers since the turn of the century, twenty-one of them in the United States. A steady series of them in the last decade fused eight former Lutheran denominations into two large bodies, joined two wings of Presbyterianism into one, and merged Congregationalists and the Evangelical and Reformed Church into the United Church of Christ. The process was gathering momentum.

In mid-1965, 102 church bodies in thirty countries were engaged in direct merger negotiations. In the United States, talks were going on aimed at a possible large-scale union of six major denominations with a total of nearly twenty-two million members—the Episcopal, United Presbyterian, Christian (Disciples), United Evangelical Brethren, and Methodist churches and the United Church of Christ. Observers of other churches, including Roman Catholics, were sitting in on the proceedings. Such projects had parallels in many countries.

Aside from reunion negotiations, the main branches of Christianity had initiated bilateral discussions on past disputes which separated them. In 1962, the Lutheran World Federation and World Presbyterian Alliance began holding regular theological parleys. The Church of England moved toward union with British Methodism, and Archbishop Ramsey launched talks between Anglicanism and the Church of Scotland (Presbyterian), and between Anglicanism and Eastern Orthodoxy, including the Russian Orthodox Church. Machinery also developed for exchanges between the Church of England and Roman Catholicism in that country. The Lutheran World Federation in 1963 set up an Inter-Confessional Research Bureau to study modern Roman Catholicism, and review the causes that divided Lutheranism and Rome.

Recalling the plans which led to the step, Lutheran leader Franklin Clark Fry said that a few years ago, "we were told that the view we had of the Roman Catholic Church was outdated, not in accord with reality, a stereotype, and sometimes a caricature, and some of us wondered if this actually could be true. Since that time it has been demonstrated a thousand times over that it was true, and it is a wonderful thing that we were ready with this kind of an interconfessional exploration."

Martin Niemoeller, the famed German Lutheran pastor imprisoned under the Hitler regime, commented after a visit in Rome: "I don't know whether the Reformation has had a greater influence on us or on the Roman Catholics." Niemoeller, a World Council president, added that it appeared that now the Protestants are the reactionaries and "are becoming petrified," in comparison with the renewal movement going on in the Church of Rome. [12]

The ecumenical activity on either side, however, had obvious reverberations on the other.

Among Protestants and Orthodox, the interchurch councils for service and evangelism had developed on the national and local levels in nearly every country, as well as on broader regional scales, such as the All-Africa Conference of Churches and the East Asia Christian Conference. Typical of the national trend was the formation in 1950 in the United States of the National Council of Churches, composed of most major Protestant, Anglican, and Orthodox denominations in the country, with a total of about forty million members. It combined thirteen formerly separate interdenominational agencies in specialized fields, such as foreign missions, Christian education, broadcasting, relief work, stewardship, and the pioneering old Federal Council dating back to the early part of the century. All of these were brought together in the comprehensive co-operative agency to "more fully manifest oneness in Jesus Christ as divine Lord and Savior."

The purpose of unity is "not bigness, but wholeness," says Samuel McCrea Cavert, a Presbyterian who led the Federal Council for twenty-nine years and who served as first General Secretary of the National Council. He observes, however, that there still is "a grievous disparity between the unity in Christ we profess in ecumenical meetings and the complacent separateness of most congregations on any Main Street in the nation." [13]

Tendencies are at work to modify that, as indicated in the proliferation of local co-operative bodies. Since 1942 the number of American communities with interchurch councils has risen from 270 to 983. In that same period the number of local chapters of United Church Women has also more than tripled, rising from 700 to 2,295. Christians of many kinds also joined in mass evangelism drives such as those led by Billy Graham, and in a variety of joint projects for "released time" religious instruction, work camps, park ministries, community service, special weeks of prayer for unity.

The most prominent manifestation of the unity movement, however, was the World Council, linking the most widely representative alliance of churches the world has ever seen in far-ranging mission, evangelism, help to the needy, and in presenting a combined front on issues of justice and international peace.

"It is a household of churches which may someday become a house-

hold of God," says Greek Orthodox Archbishop Iakovos, also one of
the council's six-member presidium. "Our times are without prece-
dent," he said in an interview. "Never in history have the Christian
churches been so much disturbed by disunity as today and so interested in establishing some kind of unity, some kind of community, so as
to break down all these walls of partition and build bridges of intercommunion. It is the most heartwarming and promising sign of Christendom today."

The World Council, however, does not see itself as an end in the
cause of unity, but only as a means, a halfway house on the road to
it. The organization repudiates the idea of becoming a "superchurch,"
as some critics have charged, but instead looks toward the time when
it will no longer even be needed. "It is our hope that one day we can
scrap the World Council as not necessary—because the church is in its
unity," says W. A. Visser 't Hooft, its General Secretary. But "much
remains to be done" in quest of that goal.

Visser 't Hooft, a wiry, dedicatedly efficient man, with deep-set, intense eyes, has offices at the council's headquarters in Geneva. He
says there is "reason to rejoice" in the fact that the Roman Catholic
Church also is "now becoming an important center of ecumenical activities and initiatives," but he cautions against considering that
church or any one church as analogous with the World Council, or
picturing a sort of tripartite Rome-Geneva-Constantinople axis. Roman
Catholicism and Eastern Orthodoxy are definitive churches, with their
own authority and jurisdiction, he points out, while the World Council is an alliance of many churches, each with its own authority. He
adds that the council has no jurisdiction over them and may act only
at their mutual direction or consent—as their servant. Thus, by its nature, the council cannot itself initiate or be a party to specific church
reunion undertakings, as can its members or Rome. But the council
does serve as a medium bringing the churches out of their former isolation and into open examination of issues for mutual correction and
mutual enrichment.

This is the key operational principle.

It is regarded as the prime process for fertilizing and nurturing the
growth toward the unified ground of one Lord where all Christians
can dwell as one. It is considered the catalyst for bringing the churches, far and near, closer to him in whom, as the Apostle Paul wrote,
"the whole body, (is) joined and knit together by every joint with
which it is supplied. . . ." [14]

Rome, whatever its future relationships may be to the World Council, has entered into that multi-denominational conversation in rapidly
expanding ways, from top to bottom.

Contrary to some casual assumptions (and anxieties), the basis of the procedure rules out any soft-pedaling or whittling down of convictions for the sake of some reduced, common-denominator agreement. Seasoned ecumenical hands of the World Council, as well as the new crop of Roman Catholic specialists in the field, stress that any scaling down or glossing over of valued convictions would undermine the whole exchange and make it unreal, deceptive, and useless. It also would deprive others of any benefits to be gained from those convictions.

"Doctrinal relativism" and "general indifferentism" are dangers, not allies, of true ecumenical effort, Visser 't Hooft says. Addressing a Protestant-Orthodox-Roman Catholic devotional service in Montreal, Canada, in July, 1963, he put it this way:

"Is this an ecclesiastical sales period in which the prices go down? Is it the night in which all cats are grey? Definitely no! The ecumenical movement is not a movement of and for the lukewarm."

Rather, the process calls for utmost integrity and candor in discussing one another's genuine positions and outlooks, seeking not to shrink them but to learn from them, to deepen and purify them through sharing insights about them. The purpose is not lesser truth, but fuller, clearer truth. Far from bargaining for the sake of unity, the underlying aim is not even to achieve unity, per se, but rather to help one another attain more closely to Christ's whole truth, thereby coming into its innate unity. Rome's "old pro" in the work, Cardinal Bea, describes it as "seeking the truth in charity."

The heart of it hangs on getting out of monologue, the introverted orbit in which a church talks and listens only to itself, and going into dialogue, the larger sphere of minds and experience where each gives as well as receives.

It is not considered an arena for triumph of one view over another, or of attempted conversions or winning arguments. Rather, it involves respectful mutual contributing and learning, seeking fresh perspectives and understanding of one another's positions and reasons for them, trying to clear up mutually misconstrued terminology and to overcome the blurring encrustations and distrusts of history. It is "like placing oneself in another's place and seeing things as he sees them," Cardinal Bea says. [15] And always one "seeks truth alone, forgetting himself, his own interest, sentiments, or resentments, keeping an open mind to the light of Christ and action of the divine Spirit who 'teaches you all truth.' " [16]

Such mutual inquiry regarding beliefs, worship, and church organization, called "Faith and Order" study, has been going on among Protestant and Orthodox bodies through a succession of national and international conferences since the first one at Lausanne in 1927. Other world gatherings of that kind have followed at Edinburgh, in 1937, at Lund, Sweden, in 1952, and Montreal, Canada, in 1963, with continuing research between them. They have been under the auspices of the World Council since its formation. Roman Catholic scholars delivered papers for the first time at the 1963 gathering. It concluded on this confident note:

"We are on the way to Christian unity. . . . Today we see openings which only faith could discern yesterday. But there is still far to go."

Originally such inquiry consisted mostly of comparing beliefs and practices, but experience has turned the emphasis to a mutual probing of common resources—Scripture and the long heritage of church thinking through the ages.

What specific form of unity is sought?

This is a central question incubating among the churches, and a complex, clouded zone between Protestantism, Roman Catholicism, and Orthodoxy.

Visser 't Hooft, the chief executive of the World Council since its founding and head of its planning committee before that, says unity "does not mean uniformity and centralization," nor merely some "vague undefined unity." Like Bea, he sees the answer in mutually illumined truth. The goal, he says, is the unity within, bestowed by one Christ, "the Lord of Lords in whom 'all things hold together' (Colossians 1:17). . . . Our task is not to create or invent, but to respond." [17]

Responses differ. To some rank-and-file Protestants, what is termed "spiritual unity" is considered sufficient, without the need for any unified, functioning apparatus to show it or carry it out in practice. However, most Protestant leaders maintain that unity must be made manifest—in concrete, working form, not merely in invisible attitudes. Some favor federations, providing a framework for common action, but leaving denominations separate. This approximates the present situation with interchurch councils, leaving denominational ministries, memberships, and worship disjoined. However, the predominant view, voiced by the Protestant-Orthodox councils, seeks closer operating connections, including mutual recognition of ministries and memberships and full sacramental intercommunion, with all branches and congregations working together on every level—locally, nationally, and world-wide.

How to achieve it organizationally remains the problem.

As described by the World Council's 1961 general assembly, unity in Christ would be manifested when all Christians "in each place" are

brought "into one fully committed fellowship, holding the one apostolic faith, preaching the one gospel, breaking the one bread, joining in
common prayer, and having a corporate life reaching out in witness
and service to all and who at the same time are united with the
whole Christian fellowship in all places and all ages in such wise that
ministry and members are accepted by all, and that all can act and
speak together as occasion requires for the tasks to which God calls
his people."

In short, the affirmed goal is one interdependent religious life
among all Christians "in each place" and between contingents of
them "in all places." That includes at home and internationally.

Determining the type of structure and doctrinal consensus necessary
to achieve that objective, however, remains the unresolved question.
For Protestantism and Orthodoxy, the difficulty lies in whether it implies an inclusive union in a single organizational network, with room
left for diverse styles, traditions, and initiatives, or whether each
branch would retain its separate administration, all existing side-by-
side but with full intercommunion, mutually recognized and trans-
ferable ministries and membership, and unstinted co-operation through
joint councils at all levels.

Although not yet agreed on "the means of achieving the goal," the
World Council said: "We are clear that unity does not imply simple
uniformity of organization, rite, or expression." But the Protestant and
Orthodox representatives added: "The achievement of unity will involve nothing less than a death and rebirth of many forms of church
life as we have known them. We believe that nothing less costly can
finally suffice."

Protestants and Orthodox draw back at any implications of "uniformity" or "centralized control." However, there is a considerable
amount of homogeneity, or uniformity, within most separate Protestant bodies. Also, most of them have tended toward closely co-
ordinated systems of church organization. A 1963 scientific study of so-
called "episcopal," "congregational," and "presbyterial" types of
church government found little difference in their actual corporate organizations, although nomenclature varied.   Orthodoxy also has moved
toward more closely unified planning and action, among its various autonomously administered branches.

On the other hand, Roman Catholicism has inclined in the other direction. It has begun spreading out its former closely centralized controls, making church government the shared responsibility of the
world-wide episcopacy, extending greater autonomy to regional units,
and giving more standing to lay people.

Thus the organizational lines of the separate Christian bodies, whatever the distance judged between them, bear to some degree toward one another.

A standard phrase of Protestant-Orthodox ecumenical parlance, "diversity in unity," finds an echo in the words of Pope Paul. The "possibility of multiplicity in unity," he described it. He said "this mystic and visible union cannot be attained except in identity of faith, and by participation in the same sacraments and in the organic harmony of a single ecclesiastical direction." However, he added, "this allows for a great variety of verbal expressions, movements, lawful institutions, and preference with regard to modes of action." [19]

Contrary to some assumptions, "single ecclesiastical direction" does not necessarily mean one-man autocracy, even on the face of it—and that canted reading of it would be incompatible with the caliber of the Second Vatican Council. Taken without any elaboration the phrase simply says that a Christian church, to be unified, must have one, harmonized direction. It must have the same, unitary rudder. At the theological taproots that means the single, rallying command, sought by all camps, of the truth of Christ, however variously conveyed to men, by many, some, or one. To the global assemblage of bishops, Pope Paul said: "Let there be no other guiding light for this gathering but Christ, the light of the world."

There again, as in other unity-minded circles, came that single, directive, summoning word.

Yet the authority vested in the pope to elucidate it, coupled with the one-sided connotations left by the unfinished work of the 1870 Vatican Council, remains a stubborn issue between Rome and other churches.

Both Eastern Orthodoxy and Anglicanism have sometimes been cited as a possible mediating ground or "bridge" between Rome's centralized structure and Protestantism's individualistic, fragmentizing tendencies. Like Rome, both Orthodoxy and Anglicanism affirm the apostolic succession of bishops and consider it a unifying bond through time and space. Both emphasize the unity among their far-flung regionally autonomous churches. Yet neither has any world-wide administrative system, other than occasional meetings of a Pan-Orthodox Conference, an Anglican Congress (of clergy and lay people), or Lambeth Conference of bishops. Leaders of both Orthodoxy and Anglicanism have indicated a readiness to recognize the pope as presiding bishop, or "first among equals," in a unified church, but without sovereign authority.

Vatican II, without removing this authority, evened the scales somewhat by making clear that the world-wide episcopacy has a part in it.

"I feel sure that reunion with Rome will one day come, though it is fair to say that both we and Rome will be a good deal changed by then," says Archbishop Ramsey, titular primate of world Anglicanism.[20]

As to what practical framework might eventually develop for "multiplicity in unity," there have been many surmises and suggestions. A Roman Catholic ecumenical expert, Abbot Laurentius Klein, head of a Benedictine abbey at Trier, Germany, sees the possibility of various Protestant "rites" being part of a reunited church—a "Lutheran Rite, an Anglican Rite, a Reformed Rite"—each with its own liturgical customs and ways of functioning, so long as there is agreement in essentials of faith.

He notes that Roman Catholicism includes, besides the Western Latin Rite, twelve Eastern Rites with their own distinctive practices, administrations, and canon laws. He points out that Roman Catholicism also includes various schools of theological thought, the Thomists, Augustinians, the modern Biblical theology, and others, each with their own nuances and emphases, aside from fundamental faith. "So why should we not also have a typical Lutheran theology?"

As he envisions it, the goal is a corporate union of Roman Catholicism with the various Christian communities "as churches, as denominations." So long as agreement is reached in essentials of faith, they would "maintain their own liturgy, their own doctrine, their own government," and "develop their own ecclesiastical life." For instance he says, Roman Catholics say the rosary, but Lutherans don't like it, and there would be no necessity for them to use that form of piety in a unified church, since it isn't an essential. He says many other disputed matters fall in this category.[21]

Similar suggestions have come from others. They note that Scripture itself uses different formulas to express the Christian faith, with the authors of the four gospels each reporting it in a different way. "Unity will not be found in uniformity," says Austria's Cardinal Koenig.[22] This seems to be the consensus in all ecumenical camps.

But the conversation has barely begun. There is opposition to it. There are fears, doubts, dismay, and puzzlement, but also hope, elation, and daring. The obstacles loom enormous. Yet both sides have asserted they have amends to make. They concede their human faultiness in representing the gospel. They declare their determination to improve. And that opens avenues to incalculable possibilities.

Hans Küng, who has become one of Rome's most widely known

theologians and who was applauded by packed audiences of thousands on an American speaking tour, says Rome has the duty of "fulfilling the justified demands of Lutherans, Calvinists, Orthodox, Anglicans, and Free churchmen in the light of the gospel of Jesus Christ." Let the gospel, he says, decide "between other Christians and ourselves which of their demands are justified and which are not." Submission to that same criterion, he says, should also apply to Protestants in "carrying out the justified demands of Roman Catholics in the light of that same gospel of Jesus Christ."

"There are expectations on both sides. Both Catholics and Protestants are gravely at fault, over the schism. They both have the grave obligation to restore church unity, this restoration being demanded not for some current opportunistic reason (e.g., fear of communism) but by the Lord of the church himself, who prayed for this unity. Protestant Christians have a brotherly right to expect a great deal from us Catholics for the sake of reunion. But Catholic Christians have a brotherly right to expect as much from Protestants: stocktaking and self-examination and self-renewal in their churches, too." [23]

The picture, however, remains in the distance—faint, hazy, uncertain. And some would say a mirage. Yet the walk, the mixed migration toward it, has started, and reaches for its stride.

"There are veritable mountains to scale," says Cardinal Bea. "With men it is impossible, but not with God."

Compared with the extent of the objective, the advance toward it so far may be small, indeed, and young. But it is only a fledgling. Measured against the centuries of Christian division, the general countermovement toward unity has gone on but briefly. It acquired extensive substance only after World War II, with the World Council's formation, and sprang up in Roman Catholicism only on the eve of the 1960's. Yet in this relatively short span, it has shaken the fixed stanchions of the ages, lit new aspirations, and given glimpses of inestimable possibilities.

Bishop Charles Helmsing of Kansas City-St. Joseph, Missouri, returning from an audience with Pope Paul in the spring of 1964, related: "We spoke of the debt we owe to the World Council of Churches for its pioneering work in ecumenism. And the Pope expressed the need for prayer and for compunction on our part for the human failures that are responsible for the divisions within Christendom." [24]

Deeply reconciling elements flowed into the new relationship.

Yet, even among the Protestant and Orthodox churches in the World Council, which have been engaged in unity efforts for sixteen years, the way remains steep, baffling, and indistinct. "The fact that we are living in division shows that we have not realized God's gift of unity and we acknowledge our disobedience before him," the inter-church organization says. "Our union with God is a mystery which pass-es our understanding and defeats our efforts to express it adequately. But as Christ has come visibly into this world and has redeemed men of flesh and blood, this union must find visible expression." [25]

Nevertheless, even as the Protestant-Orthodox aggregation of churches still hunted for unifying ground, Rome has added the new, amplifying, and even more intricate dimension to the movement. Visser 't Hooft, doubtlessly the most widely experienced professional of ecumenical work, looks at the situation with hope and realism. "A great change is taking place. . . . What we need is men who under-stand on the one hand that the Spirit is at work in the new self-examination and self-correction of the Roman Catholic Church and that all churches can learn from this, but who understand also that while this creates new opportunities for conversation and collaboration, the fun-damental issues which have kept us apart remain stubborn realities." [26]

From his World Council offices in a cluster of converted army bar-racks and vine-matted houses in Geneva, Visser 't Hooft has roved the world, by correspondence and in person, building mutual concern among once insular churches. And the cause has waxed strong, with theologians, educators, and prelates around the world giving their time and energies to it. In 1965, with Visser 't Hooft scheduled to re-tire by the end of the following year, the organization moved into a new three-million-dollar headquarters at 150 route de Ferney on the edge of Geneva. With the physical symbol completed, the man who had done so much to nurture the ideal for which it stands was soon to leave his post. It had been an obscure venture at first, but a swiftly widening one. Visser 't Hooft had labored in inter-Christian activity since his youth, as a leader of the Student Christian Movement in Holland, rounding up cargoes of food and clothing for relief in World War I. He became head of the provisional committee set up in Utrecht in 1938 to plan the formation of the World Council. World War II delayed the project, but through those years, from the make-shift Geneva quarters, he managed to maintain precarious communi-cations between church leaders outside the crush of Hitler's war ma-chine and those within it, extending aid and sympathy to them.

Then, out of the terrible alchemy of that experience which bound Christians of many kinds closer together, the movement for unity emerged with renewed force.

John L. McKenzie, a Jesuit Biblical scholar, appraising the stir in

Protestantism and Orthodoxy and that unleashed by the Vatican Council, compares it "with the restlessness which preceded the Reformation. Luther did not appear out of a vacuum. With him tensions which had long been building up were released. . . . But the restlessness of our own day moves toward unity, not disunity. It would be rash to predict that the movement will attain its goal; it seems now equally rash to predict that it will not." [27]

An unpredictable and almost uncanny aspect of the movement lies in the powerfully leavening effect of its key technique—discussing frankly and working loyally together, even while still seeking the means of unity. It yields some remarkable presentiments.

Admittedly, the tangible answers remain beyond sight or specification, and jagged rifts between the churches still keep Christians apart at the very heart of worship, the Eucharist, and perpetuate shadows of separateness, alienation, and competitively duplicated churches among followers of one Lord. Yet, as leaders of these divided churches engage in earnest communication and shared tasks, something strange begins to happen. Those involved frequently speak of it. They realize the divisive issues remain unsolved, that the churches still are largely fragmented, that Christians who proclaim reconciliation in one Lord and each other remain manifestly separated. Yet, they say, even while definite solutions elude them, the very process of contact, of honest encounter and common service seem to produce semblances of the goal, even before it is technically decipherable.

Roman Catholicism has barely entered the process, to partake of, and add to that experience and its compelling overtones. The World Council has discussed this curious quality. Church representatives say that through the trans-denominational fellowship, something more than the sum total of their individual churches comes into being, a richer reality, a plus. And it beckons them on.

The journey faces rocky, difficult, and clouded terrain, and unknown jolts and challenges, over an unmarked course. The coming together of long-separated Christians produces its share of frustrations, setbacks, and perplexity, as well as surprises and expectations. But while the goal remains latent, hidden, there comes that other sense, that extra, that foretaste of a destination before it is reached or even clearly discerned. Visser 't Hooft, after years of involvement in the process, speaks of that something else, that absorbing, strong, but elusive element.

"As churches live, speak, act together, a new reality begins to emerge. What is this new reality?" It is not a unified Christian church; the churches remain divided, the issues unresolved. Yet even so, in the moments and places where two, three, or many churches gather together in one Lord's name, that cohesive, universal reality invades the air, an enrichment, a promise, a stimulating new dimension, a thing that begins to exist before it can be described. It is as if by the very moving, the raising of the purposeful signs of unity "through exchange in thought and life and through common witness and common service to the world," there come intimations and essences of that further prospect in store, even before it can be calculated or named.

"It is better," Visser 't Hooft philosophizes, "to live with a reality which transcends definition than to live with a definition which claims more substance than we have in reality."

That impalpable phenomenon also was being felt elsewhere, in the places of everyday Christianity.

CHAPTER *13*

Hometown Intersections

"O Lord Jesus Christ, who on the eve of thy passion didst pray that all thy disciples might be one . . . grant that we may suffer keenly on account of the infidelity of our disunion." The prayer poured from the lips of a mixed company of Christians. "Grant us the loyalty to recognize and the courage to reject all our hidden indifference and mistrust, and our mutual hostility." Side by side stood Roman Catholics, Baptists, Greek Orthodox, Presbyterians, Methodists, Episcopalians, Lutherans, and others, their voices blending in supplication. "Grant that we may find each other in thee. . . ." About eight hundred church people—men and women, clergy and laity—had assembled that evening in a hall in Worcester, Massachusetts, beseeching their Lord for unity "such as thou willest and by the means that thou willest."

The local "Ecumenical Convocation," held January 25, 1963, under joint sponsorship of the Roman Catholic Diocese of Worcester and the Worcester Area Council of Churches, gave expression to a mood and manner which has swirled throughout America, as well as other lands around the globe. There has arisen a "spirit of reconciliation that the world has not known for centuries," Catholic Bishop Bernard J. Flanagan told the interdenominational gathering. Declared Ralph L. Holland, Executive Secretary of the Protestant-Orthodox Council: "We can never again shrink back into our divisiveness." Vigorously the throng sang, "Faith of our fathers, living still . . ." They then joined in a litany led by Episcopal Bishop Robert M. Hatch.

"In spite of our ignorance, our prejudice and our enmities," he intoned.

"Unite us, O Jesus," mingled Protestant, Roman Catholic, and Orthodox believers responded.

"O God, for thy greater glory," the bishop spoke.

And the people said, "Gather together all separated Christians."

Then they prayed in unison for that cause "in obedience to thy love and truth."

It was not a unique affair, but it represented the vanguard of a style which has blossomed in many communities in many ways, as Roman Catholics engaged with other Christians at the hometown level in discussions, church visits, exchange of speakers, symposiums, re-treats, and joint devotions of hymn-singing, prayer, and litanies of hope and praise. The trend also had its lighter side, with such events as Canada's "Ecumenical World Series," in which Catholic priests narrowly outscored a team of Protestant ministers and one rabbi, 21 to 20, doing so, it is said, by stealing bases. Evidence to "vigilant" Protestants, perhaps, of Rome's "devious methods." "Throw out the umpire!"

With or without gimmicks, however, Roman Catholics, spurred by Vatican II, entered into associations with other Christians to an extent never achieved before. Local Catholic congregations and laymen "will have to get accustomed to a new type of inter-Christian and inter-church relations," says Catholic theologian Bernard Lambert.[1]

In the United States, the late John F. Kennedy, as an earnestly religious man and a popular, luminous, and even-handed President, doubtless did as much as, or more than, anyone to bring about an open confrontation, to puncture anti-Catholic fraud, and to create a sense of interreligious mutuality and confidence. As the first Roman Catholic to hold the nation's highest office, he brought to a new plateau the image of a united citizenry. It was an unspoken thing, by and large, but he served as an "outward sign" of a maturing inward grace knit-ting the people, a symbol of an abandonment of the enclosed religious battle trenches and of a freshly found comradeship of trust in a soci-ety growing up to its religiously plural character.

Remnants of prejudice remain, of course, still a subtle stock-in-trade for its professional exploiters. But the blaze of events and information cuts through the most flagrant hoaxes which used to thrive under the cloak of religious isolation. As the separating walls dissolved, and men came to know their neighbors in a mobile, mingling population, the lie had fewer crannies in which to hide and fester. The emergence from beneath the mildewing timbers of interreligious suspicion and hostility was inevitably abetted by the cross-flowing patterns of mod-ern life. Aside from the churches, secular history helped fashion the change.

Whether by Providence or coincidence, Pope John at the same time let loose the tides of the Vatican Council, stirring the new hum of concourse among the congregations, pastors, and professors of the churches themselves. "A year ago we hardly knew one another," a Methodist minister remarked of his newly acquired friends among the Catholic clergy in Newport, Rhode Island. There, Roman Catholic and Protestant clergy alternately play hosts at joint dinners. "We have learned we can co-operate without compromising our positions," a Catholic priest said. "We have grown up."[2]

The new interchange went on in sundry forms, building up through the mid-1960's, in the academic halls of learning, in intimate dialogue groups, in print, on the air, in a swelling colloquy between separate congregations on innumerable Main Streets across the map.

Some assorted examples:

"Fellowship Forums" in the Kansas City-St. Joseph, Missouri, area, where Roman Catholic-Protestant panels rotated from church to church in a series of discussions before mixed gatherings.

"Operation Understanding" in New Orleans, a project in which Roman Catholic, Protestant, and Orthodox churches and Jewish synagogues exchanged visits to get acquainted with one another's customs.

"Your Neighbor's Faith," an eight-part lecture series sponsored by Roman Catholics and Episcopalians in Buffalo, New York, and drawing an average of more than one thousand people to each meeting.

An "Ecumenical Procession" through the streets of Meriden, Connecticut.

Protestant-Roman Catholic "Colloquiums" at Harvard University, where Cardinal Bea took part; at the University of Chicago Divinity School; at Kenrick Seminary in St. Louis; at Ambrose College in Davenport, Iowa; at Notre Dame University in Indiana; and elsewhere.

"Faith to Faith," a television series over Baltimore's Station WMAR-TV, in which a Presbyterian minister, John Middaugh, and a Roman Catholic priest, Joseph M. Connolly, discussed their respective church concepts in lively, forthright, and friendly fashion.

For the first time in Methodist Church history, its 1964 quadrennial general conference had a Roman Catholic bishop on the program as a speaker: John J. Wright, of Pittsburgh. Nine hundred Methodist delegates gave him a standing ovation. He also addressed the 1964 biennial convention of the Lutheran Church in America. Cardinal Cushing spoke in Denver at Greek Orthodoxy's biennial congress in June, 1964, and the Protestant Episcopal Church invited a hundred Roman Catholics to attend its triennial general convention in St. Louis in October, 1964. Never before had the programs of any of these denominational policy-making assemblies included Roman Catholic prelates. Catholic Archbishop (now Cardinal) Lawrence J. Shehan of Baltimore, appearing before a meeting of one hundred Protestant Episcopal clergymen, remarked: "Ten years ago I can't imagine being invited to address a group like this. And I can't imagine having accepted." But the uncommon became common.

In Steubenville, Ohio, Catholic Bishop John King Mussio, speaking for the first time before the local ministerial association, called its members "fellow ministers of the Word of God." He said his presence was "expressive of that tremendous impetus that is moving men everywhere to approach one another with an open mind and a heart vivified with Christian charity." [3]

Around Boston, Cardinal Cushing became a familiar figure at Protestant and interchurch meetings. As a side feature he arranged get-togethers for members of the Roman Catholic Dominican Sisters of Bethany and the Protestant Episcopal Sisters of the Society of St. Margaret. "On the occasion of their first meeting," he related, "they were so attached to one another you would think that they were long lost sisters." Then he added, "That's just what they were." [4]

These affairs were simply illustrative of the general conciliatory gestures on the local scene in the United States. Similar activities—"open houses" for exchange of visits, ecumenical meetings, interreligious panels and programs—occurred in countless communities: in San Antonio; Springfield, Ohio; Minneapolis; Santa Fe; Houston; Philadelphia; San Francisco; and also in small villages. Roman Catholic priests appeared in Protestant pulpits, and vice versa. They taught special courses in one another's classrooms, and attended one another's ceremonial occasions. In Tulsa, Oklahoma, the Church of the Madalene joined the local Council of Churches in 1964, the first Roman Catholic church to affiliate with an interdenominational council of Protestant and Orthodox bodies. In Dallas the Pastors Association elected its first Roman Catholic member to the executive board. With approval of their bishops, Roman Catholic priests joined the community ministerial associations in Alexandria, Louisiana; Alpina, Michigan; and elsewhere. In Grand Rapids, Michigan, St. Andrew's Catholic Cathedral entered the area Council of Churches. New Mexico's State Council of Churches, previously made up of various Protestant denominations, became the first state-wide interchurch council to include Roman Catholics when the Santa Fe, New Mexico, archdiocese joined late in 1964. The movement spread.

Trying to survey the extent of Roman Catholic-Protestant interchange, a National Lutheran Council research team figuratively threw up its hands, reporting: "The source material for a study of this nature is virtually inexhaustible." [5]

The most substantial aspect of the new encounter, and the backbone of all the public displays of good will and amiable hand-shaking, was the quiet, serious, theological dialogue going on increasingly between Roman Catholic, Protestant, and Orthodox scholars. Laymen often participated in this interreligious give-and-take.

The first such officially and publicly authorized program in this country was launched in 1961 by then Archbishop Shehan, of Baltimore (elevated to the cardinalate in 1965), who set up a lay-clergy commission on Christian unity to arrange discussion meetings with other church groups. The program has grown into numerous dialogue circles throughout the diocese. Presbyterian minister William R. Sengel, describing the group of Roman Catholic, Baptist, Methodist, Disciples, Presbyterian, and Assembly of God pastors in which he participated, says: "The elaborate Roman Catholic adoration of Mary and papal infallibility became subjects of lively debate. So did the problems of the lack of discipline among Protestants and their confusion about the meaning of worship. And time and again our discussions brought us to the Bible. . . . It was a tremendous experience in that setting to sing together, 'Praise to the Lord, the Almighty, the King of creation. . . .' The Holy Spirit has far more to say to the churches than either Protestants or Roman Catholics have been willing to hear." [6]

By the end of 1962, similar programs had been launched by Roman Catholic Bishop John J. Russell, of Richmond, Virginia; by Archbishop Edward D. Howard, of Portland, Oregon; and by Archbishop Paul J. Hallinan, of Atlanta, Georgia. After that, through 1963 and 1964, the pattern literally snowballed. Such projects, on a diocesan-planned and assigned basis, were started by the Roman Catholic ordinaries in Boston; St. Louis; Pittsburgh; Pueblo, Colorado; and Bridgeport, Connecticut, among others. But beyond the extensively organized systems, the far larger facet of the new dialogue was in the spontaneously formed groups in scholarly circles and in little rings of pastors in neighborhoods throughout America as well as Europe. The Roman Catholic position in the past had variously limited, discouraged, or forbidden such activity.

Some of it had gone on before, of course, in private, unofficial sectors of the church. Although not directly approved, it was tolerated by church authorities in some regions, chiefly in western Europe. There the impact of two world wars had forged deep and irreversible inter-Christian bonds. The Una Sancta movement developed in Germany, led by the heroic priest Max Joseph Metzger, who was executed by the Nazis, and the great Roman Catholic scholar Karl Adam. It spread into France and the Low Countries. It was not an organization, but an impulse and contagion which brought Catholic and Protestant theologians together in homes and universities for probing conversation and friendship. In a similar spirit and period, a gentle French Catholic professor, the late Abbé Paul Couturier, started the Association Unité Chrétienne at Lyons, France, which also brought together thinkers of the various churches for discussion and prayer. His approach generated profound influences which only now—a decade after his death—have gained standing in the church.

Previously, however, it was a lonely occupation, an exception to the rule, carried on behind the scenes by bold, visionary individuals, their work often opposed and treated by church officials as odd or questionable. It had penetrated Catholic-Protestant relationships in western Europe long before it spread throughout the church at large.

Interestingly, the efforts of the European forerunners began when Protestant and Orthodox churches were organizing into council. Many of that movement's leaders, including Visser 't Hooft, became friends of Germany's Karl Adam and France's Abbé Couturier. American Catholicism also had a few pioneering ecumenical advocates, notably the diligent Gustave Weigel, a big-framed, always obliging Jesuit professor of Woodstock College in Maryland, and a consultant at the Vatican Council until his death early in 1964.

However, direct Protestant-Catholic theological exchange in this country had been an extremely rare thing heretofore, compared to the European activity, and had been limited mostly to highly specialized fields, such as Biblical research. By and large, Catholic ecumenical effort had remained an orphan, a peculiarity of individuals, which was permitted in Europe but not generally elsewhere. Then Rome, through its Christian Unity Secretariat in 1960, made it regular policy. Since then it has filled out and spread like streaks of daybreak. It has burnished the tone of church publications, stimulated new ones, and lit wider fields in institutions of learning.

Mutual exposition of positions and examination of issues became common practice in print. Protestant journals increasingly ran material by Roman Catholics, and Catholic periodicals carried articles by Protestants. Both included commentaries by Jewish and Orthodox thinkers. New joint Protestant-Catholic publications also developed, including the *Journal of Ecumenical Studies,* launched in 1964 at Pittsburgh's Catholic Duquesne University Press, with an interreligious staff including Catholic theologians Gregory Baum, Hans Küng, and George Tavard, and Protestants Robert McAfee Brown, Elwyn Smith (Presbyterians), and George Lindbeck (Lutheran). The lay-edited Catholic weekly, *The Commonweal,* enlisted Brown, of Stanford University, to write a regular column, "A Protestant Viewpoint." "Not many years ago, it would have been unthinkable," the editors observed in an introductory note. "Those days, happily, have now passed."

Lutheran Jaroslav Pelikan became a columnist for Denver's Catholic diocesan weekly, *The Register.* The *St. Louis Review,* another diocesan weekly, carried parallel discussions, by Protestant and Catholic scholars, on various interchurch issues. A Jesuit monthly, *Social Order,* devoted an issue to an exchange of ideas between Jewish and Catholic thinkers. The American Lutheran Church started a new quarterly, *Dialogue,* offering a channel for Catholic, Protestant, and Orthodox views. The Paulist Fathers started a new monthly in 1962, *The Ecumenist,* edited by Baum, analyzing various sides of church unity problems. Books also reflected the theological cross-currents, and increasingly had joint Catholic-Protestant authorship. After fifty-five years of calling itself a "nondenominational weekly," *The Christian Century* changed its description in 1963 to "an ecumenical weekly."

It was the temper of the day.

In the "new age of ecumenical understanding," says Monsignor Daniel Moore, editor of the *St. Louis Review,* religious publications have a duty to include varying viewpoints, "responsible criticism and dialogue," not only as a matter of fairness, but for "completeness of education" of the readers on the subjects presented.

In the academic world, where the spadework of solving doctrinal and historical problems often begins, teaching perspectives widened. Protestant-founded Yale University added a new chair for Roman Catholic studies in 1963. Harvard Divinity school had set up a visiting chair for Roman Catholic professors in 1959. Harvard's noted Protestant scholar, Krister Stendahl, in 1964 lectured at the Roman Catholic Divine Word Seminary. Lutheran theologian Arthur Carl Piepkorn helped teach a summer session for nuns at Webster College. Three seminaries in Iowa, one Roman Catholic, another Presbyterian, and the third Lutheran, formed a joint faculty association to handle religious instruction at the University of Iowa. The method invaded parish congregations as well. A nun, Sister Mary John, a Biblical scholar of Marylhurst College, taught a six-week seminar at Moreland Presbyterian church in Portland, Oregon. A Jesuit, Michael J. Taylor, taught a twelve-week adult class on Roman Catholicism for a Protestant congregation in Seattle's University Christian church.

The most intensive analysis of issues and relationships went on at a new kind of institution, nonexistent in other generations—the special "ecumenical" centers. Among the earliest and best known are the center founded by Abbé Couturier at Lyons; the Roman Catholic *Istinia* center near Paris; the Protestant center at Taizé, France; and the World Council's Ecumenical Institute at Bossey, Switzerland; with a half dozen related branches in other cities, including Evanston, Illinois. Additional institutions of this kind for interchurch study were being set up by Cardinal Cushing in Massachusetts and by Cardinal Léger in Montreal. Many universities and theological schools also have set up special chairs on ecumenism, about a score of them in America and Europe.

Competent, exacting scholarship, says Cardinal Bea, serves as the main implement of unity work. And, he adds, it necessarily concentrates on "the common ground of all Christians"—the Bible. "If we are to unite, we must go constantly to the Word of God, and try to penetrate more deeply into the mystery of his revelation." [8]

Significantly, the entire ecumenical movement has paralleled a mounting emphasis on the Bible and the resurgence of "Biblical theology" both in Protestantism and Roman Catholicism. Collaboration in that field developed early, setting the pace for later associations in other ways. Nowadays, says Lutheran leader Franklin Clark Fry, when "you get Roman Catholic Biblical scholars and Protestant Biblical scholars together, it's very difficult to sort them out after the first half hour, because they are proceeding on the same basis." [9]

A common Bible for Protestants, Orthodox, and Roman Catholics came into being in Great Britain in 1964, after Catholic authorities there approved an edition of the Revised Standard Version, a translation produced by an interdenominational Protestant-Orthodox team of the National Council of Churches of Christ in America in 1952. "The Bible is coming to be, as it should be, a bond of Christian unity rather than an instrument of division. . . ." says Luther A. Weigle, Yale Divinity School's dean emeritus who headed the twenty-two-year translation project. Catholic and Protestant scholars in Germany and the Netherlands were working on common versions. In the United States, an official Catholic edition of the Protestant-produced Revised Standard Version of the New Testament was published in July, 1965, and a complete Revised Standard Version of the Bible for Catholics is ready for issue early in 1966. A cause for "great joy," said Boston's Cardinal Cushing. The late Cardinal Meyer says in a preface: "The present edition of the New Testament should help usher in a happier age when Christian men will no longer use the word of God as a weapon, but rather, like our forefathers before the time of the Reformation, will find God and Father of our Lord Jesus Christ speaking to them within the covers of a single book." Without church sponsorship, a group of Protestant, Roman Catholic, and Jewish experts were working on another joint version under chairmanship of the noted Biblical archaeologist William F. Albright, of Johns Hopkins University.

Already certain Catholic educational institutions used Protestant translations, either the Revised Standard Version or others that had been translated from original manuscripts, in preference to Catholicism's archaically worded Douay Version of 1610. It and the Catholic

Knox Bible were drawn from the Latin Vulgate of the fourth century, when many early manuscripts and other data were not available. A new Catholic Biblical Association version, using original sources, was in the works, and partly done. The highly interwoven picture was especially exemplified at Seattle University, a Roman Catholic institution, where students in Old Testament used the Protestant Revised Standard Version in a course taught by a Jewish rabbi.

The legacy of a book convened its sundry stockholders.

Not only in mind, but also in deed, the partnership grew. Catholics, Protestants, and Jews entered into common action. In the United States a graphic case had to do with the nation's most troubling issue of the 1960's, racial justice. Uniting for the first time in history on a nationwide basis, the major representative organizations of Catholicism, Orthodoxy, Protestantism, and Judaism joined in the National Conference on Religion and Race; this took place in Chicago, in January, 1963. They set up a continuing council for co-operative effort in behalf of racial integration. Local interreligious branches sprang up afterward in more than forty-five cities, and the number increased.

Nuns, priests, ministers, and rabbis walked together on picket lines and in desegregation demonstrations. At a congressional hearing on the subject, Presbyterian leader Eugene Carson Blake served as joint spokesman for the country's four main religions. More than 6,500 Jews, Protestants, Roman Catholics, and Orthodox assembled at a National Interreligious Convocation on Civil Rights in Washington, D.C., in April, 1964; and for two months afterward kept up a joint "prayer vigil" at the Lincoln Memorial until a new Civil Rights Bill became law.

The broken voice, in crisis, steadied.

Collaboration in other areas developed gradually, although on a lesser scale for the time being. In some communities, the various groups worked together in religious census-taking, and contributed to one another's building projects. Regionally and nationally, their specialists conferred on various matters: religious liberty, alcoholism, psychological counseling, education, interfaith marriage. The late Cardinal Meyer of Chicago said there are many "questions on which we could co-operate: the problems of unemployment, public welfare, religious education, general education, and population expansion." [10] Inclinations and events pointed toward expanding co-operation in programs of social concern.

The most extraordinary and intimate feature of the changing relationship, however, was in the united participation in religious devotions—something generally taboo for Roman Catholics since the

Protestant Reformation. These joint public services, unheard of in English-speaking countries before the 1960's, have become increasingly frequent, both in small settings, like the one in Boston's University chapel, and the large kind, such as Worcester's "Ecumenical Convocation," and San Antonio's Municipal Auditorium gathering, where 5,500 Christians of all kinds prayed together and sang hymns on Pentecost evening, 1963. One stirring service in Montreal had an international makeup. Arranged by the city's church leaders, including the Catholic archbishop, Cardinal Léger, it took place on July 21, 1963, in conjunction with the Faith and Order Conference there of the World Council of Churches. About fifteen hundred Christians from around the globe, Protestant, Orthodox, and Roman Catholic, joined in hymns, prayers, and litanies. On these occasions, Christians reclaimed a basic kind of relationship which previously had been wanting.

Roman Catholic discipline forbids *communication in sacris*, a technical term meaning participating in the *sacramental life* of other churches. Canon 1258 makes it illicit. The reason is that worship, as a "sign of unity" in faith, should be limited to contexts in which that unity exists. And in the past, even passive attendance at solemnities of other churches, such as weddings or funerals, has been considered permissible only for grave reasons. (For the first time, New York's Cardinal Spellman in 1964 attended a Protestant funeral—the Presbyterian services for the wife of Mayor Robert F. Wagner.)

However, Vatican rulings have allowed for other exceptions in administering or receiving the sacraments in emergencies, and some Catholic scholars say the present ecumenical situation justifies modified approaches in special circumstances. They point out that worship, besides being a "sign of unity," also is a "means of grace," and that the latter purpose may override strict application of the rules in settings which further love among separated Christians, and manifest such unity as exists. Moreover, the widening Catholic view of the church as a fellowship, surmounting sharply defined institutional lines, has tended to lessen the devotional barriers. The 1964 Decree on Ecumenism specifically enjoins common prayer with other Christians, and also permits "worship in common (*communication in sacris*)" although admonishing that it should not be "used indiscriminately for the restoration of Christian unity."

An American Jesuit, Daniel J. O'Hanlon, has suggested it might be "theologically possible" to permit other Christians to receive communion with Catholics "in exceptional circumstances." He notes that this happened in moments of danger in World War II, and surmises that it might be justified "in the equally real emergency of a scandalously divided Christianity" if "other Christians were invited on rare occasions to communion at a Catholic Mass." He says it would not be an "honest sign" if it occurred frequently or normally, but suggests it would be honest if limited to exceptional events. Such limitation in itself would make clear the lack of unity, and at the same time foster the yearning for it.[11]

The question, however, touches an acutely delicate zone: the core of worship. Different understandings of the Eucharist, the Lord's Supper, are the difficulty. Even between some Protestant denominations, it remains an obstacle. Some of them avoid mixed or "open" communion, except in rare instances. Eastern Orthodoxy does not authorize intercommunion with Protestants, although it works with them in interchurch councils. Bernard Cardinal Alfrink of Utrecht, Holland, says that "undoubtedly it would be a striking expression of the desire for unity if the faithful of the different Christian churches celebrated communion together, but in so doing they would be giving a semblance of a unity which does not really exist."[12]   There have been no weighty indications toward permitting it generally.

The United States Bishops' Commission, in its 1965 guidelines for interdenominational worship, said, "Restoration of Eucharistic communion is the goal of our ecumenical effort. At the present time, however, except in particular cases of members of the Eastern Orthodox Church, intercommunion with Christians of other denominations should not be permitted. Our separation is most keenly felt at the Table of the Lord and the sense of sorrow awakened by a deepening realization of the meaning of the tragic separation should in itself provide a powerful stimulus to ecumenical concern. . . ."

In other respects, the commission recommended broad participation in interchurch services to the one-hundred-and-forty-nine United States dioceses, saying: "With the approval of local bishops, priests are to be encouraged to take an active part in the conduct of the services, e.g., by reading Scripture lessons, preaching homilies, offering prayers, and giving blessings." Catholic laymen also may take active parts in the ecumenical services, the commission said. They also may attend regular Protestant and Orthodox worship, but should not take official roles unless it is a specifically ecumenical occasion. Other Christians also should be made welcome in attending Catholic liturgical celebrations, including the Eucharistic Communion (the Mass), and may be invited to join in accompanying prayers, litanies, and hymns, the commission said, but should not be asked to take leading roles in official Catholic worship. However, concerning specifically interdenominational worship, the commission said the effort for unity must move beyond theological discussions and the practical realms of co-operative social and educational efforts and enter into "spiritual ecumenism." For the present, the main reservation involved is sharing in the Lord's Supper.

Nevertheless, with Rome's thrust into ecumenical affairs, many of its leaders eased the restraints against other kinds of worshipful inter-Christian services. The phenomenon, because of its newness, offered no fixed outline or settled format. It belonged to that evolutionary stage in which the design still was forming. It varied from country to country and diocese to diocese, according to local episcopal temper. Conditions shifted, and new customs arose to meet new circumstances. "We have to symbolize our unity," Father Baum, director of the ecumenical center in Toronto, told me. "We also have to symbolize, alas, our separation." In the past, only the latter seemed in evidence. But now both were recognized and attested to as real, in worshipful acts together. It was a distinct change.

Under a 1949 Vatican decree, Catholics had been permitted to join in saying the "Our Father" with other Christians. But the new joint services went considerably beyond that, including gospel readings, discourses, extensive prayer, hymn-singing, litanies recited in unison—all marks of worship not taken from the rites of any one particular church. Some prelates objected to the new activities, calling them disconcerting to Catholic laymen. They "can well be excused for asking what is happening," says Archbishop John C. Garner of Pretoria, South Africa. "Where bishops and priests formerly warned them against taking part in the services of other churches, or interdenominational services, they themselves are going out of their way to take part in the once-banned functions. Can they be blamed for asking: Illicit before, are they licit now? Or even (in their perplexity) sinful before, are they virtuous now?" [13]

As in any new and unfamiliar atmosphere which demands adjusted methods and roles to suit the altered needs, there were bound to be moments of puzzled uncertainty and awkwardness. Even in saying the Lord's Prayer together, there was some fumbling. In the usual Catholic version, the prayer ends with the phrase, "But deliver us from evil." The common Protestant version adds a concluding line, "For thine is the kingdom, and the power, and the glory, forever." At some Protestant-Catholic meetings in Rome, with each group trying to be considerate of the other, it happened that Protestants stopped with "deliver us from evil," while the Catholics went on to include the final doxology. Jesuit Gustave Weigel later remarked, "Why shouldn't we Catholics say the final lines? After all, they're nothing but a Catholic addition to the original text."

Amid the stumbling and the discoveries, the inter-Christian "conversation" spread, reaching even into areas with a background of especial antagonisms, Spain and Latin America. In Colombia, scene of previous sharp conflicts, Catholic and Protestant clergy held friendly discussions. "The bell of reconciliation has sounded in Colombia," editorialized the country's largest daily, *El Tiempo*. [14] In Bogotá in early 1964, more than a thousand Roman Catholics and Protestants joined in a two-hour interconfessional service of prayer and hymns. Similar ecumenical meetings took place in Madrid. Methodist, Lutheran, and Jesuit theological schools in Brazil exchanged lecture invitations and other courtesies. Protestant and Catholic scholars conducted common Bible study meetings in Buenos Aires. "We are beginning to see strange and marvelous things happen," observes Jorge Lara-Braud, dean of Mexico City's Presbyterian theological seminary. [15] That impression extended through the Christian domain nearly everywhere.

It was not simply a polishing up of interreligious etiquette. Its basic dynamism hinged on concern for one another, on attentiveness to one another's values, and on sharing them to the end that all might serve more rightly their mutual, avowed cause. It involved the far-going reassessments of the Vatican Council, and the kindred conciliar probings of Protestantism and Orthodoxy. Ultimately "some sort of synthesis of all that is good and true in all camps must find a common expression," says French Catholic theologian Yves Congar. "This may eventually lead to the discovery of spiritual riches among our neighbors which we ourselves may not possess, and some day all will meet in a church organism where the beliefs of all Christians can converge." [16] That was the far-off hope, beyond the still imponderable institutional obstacles. The immediate purpose was to begin clearing the debris of bias and misrepresentations about "others," to recover the chords of understanding. Even that task met roadblocks.

In some Catholic quarters, there were fears that the work would cause religious "indifferentism"—an attitude that any and all ideas of faith are equally valid. Yet the undertaking proceeds on a directly opposite premise—the conviction that only through a clearer, non-competitive hearkening to Christ's truth, unclouded by self-obsessed defensiveness and rivalry, can valid unity be found. Ecumenism, says Catholic Bishop John King Mussio, "is renewed respect for the conscientious adhering to what one seriously considers the will of God in his regard. It is a re-evaluation of past history, putting things in their proper perspective, separating the human from the divine, passion from intent, the spirit from the human failings in expressing it." [17]

Among some Protestants, there also were suspicions that all the gracious behavior merely amounted to maneuvers for a "return to Rome." Yet this disregarded the basic nature of the whole endeavor— its character of movement, change, and advance toward a new area of encounter. To reach it, all will have "to go a part of the way," says Jesuit Bertrand de Margerie.[18] The objective was not yesterday's Rome, or Wittenberg Castle, or Constantinople, but that ever-summoning region of universal Christian aspiration, Calvary, where self is given up in love for others.

That impulse and the transformations stemming from it already had yielded tangible results. Differences between Protestants and Catholics "will be unrecognizable in fifty years" if the ecumenical progress in that time equals advances of the last five years, says Douglas Horton, Dean Emeritus of Harvard Divinity School and observer at the Vatican Council.[19]

Horton, chairman for nearly a decade of Faith and Order studies of the World Council of Churches, told me in a lengthy interview that the entry of Rome into reciprocal discussions with other churches was the vitalizing factor. "Conversation, the attempt to solve problems, that is the beginning of revolution," he said. "The most important exchange is probably at the theological level, but laymen are doing it and having a great time doing it."

Some Protestant denominations issued guides for participation in the "dialogue" with Roman Catholics. The United Presbyterian Church, in an advisory to members, approved by its 1963 general assembly, said the discussions should not "be regarded as encounters of wit or debates to tear down opposing arguments. Rather, they should be approached as opportunities for increasing mutual understanding and for joining together in seeking more complete comprehension of the obedience to God's truth and its meaning for his church and his world." After the years of suspicion and tension, it is a long road to "true Christian fellowship," the guide says. "It is a still longer way to the agreements that would be prerequisite to any kind of churchly unity. But we should neither discount the importance of progress in mutual understanding nor doubt that in each new situation, God will show us the next steps to take."

As to what those steps might be, Christians of all kinds around the world began in 1964, for the first time, to pray for light in one accord. Until then the annual week of prayer for Christian unity had contained a somewhat discordant note.

The observance first was started in 1908 by an Episcopal minister, Lewis T. Wattson, who entered the Roman Catholic Church the following year together with a small band of Anglican friars; they dedicated themselves to the conversion of all Christians to Roman Catholicism. He took the name Father Paul James Francis. The order which he founded, the Society of the Atonement, with headquarters at Graymoor, New York, sponsored the annual "Chair of Unity Octave" in which the intention of the prayers was the return of other Christians to the Roman fold. Pope Benedict XV in 1916 extended the observance throughout the Roman Catholic Church. But to other folds the movement could not help but seem particularized.

However, another influence arose, that of the late Abbé Couturier of Lyons, France, in the late 1930's. He urged use of a different formula of prayer, in which all Christians could join, that unity "may come, such as Christ wills, and by the means he wills." This approach caught on among many Catholics in Europe, and also appealed to Protestant and Orthodox churches. It left the terms of unity open, in God's hands. On that basis all Christians could pray for it in harmony. As a result, Protestant and Orthodox churches in 1940 shifted their own annual week of prayer for unity from spring to January 18-25, coinciding with the Catholic observance. Under sponsorship of the World Council of Churches, plans for the period were co-ordinated with that of the Catholic Christian Unity Association of Lyons. In 1963, for the first time, both used identical materials for the observance. Some Catholic parishes shifted to the joint theme, praying for unity "according to Christ's will, in his way and in his time." Other Catholics, however, continued that year to use the Graymoor program materials, praying for "the return" of all Christians to "union with the Chair of Peter . . . in the one true church."

But in 1964, after fifty-five years and with churchly antennae sensitized to the new and unforeseen signals of the spirit, sponsors of the original Graymoor program also ceased scheduling prayers for the prescribed-in-advance route to reunion. The new intentions of the prayers, like those of the Catholic Christian Unity Association of Lyons and the World Council of Churches, simply implored "the unity of all Christians in the church," without specifying the method by which it might come about.

Thus, across the board, Christians now prayed as one and kept themselves patiently and humbly open to what still remained beyond their ken—the plan.

One man had much to do with harmonizing these supplications.

On March 24, 1953, in a small apartment on the Rue du Plat in Lyons, he lay on his bed, a slight, slender Catholic priest, fatally ill. Nearby hung a white chasuble, given to him by Anglicans. On a table were mementos from Lutherans and Presbyterians. On the wall were many crosses, Latin and Orthodox, some Russian icons, and above his head, a "Week of Prayer for Unity" picture poster. It showed the allegorical figure of Humility, whose delicate hands moved among brambles and reptiles to "open the ways that are barred." That was the scene, as described by visitors, when Abbé Couturier died at the age of seventy-one.

In no small measure, this gentle, sympathetic "apostle of unity" had lighted the way out of the murky anachronism of "rival prayers" for unity. A revered friend of all kinds of Christians in a period when that was not a particularly popular role, he sensed and conveyed a single, vibrant note in regard to unity—that God's "will be done." On that motif, the world-wide orchestration of prayer came in tune.

This did not mean that the course was charted, that preliminaries were agreed on, that prospects were in sight; rather it meant just the opposite: that at this point the future steps were unknown, the dilemmas deep, the answers inscrutable, and the way ahead hidden.

As Abbé Couturier saw it, it meant a "total renunciation, a plunge into a mystery where much is obscure and which transcends all the ideas that we can present to our Lord in the name of our faith; it is the attitude of a soul open to the one sovereign will of Christ, saying 'yes' to his prayer for unity. Then it is Christ who prays within us, without the burden of our fallen nature." [20]

In that vein, Christians finally could pray together. Acknowledging their deficiencies, recognizing that all their varied computations fall short, and submitting to a will and wisdom exceeding their own, believers of many kinds had found rapport on their knees.

And that was a profound difference; something they had not experienced before—an affinity at the heart of the matter.

In that vein, Pope Paul in January, 1964, urged observance of the week of prayers which "brings together Christians of every denomination in a single effort of intercession for the unity desired by Christ for all those with the name of Christian." [21]

In that vein, the late Cardinal Albert Meyer of Chicago joined in a service of prayer that week with two hundred Protestant clergymen. A United Church of Christ minister introduced the devotions with the words, "Save us, O Lord our God." Cardinal Meyer, together with Douglas Horton, the veteran Protestant ecumenical statesman, responded along with the assembly, "And gather us from among the nations."

After a Scripture reading and recitation of the Nicene Creed, Cardinal Meyer led a three-part litany, part of the special order of devotions distributed both by the World Council and the Christian Unity Association of Lyons.

"We thank thee, Father," the cardinal recited, "for the benefits which thou dost grant us in the ecumenical movement; for opening minds and hearts to the understanding and sharing of thy gifts in us and in our brethren, through the Holy Spirit."

The Protestant ministers responded, "Glory be to thee for ever and ever."

The cardinal resumed, "For our controversies, sometimes full of irony, narrow-mindedness, or exaggeration with regard to our Christian brethren, for our intransigence, our harsh judgments . . ."

"We beseech thee to pardon us, O Lord," the assembly responded.

"For all self-sufficiency and pride which we have shown our Christian brethren over the centuries," the cardinal went on, "and for all our lack of understanding towards them . . ."

"We beseech thee to pardon us, O Lord," the others answered.

"Beyond the frontiers of language, race, and nation . . ." the cardinal said.

"Unite us, Lord Jesus," the voices came back.

"Beyond our ignorances, our prejudices, and our instinctive enmities . . ."

"O God, for thy greater glory," the Catholic prelate spoke in resonant tones.

"Gather together all separated Christians," chorused the Protestant throng.

"O God, that goodness and truth may prevail." The lone voice.

And then the many, "Gather together all separated Christians."

"O God, that peace may at last reign on earth."

"Gather together all separated Christians."

CHAPTER *14*

EPILOGUE

"Sic transit gloria mundi." On the way to the altar for the coronation of a pope, a friar moves beside him, burning a piece of flax. Three times, as the smoke rises - and disappears on the air, the friar calls out loudly, "So passes the glory of the world!"

The mundane splendors flame and fade, vapors on the wind of time. And the forgotten monuments crumble even as the wearied old cling to them and cry against the day. But history races on. Change is its law. And that which stands still is cast aside and noticed no more.

Once the Church of Rome sat in the courts of the world's mighty, wielding thrones and powers, and it put on the royal robes, the scepters and jewels. Ah, for that magnificence, that lustrous yesterday, the nostalgic ones lament, and gaze in dismay on the new world of steel, democracy, and astrophysics. Hold on, hold fast against the dangerous now; clasp firm the formerly and heretofore.

"Sic transit . . ." So that animating force, that enduring inner fire, leaps up again. And the pilgrim church moves on into the habitations of today.

It is a different world; the old uniformities and isolated citadels have gone; Christendom no more reigns by crowns and jurisdictions, but walks the earth scantily regarded. It is a world of many voices, of many equations, of many newly discovered truths, a world of exploration into space, into the depths of the earth, the seas, the psyche, and the atom. Other schools besides the ecclesiastical institutes teach; some teach well, and monopolies of thought and theory could not continue. Churchdom, bereft of its temporal suzerainty, is left with a Christianity as it was in the beginning—a few among many, a diaspora among larger societies and other dominions.

It is a risky, variegated world, unlike the protected religious dwelling places of the past.

And it was into this challengingly real world, into this electric new environment, that Roman Catholicism progressively moved, aroused by the charisms of that gentle, witty old prelate, Pope John, emboldened by the acumen of Pope Paul, and powered by that ebullition of bishops and planners from around the globe who brought

238

to the Vatican Council a fuller, sharper vision of the conditions and duties of Christianity in the present hour of this planet.

There was a key, a theme, to what they did, and to what the church was doing: it was shedding preoccupation with itself, with its own stature and majesty, and turning its attention to others—to other methods, other peoples, other Christians, other religions, other fields of knowledge, to science, art, technology, to the vast, varied realities that make up the actual world in which men live, a world which could not be served by a church apart from it.

To close the gaps, to build bridges, to find the mortise joints and unifying cement between the old faith and the new age, that was the immense renewal project undertaken.

Let there be no closed frontiers between religion and science, said Pope Paul. "Where there is research, discovery, conquest, increasing knowledge, and action . . . there is the penetration of the work of God and the use of the resources hidden in it." Let friendship, he said, be re-established between church and the artists on whom it has tended formerly to lay a restricting "cloak of lead" while they went apart to "drink from other fountains." "We must return to being allies." Crossing the religious borders between East and West, he went forth to embrace Athenagoras, to set his feet on the ground of all Christians and Jews. In India, he sought co-operation with the ancient Oriental faiths—Islam, Hinduism, and Buddhism.

Against other separations and barriers, the voices of the church resounded. They acted to bind up, to heal, to join tradition to the Bible, to couple papal authority with that of other bishops, to bring laity and clergy into closer collaboration, to strengthen the bonds between Christian and Christian, between Christians and Jews, between Judeo-Christianity and other religions. The work was to renew connections, to begin dialogue, to vitalize relationships.

It was strange how that unifying thread ran through the entire enterprise.

Yet it was not a fixed, narrow seam, but rather a fluid, growing weave, wrought in respect for sincere differences, in liberty of conscience, in diversity of custom and cultures, leaving breadth for new modes and ideas, and recognizing that even the church's own doctrine should not be immobilized in set formulations, but should be open to ever new clarifications in the mutual search for truth and for that gracious understanding among men born of the truth of love.

In the modern era, churches of every stamp realize the minority status of Christianity, not only as being but a third of the earth's population, but as being overshadowed by the giants of technology and the paternal state. Once, churches tended to look resentfully on the ascendant secular organizations and achievements, pining for the days of religious hegemony. But a deep reassessment, the new awareness, has come about.

As displayed by Rome and by other major churches, the realization is that Christians are confronted with a basic and crucial unity in order to represent their faith clearly in this new kind of world. Their supplementary role makes their rivalries seem equivocal and irrelevant in a society dominated by other establishments. A further realization is that instead of glowering at these overruling institutions and accomplishments, Christianity must function in and through them, for they are the shape of life today.

It is this role for which Roman Catholicism was gearing itself.

The day had decreed its demands. "For everything there is a season," Ecclesiastes mused, "a time for every matter under heaven. . . ." And the time of transition had struck in the ancient fold of Rome. It no longer held itself apart, but went forth to embrace its brothers, and to work as the leaven in a world not its own, but which it now affirmed with affection and good heart.

No matter what attitude the world has toward Christianity, Paul said, the church looks on that world with "immense tenderness," concerned for its poor, its afflicted, and its sorrowing, appreciating its culture, learning, and science, esteeming it with an "inexhaustible love"—a universal love emanating from Christ and which "thinks of others even before it thinks of itself."

That was the spark, the life-giving ferment which kept the faith going, which roused it from its sleeps. That selfless love was what put the apostles on the road. That was the "salt" given them to season the days of men with peace. Its advocates have faced all kinds of worlds, worlds that honored and exalted them, worlds that hated them. "Sic transit . . ."

Sometimes the human bearers of that mandate of love have faltered and failed it. Sometimes its external conveyances lagged or slumbered. "Sic transit . . ." The genuine thing abided. It went on, through all kinds of landscapes, of ease or storm. It was not fixed to one period or place or circumstance. It was not restricted to changeless structures. It was a traveler. It was the energy of a voyage, living and trimming itself to any time or clime. And it was on the wind as the church set sail for twentieth-century weather.

NOTES

CHAPTER *1*

1. *Epocha*, Rome, Jan. 12, 1964.
2. *The Sign*, February, 1965.
3. *Catholic Messenger*, Jan. 23, 1964.
4. National Lutheran Council News Bureau, Sept. 30, 1963.
5. *The St. Louis Review*, Aug. 16, 1963.
6. *The Pilot*, Fez.
7. Address, Vatican Council, Sept. 29, 1963.
8. Pastoral Letter, Jan. 26, 1959.
9. Council Address, Sept. 29, 1963.
10. Hans Küng, *The Council in Action* (New York, Sheed and Ward, Inc., 1963), p. 276.
11. Mark 3:25.
12. *Catholic World*, Feb. 1963.
13. *The Lutheran*, Dec. 4, 1963.
14. *America*, Jan. 14, 1961.
15. Address, Pro Deo University, Rome, Jan. 31, 1963.
16. *Jubilee*, July, 1963.
17. *Catholic Mind*, April, 1963.
18. *Catholic World*, Feb., 1963.
19. John 17:21.
20. Romans 12:5.
21. George H. Tavard, *Two Centuries of Ecumenism* (New York, The New American Library, 1962), p. 106.
22. Address, Sept. 29, 1963.
23. N.C.W.C. Bureau of Information, Dec., 1963.
24. *Christianity Today*, Feb. 28, 1964.
25. *The Pilot*, Jan. 19, 1963.
26. Address, Vatican Council, Sept. 29, 1963.
27. *America*, Feb. 29, 1964.
28. *The Ecumenist*, Oct. 1962.
29. *Catholic Mind*, May, 1962.
30. *Time*, Feb. 7, 1964.
31. *The Catholic Reporter*, Jan. 3, 1964.
32. *Catholic Messenger*, Jan. 25, 1962.
33. *Christian Beacon*, Nov. 7, 1963.
34. *Action*, January, 1964.
35. *The Dialogue*, N.C.C.J. Bulletin No. 27, Jan. 1964.

36. N.C.W.C. Bureau of Information, Sept. 20, 1963.
37. *The Ecumenical Review*, July, 1963.
38. *The Pilot*, March 9, 1963.
39. *Catholic Messenger*, Oct. 10, 1963.
40. *Christianity and Crisis*, Oct. 14, 1963.
41. *America*, Jan. 19, 1963.
42. *St. Louis Review*, Nov. 22, 1963.
43. *Christianity and Crisis*, Dec. 9, 1963.
44. Acts 2:5,7,11.

CHAPTER *2*

1. John G. Clancy, *Apostle for Our Time* (New York, P. J. Kenedy and Sons, 1963), p. 94.
2. Address, Vatican Council, Oct. 11, 1962.
3. Papal bull, Dec. 25, 1961.
4. *The Commonweal*, Jan. 8, 1962.
5. *America*, June 19, 1963.
6. *Catholic Messenger*, May 17, 1962.
7. *Ibid.*
8. *Catholic Mind*, November, 1963.
9. Address, Vatican Council, Oct. 11, 1962.
10. Clancy, *op. cit.*, p. 149.
11. *Ibid.*, p. 146.
12. *Ibid.*, p. 145.
13. Colossians 1:17.
14. Address, Vatican Council, Sept. 29, 1963.
15. Address, Vatican Radio, June 22, 1963.
16. Philippians 3:13-14.
17. I Corinthians 16:23-24.
18. Andre Fabert, *Pope Paul VI* (New York, Monarch Books, Inc., 1963), p. 74.
19. Reported by Abbé René Laurentin in *Le Figaro*, June 22–25, 1963.
20. Address, June 7, 1963.
21. *St. Louis Review*, July 5, 1963.

22. *Catholic Reporter,* July 5, 1963.
23. Address, Sept. 21, 1963.
24. *The Pilot,* Feb. 2, 1963.
25. *The Catholic News,* Nov. 14, 1963.
26. *Ibid.*
27. Text, *The New York Times,* Sept. 22, 1963.
28. *St. Louis Review,* Nov. 15, 1963.
29. Related by a nephew and namesake, Giovanni Battista Montini, in *Look,* Feb. 25, 1964.
30. Address, Sept. 29, 1963.
31. Acts 12:7-9.

CHAPTER 4

1. Ephesians 2:13-14.
2. Address, Vatican Council, Dec. 4, 1963.
3. Christmas message, 1963.
4. *Ibid.*
5. *Ibid.*
6. John 10:16.
7. Christmas message, 1963.
8. *Ibid.*
9. Luke 4:18-19.
10. Departure statement, Fiumicino Airport, Jan. 4, 1964.
11. *The Eucharist,* Oct. 1962.
12. Address, Vatican Council, Sept. 29, 1963.
13. Genesis 18:18
14. Genesis 28:16-17.
15. II Chronicles 3:1.
16. Galatians 4:4.
17. John 10:10.
18. John 16:33.
19. Psalms 122:1-2.
20. 1 Peter 2:17.
21. Psalms 46:4.
22. Deuteronomy 8:7-8.
23. Luke 3:21-22.
24. Joshua 6:20.
25. Luke 19:9-10.
26. Luke 4:4,8.
27. John 11:43-44.
28. Isaiah 52:1.
29. From Psalm (122:2) as cited in Pope Paul's text for use on reaching the Damascus Gate in ceremonies which were disrupted.
30. Psalm 122:6-7.
31. Luke 19:42.

CHAPTER 5

1. Christmastide talk to cardinals, *Catholic Messenger,* Jan. 2, 1964.
2. Airport departure remarks, Rome, Jan. 4, 1964.
3. Luke 23:5.
4. Luke 16:20-21.
5. Matthew 25:40.
6. Matthew 16:24-25.
7. John 16:20.
8. *Catholic Messenger,* Feb. 16, 1964.
9. Matthew 9:12.
10. Luke 6:20-21.
11. John 15:13.
12. Matthew 18:22.
13. Luke 23:34.
14. John 3:16.
15. John 20:16.
16. Matthew 28:7.
17. John 19:30.
18. Matthew 27:54.
19. An audience, Rome, *Catholic Messenger,* Jan. 16, 1964.
20. John 18:4-5.
21. Matthew 26:52.
22. Matthew 26:38.
23. Luke 22:42.
24. John 17:1.
25. John 17:11.
26. John 17:23.

CHAPTER 6

1. Luke 7:26,28.
2. Revelation 16:18.
3. John 1:46.
4. Luke 4:24.
5. Luke 1:28,30,31,32,34,35,38.
6. Matthew 4:23.
7. Matthew 14:20.
8. Matthew 14:30.
9. John 21:15-17.
10. Matthew 8:26.
11. Mark 4:39.
12. Matthew 4:13.
13. Matthew 5:3-10.
14. Matthew 5:44.
15. Matthew 6:21.

16. Matthew 6:24.
17. Matthew 7:1.
18. Hosea 5:1.
19. Luke 9:29–30.
20. Matthew 17:5–7.
21. Matthew 6:29–34.
22. Matthew 26:22–23,26–28.
23. John 13:16.

20. *Catholic Register,* Oct. 20, 1963.
21. *Catholic Messenger,* Jan. 9, 1964.
22. *American Review of Eastern Ortho-doxy,* Dec. 1963.
23. Statement of Jan. 3, 1964.

CHAPTER 9

1. John 15:12.
2. *Time,* Jan. 17, 1964.
3. John 12:32.
4. *Catholic Messenger,* Jan. 23, 1964.
5. *Christian Century,* Jan. 29, 1964.
6. *Catholic Messenger,* May 6, 1964.
7. *Catholic Register,* Feb. 14, 1964.
8. *The Catholic Reporter,* Jan. 26, 1964.
9. *The Pilot,* Jan. 11, 1964.
10. Ecumenical Press Service, No. 18, May 14, 1964.

CHAPTER 7

1. Micah 5:2.
2. Luke 2:10–11.
3. Luke 2:12.
4. Ephesians, 4:31–32.
5. *United Church Herald,* Jan. 15, 1964.
6. *Catholic Messenger,* Jan. 9, 1964.
7. *Catholic Messenger,* Jan. 16, 1964.

CHAPTER 8

1. *The Living Church,* Aug. 1, 1954.
2. John 1:6.
3. *American Orthodox Review,* May, 1960.
4. *Catholic Messenger,* March 18, 1962.
5. Mark 10:43–44.
6. Alexander Schmemann, *The Historical Road of Eastern Orthodoxy* (New York, Holt, Rinehart and Winston, 1963), p. 246.
7. John 14:17, 26.
8. *Catholic Register,* Oct. 20, 1963.
9. *Jubilee,* January, 1961.
10. *St. Louis Review,* March 15, 1963.
11. *The Christian Beacon,* April 18, 1963.
12. *The Pilot,* Sept. 21, 1963.
13. Clancy, *op. cit.,* p. 228.
14. *The Pilot,* Oct. 19, 1963.
15. Philippians, 3:13–14.
16. Ecumenical Press Service, No. 44, Nov., 1963.
17. *Catholic Messenger,* Sept. 26, 1963.
18. *St. Louis Review,* Sept. 20, 1963.
19. *The Commonweal,* Nov. 15, 1963.

CHAPTER 10

1. Address, Rome, *Catholic Messenger,* Jan. 9, 1964.
2. *L'Espresso,* Dec. 2, 1962.
3. *The Register,* Jan. 19, 1964.
4. Lenten Pastoral, 1964.
5. *America,* June 29, 1963.
6. *The Sign,* May, 1964.
7. *Catholic Mind,* June, 1963.
8. *St. Louis Review,* Jan. 10, 1964.
9. *United Church Herald,* March 15, 1964.
10. Address, Fourth anniversary of John's coronation, Nov. 4, 1962.
11. *The Catholic World,* May, 1963.
12. *Theology Digest,* St. Mary's College, Kansas, Autumn, 1963.
13. 2nd Corinthians 4:7.
14. *Catholic Mind,* May, 1962.
15. *America,* Jan. 19, 1963.
16. Commentaries by theologians in various church journals, including those by Paulist John B. Sheerin, editor of *Catholic World,* in Feb. 1963,

issue, and by Augustinian ecumenist Gregory Baum, in *Commonweal*, Dec. 21, 1962.

17. *American Lutheran*, Nov. 1963.
18. *Ave Maria*, Nov. 26, 1963.
19. *America*, Dec. 1, 1963.
20. *Catholic Mind*, Sept. 1963.
21. Address, Harvard University Divinity School, March 28, 1963.
22. *The Catholic World*, Oct. 1963.
23. *Catholic Messenger*, Jan. 21, 1965.
24. *Commonweal*, Dec. 21, 1962.
25. *New York Times*, Oct 21, 1963.
26. *The Register*, Feb. 14, 1964.
27. *Presbyterian Life*, Jan. 15, 1964.
28. *Catholic Reporter*, Oct. 18, 1963.
29. *Catholic Messenger*, Feb. 28, 1963.
30. John 14:16,17,26.
31. Hans Küng and other editors, *Council Speeches of Vatican II* (Glen Rock, Paulist Press, 1964), p. 69.
32. *New York Times*, Nov. 12, 1963.
33. Küng, *Council Speeches of Vatican II*, op. cit., p. 132.
34. *Ibid.*, p. 135.
35. *The Pilot*, Nov. 9, 1963.
36. *Ibid.*
37. Divine Word News Service, Nov. 13, 1963.
38. *Ibid.*, Nov. 6, 1963.
39. *St. Louis Review*, March 6, 1964.
40. *Catholic Messenger*, Jan. 20, 1964.
41. *St. Louis Review*, Feb. 7, 1964; *Catholic World*, Jan. 30, 1964.
42. *Catholic Messenger*, Jan. 30, 1964.
43. *America*, Feb. 29, 1964.
44. *Ibid.*
45. *Commonweal*, Feb. 14, 1964.
46. *United Church Herald*, June 15, 1964.
47. *St. Louis Review*, May 8, 1964.
48. *Cross Currents*, Fall, 1963.
49. *America*, Feb. 29, 1964.
50. *The Catholic News*, March 12, 1964.
51. Report, World Council Central Committee, Rochester, N.Y., Aug. 1963.
52. *La Croix*, Paris, quoted in *Catholic Messenger*, Jan. 14, 1965.

3. Address, Washington, D.C., Nov. 18, 1962.
4. Luke 6:37.
5. *America*, Nov. 30, 1963.
6. Council address, Sept. 29, 1963.
7. *The Pilot*, Feb. 1, 1964.
8. *The Pilot*, March 7, 1964.
9. *New York Times*, Sept. 24, 1964.
10. *Ibid.*
11. *Ibid.*
12. Address to Italian Jurists, Rome, Dec. 13, 1963.
13. National Institute on Religious Freedom and Public Affairs, Washington, D.C., Nov. 18–21, 1962.
14. *Catholic World*, Sept. 1963.
15. *Catholic Mind*, March, 1964.
16. Romans 11:18.
17. Romans 11:25.
18. An editorial, *The Providence Visitor*, Nov. 15, 1963.
19. Council address, Nov. 19, 1963.
20. Address, Lutheran World Federation, "Consultation on the Church and the Jewish People," Logumkloster, Denmark, May 12, 1964.
21. *New York Herald Tribune*, Nov. 21, 1964.
22. Statement issued on Oct. 16, 1965.
23. *Catholic Messenger*, Jan. 2, 1964.
24. *The Ecumenist*, Oct. 1962.
25. Küng, *Council Speeches of Vatican II*, op. cit., pp. 83, 84, 85.
26. *Catholic Reporter*, Oct. 25, 1963.
27. *St. Louis Review*, Jan. 22, 1965.
28. *St. Louis Review*, Nov. 1, 1963.
29. *Catholic Messenger*, Jan. 17, 1963.
30. *Ibid.*, Dec. 5, 1963.
31. Luke 1:42.
32. *St. Louis Review*, Jan. 31, 1964.
33. Address, Catholic University of America, *St. Louis Review*, May 8, 1964.

CHAPTER 12

1. Report, World Council of Churches Central Committee, 1963.
2. "Christian Unity—the Present Stage," adopted by W. C. C. Central Committee, Odessa, Russia, Feb. 1964.

CHAPTER 11

1. *Catholic Reporter*, April 24, 1964.
2. Text, *Catholic Messenger*, Dec. 12, 1963.

3. Address, Fourth Assembly, Lutheran World Federation, Helsinki, Finland, July 31, 1963.
4. Address, U. S. Conference for the World Council, Buck Hill Falls, Pa., April 27, 1961.
5. Nils Ehrenstrom and Walter G. Muelder, editors, *Institutionalism and Church Unity*, Faith and Order Commission, W. C. C. (New York, Association Press, 1963), pp. 370, 158.
6. Rouse and Neill, *A History of the Ecumenical Movement* (Philadelphia, The Westminster Press, 1954), p. 359.
7. Henry Pitt Van Dusen, *One Great Ground of Hope* (Philadelphia, The Westminster Press, 1961) pp. 116, 131.
8. Kenneth S. Latourette, *Christianity in a Revolutionary Age*, Vol. 5, *The Twentieth Century Outside Europe* (New York, Harper & Row, 1962), p. 503.
9. Commentary-Documentation, Rome, Jan. 1963.
10. *Catholic Messenger*, May 14, 1964.
11. Ecumenical Press Service, No. 17, May 7, 1964.
12. *Catholic Reporter*, March 27, 1964.
13. Samuel S. Cavert, *On the Road to Christian Unity* (New York, Harper & Brothers, 1961), p. 136.
14. Ephesians 4:16.
15. Address, Pro Deo University, Rome, Jan. 31, 1963.
16. Documentary, Apostleship of Prayer, Rome, Jan. 1963.
17. Address, W. C. C. General Assembly, New Delhi, Nov. 19, 1961.
18. Study by Sociologist Paul M. Harrison, of Princeton, for 1963, "Consultation on Church Union."
19. Küng, *Council Speeches of Vatican II, op. cit.,* p. 145.
20. *American Church News*, October, 1963.
21. *Catholic Reporter*, July 19, 1963.
22. *St. Louis Review*, April 10, 1964.
23. *Christianity and Crisis*, Sept. 16, 1963, reprinted from Küng, *The Council in Action, op. cit.*

24. *Catholic Reporter,* March 20, 1964.
25. W. A. Visser 't Hooft, editor, *The New Delhi Report* (New York, Association Press, 1963), p. 118.
26. Report, W. C. C. Central Committee, Aug. 1963.
27. Dialogue, Autumn, 1963.

CHAPTER 13

1. *The Pilot,* Feb. 1, 1964.
2. *American Review of Eastern Orthodoxy,* Dec. 1963.
3. *The Pilot,* Jan. 19, 1963.
4. Religious News Service, Jan. 22, 1963.
5. Study Report, Department of Theological Co-operation, National Lutheran Council, Mar. 10, 1964.
6. *Presbyterian Survey,* Nov. 1962.
7. *Commonweal,* Jan. 4, 1963.
8. *The Living Church,* Nov. 1963.
9. "The Christian Revolution," an international television roundtable, produced by the Columbia Broadcasting System, via Telstar, Oct. 15, 1963.
10. Lenten Pastoral Letter, 1964.
11. *Catholic World,* April, 1964.
12. Ecumenical Press Service, No. 9, March 5, 1964.
13. *Southern Cross,* Capetown, quoted in *Catholic Messenger,* April 14, 1964.
14. Ecumenical Press Service, No. 9, March 5, 1964.
15. *Presbyterian Survey,* June, 1964.
16. *St. Louis Review,* Feb. 14, 1964.
17. *Ibid.,* April 10, 1964.
18. *American Church News,* Oct. 1963.
19. *St. Louis Review,* May 29, 1964.
20. Maurice Villain, S.M., *The Life and Work of Abbe Paul Couturier* (Lyons, Christian Unity Association, 1954), p. 7.
21. *The Pilot,* Jan. 18, 1964.

INDEX